ROUTLEDGE LIBRARY EDITIONS:
ECONOMICS AND SOCIETY

Volume 14

GOVERNMENT POLICY AND INDUSTRIAL CHANGE

GOVERNMENT POLICY AND INDUSTRIAL CHANGE

Edited by
DAVID GIBBS

Routledge
Taylor & Francis Group
LONDON AND NEW YORK

First published in 1989 by Routledge

This edition first published in 2026
by Routledge
4 Park Square, Milton Park, Abingdon, Oxon OX14 4RN

and by Routledge
605 Third Avenue, New York, NY 10158

Routledge is an imprint of the Taylor & Francis Group, an informa business

British Library Cataloguing in Publication Data
A catalogue record for this book is available from the British Library

ISBN: 978-1-032-97576-4 (Set)
ISBN: 978-1-041-13159-5 (Volume 14) (hbk)
ISBN: 978-1-041-13161-8 (Volume 14) (pbk)
ISBN: 978-1-003-66837-4 (Volume 14) (ebk)

DOI: 10.4324/9781003668374

Publisher's Note
The publisher has gone to great lengths to ensure the quality of this reprint but points out that some imperfections in the original copies may be apparent.

Disclaimer
The publisher has made every effort to trace copyright holders and would welcome correspondence from those they have been unable to trace.

Government Policy and Industrial Change

Edited by David Gibbs

Routledge
London and New York

First published 1989

by Routledge
11 New Fetter Lane, London EC4P 4EE
29 West 35th Street, New York, NY 10001

Typeset by Photoprint, Torquay, Devon
Printed and bound in Great Britain by Mackays of Chatham PLC

British Library Cataloguing in Publication Data

Government policy and industrial change.—
(Geography & environment).
1. Industries. Policies of governments
I. Gibbs, D.C. (David C.), *1955–* II. Series
338.9

ISBN 0–415–01032–2

Library of Congress Cataloging in Publication Data

Government policy and industrial change.

(Routledge series in geography and environment)
Papers presented at a conference sponsored by the Industrial Activity and Area Development Study Group of the Institute of British Geographers and held March 1987 in Manchester.
Includes index.
1. Industry and state—Great Britain—Congresses.
2. Industrial organization—Great Britain—Congresses.
2. Industry and state—United States—Congresses.
4. Industrial organization—United States—Congresses.
I. Gibbs, David, 1955– . II. Institute of British Geographers. Study Group on Industrial Activity and Area Development. III. Series.

HD3616.G73G68 1989 338.941 88–29714
ISBN 0–415–01032–2

Contents

List of figures

Figure

List of figures

List of tables

Table

Preface

This book has its origins in a conference organized under the auspices of the Industrial Activity and Area Development Study Group of the Institute of British Geographers, held in Manchester in March 1987. The conference was specifically concerned with the relationship between industrial change and government policy at the local, national, and supra-national level. This volume has been compiled from a number of papers presented at this conference, plus two additional papers which provide a US perspective. The book is edited on behalf of the Industrial Activity and Area Development Study Group and represents part of the Study Group's continuing contribution to the debate on policy issues, industrial change, and restructuring.

In many ways the late 1980s is an appropriate time to take stock of policy issues. The crisis of the late 1970s and early 1980s appears to have given way to a period of restructuring and experimentation as firms adapt to, and themselves create, new forms of capital accumulation. At the same time, policy initiatives at all spatial scales have come under review. In the USA and UK in particular, this has been closely associated with the accession to power of conservative governments. There is a clear need to improve our understanding of the changing relationship between economic restructuring and the policies of the state that are emerging in the 1980s. Thus the work of the French regulation school suggests that a 'new regime of accumulation' is interlinked with a 'new mode of regulation'. Geographers have only recently started to come to grips with the issues raised by the new forms of flexible accumulation, and there is only a limited body of work which attempts to make the connection with policy changes. The collection of papers in this volume provides some pointers as to the character of the regulatory apparatus and policy initiatives that are emerging, and relates these to the process of restructuring.

Preface

I would like to thank Peter Sowden of Routledge and Mike Bradford for their advice and assistance in editing this volume. I am also extremely grateful to Jamie Peck and Andy Gillespie for their advice and comments on an earlier draft of the introductory chapter.

David Gibbs
Manchester Polytechnic, April 1988

Acknowledgements

Jeremy Howells and David Charles' work is associated with a wider study co-ordinated and directed by Professor John Goddard and Alfred Thwaites on Research and Technical Development in the Less Favoured Regions of the European Community, funded by the Regional Policy Directorate of the European Commission. The views they express in the chapter are, however, entirely their own.

Barry and Lorraine Moriarty acknowledge the financial or institutional support of the University of North Carolina R.J. Reynolds Research Fund, National Science Foundation (grant number SES – 8600654), Chapel Hill – Carrboro City Schools, the University of Newcastle upon Tyne, Centre for Urban and Regional Development Studies, and the Rheinisch Westfalischen Technischen Hochschule (Aachen) Geographisches Institut.

Howard Stafford acknowledges the support of grant number SES – 8608128 from the National Science Foundation.

John Bachtler and Phillip Davies would like to acknowledge the helpful comments of Kevin Allen, Richard Rose, and Douglas Yuill.

David Hitchens and Patrick O'Farrell would like to thank all those persons who helped in the comparisons made in their study, especially those firms which agreed to be interviewed. Background information and help were received from the Department of Economic Development, IDB, and LEDU in Northern Ireland, and from the WDA, Cwmbran, and Welsh County Councils in South Wales. The research was made possible by a grant from the Economic and Social Research Council, the Department of Economic Development, Northern Ireland, and the Welsh Development Agency. The authors also wish to thank Professor Billy Black for his helpful comments on an earlier draft.

Bill Lever would like to thank U. Kuppes and G. Uhlig of the

Amt für Stadtentwicklungsplanung, Stadt Köln, and Professor A. Cassone and Professor A. Tasgian of the Universita di Torino for their assistance with his chapter.

John Philpott would like to thank Simon Speller, Employment Co-ordinator, and his colleagues in the Development Group of Stevenage Borough Council for providing information for the research on which his chapter is based.

Michelle Lowe thanks Ron Martin and Chris Philo, who commented on an earlier draft of the chapter, together with all those mentioned in the text who helped with the research.

1

Government policy and industrial change: an overview

D.C. Gibbs

Introduction

Policy makers have come under increasing stress in recent years as the received wisdom upon which their policies were traditionally based has undergone substantial change. Thus the processes of deindustrialization, internationalization and technological change have largely broken down the long-standing relationship between new investment, output, and employment growth (Amin and Goddard 1986). In consequence, the traditional tools of policy-making, such as capital subsidies to attract mobile investment, are no longer adequate to counter widening regional disparities. The basic economic argument sustaining regional policy was that a balanced inter-regional distribution of resources would facilitate economic demand management. Uneven inter-regional development made it difficult to operate blanket macroeconomic policies, and hence regional policies made the Keynesian demand-management policies of the 1960s and 1970s more effective (Jones 1986). While this argument provided the consensus upon which many Western European governments based their spatial economic policies, in the United States governments have assigned a fairly low priority to the issue of assistance to specific geographical areas. Instead there has been a focus on designating 'growth centres' with associated investment in public works in order to attract further investment by the private sector (Rees and Weinstein 1983).

The justification for these types of spatial policies, reliant upon mobile investment, received severe blows from the economic crisis into which the world was plunged between 1973–1982. Perhaps the most appropriate framework within which to place these developments is the work of the French regulation school (Boyer and Mistral 1978; Boyer 1979; Aglietta 1979; Lipietz 1979) who have attempted to periodize capitalism in terms of interlocking 'regimes of accumulation' and 'modes of regulation'. It would appear that the capitalist system is emerging from this period of crisis by moving towards a new regime of capital accumulation, although this new regime of 'flexible accumulation' is at present only a tendency rather than a fully-implemented model of production and consumption. This new model is reliant upon the transformation of capital-labour relations, a new international and inter-regional division of labour, and a new role for the state and the public sector (Castells 1985). The consequence of these changes has taken a similar form with regard to spatial economic problems in many western developed nations, including economic decline in older industrial regions and cities, with particular concentrations of unemployment and decay in inner city areas. In turn, these problems are related to wider social and economic trends including the urban-rural shift, the growth of the service sector, and the decline of manufacturing (Hausner 1986). While the specific outcomes have been local, the broader scale forces have created pressures for whole economies to reshape themselves according to international conditions, particularly the increasing internationalization of both production and finance (Storper and Scott 1986). These external pressures on national economies have been instrumental in leading to changes in state economic policies, as the Keynesian regulatory apparatus came under increasing stress. Indeed, these processes were both a cause and a consequence of a resurgence in political conservatism which led to the election of a number of conservative governments throughout western nations, most notably the Reagan and Thatcher administrations.

The changing role of the state

The changing role of the state is perhaps typified by the monetarist governments elected in the UK and the USA in 1979 and 1980, respectively. The emergence of a new regime of economic accumulation has necessitated restructuring by states in order for this accumulation to proceed. At the national level, obviously states seek to reproduce in their depressed areas the positive growth factors associated with restructuring, which are present in more favoured regions. The US and UK governments have largely sought to achieve this by removing impediments to the workings of the free market. In the US, the Reagan administration initially sought substantial reductions in government and an emphasis on the free market to restore competitiveness. In terms of business-oriented policies this meant: cutting business taxes, lightening the burden of regulation, and encouraging freer trade (Quick 1984). Similar supply-side issues were paramount in the UK where slow job growth was attributed by government to a lack of flexibility, mobility, and adaptation to change in the labour market. Thus the UK government has attempted to improve the functioning and flexibility of the labour market by curbing what is seen as excessive wage growth and distorted pay relativities (Martin 1986). This has been attempted by a range of measures intended to encourage greater wage flexibility, including industrial relations legislation, weakening employment protection, and changes in the tax system, plus changes such as multi-skilling and new training schemes which undermine craft apprenticeships. Thus both administrations have responded to a transitional regime of accumulation by seeking to alter the mode of regulation (Lipietz 1986).

Both governments have sought to alter more than the quantitative factors influencing business health. Indeed, Reagan and Thatcher have declared aims of breaking the cycle of negative expectations, renewing national optimism and confidence, and creating a 'general climate' which is conducive to efficient and competitive production. However, macroeconomic policies pursued by both governments have tended to hinder rather than aid recovery, at least in the short term. In the US a rise in real interest rates led to an increase in the cost of capital which discouraged production and consumption of consumer durables and capital goods. Thus the rising value of the dollar in the period 1981–82 put US manufacturers at a sharp disadvantage, which was compounded by world-wide recession. The 'Triple Squeeze' of recession, high interest rates, and deregulation led to significantly reduced profitability, outright losses, worker layoffs and company failures (Quick 1984). In the UK public expenditure (on certain social programmes) was sharply reduced. A tight monetary policy was introduced which led to high interest rates, an adverse exchange rate and consequent large-scale job losses in manufacturing, and a dampened pace of recovery in the depressed periphery.

While the declared aim of governments has been non-intervention, in reality intervention has been restructured to take new forms. Thus withdrawal from social provision (particularly in urban programmes and community services) by the US government has been accompanied by increased intervention through defence procurement policies. A similar shift in resource allocation has occurred, albeit to a more limited extent, in the UK (Breheny *et al.* 1985). Investment in defence has mitigated the short-term costs of both governments' macroeconomic policies, particularly through the boost it has given to high technology sectors. Indeed, several authors point to the role of defence spending as being the core of high tech development in the US (Castells 1985; Markusen, Hall, and Glasmeier 1986; O'hUallachain 1987). Moreover, these declaredly aspatial policies have had a considerable impact upon spatial structures (Malecki 1987). The high level of spending on defence, coupled with the dismantlement of the welfare state, is directly associated with the decline of inner cities and growth in new regions, particularly suburban locations in small and medium sized cities in California, Texas, and some of the New England states (Glickman 1983; O'hUallachain 1987). Similarly, it has been argued that the development of much high technology industry in the southern half of England is predicated upon government demand for military hardware (Breheny *et al.* 1985; Lovering 1985; Lovering and Boddy 1988).

The geography of 'recovery' from recession has been spatially uneven, therefore, with certain regions and areas benefitting while depressed areas have lost out. If anything macroeconomic policy has increased and heightened existing spatial disparities within countries. At the same time there has been a review of the effectiveness of traditional spatial policies including the role of regional policy, the relationship between regional and urban economic development, and the development of new policy areas. Several of these are common to both the US and UK (Hausner 1986; Marshall and Bachtler 1987).

The demise of regional policy

Despite a degree of commonality, one policy area specific to western European countries is regional policy. Indeed, regional policy formed the mainstay of UK industrial policy up to the election of the first Thatcher government in 1979. A reduction in areal coverage in 1979 was followed by moves away from automatic schemes of assistance (Regional Development Grants (RDG)) towards selective assistance in 1984. This was intended to ensure 'value for money' whereby it was thought that many projects would have gone ahead without assistance and, by politicians, that 'objectively' regional policy did not work. Reductions in assistance were also part of the government's attempt to reduce both public expenditure and the role of the state in industrial decision making. The 1984 policy changes also made services eligible for assistance. In part these changes involved recognition that manufacturing industry's record of job creation was worsening and that jobs were more likely to be found in this sector (Marshall 1985). Indeed, grant aid was linked to job creation for the first time rather than to capital investment. A more far-reaching change was the redefinition of regional policy as social policy, rather than an economic measure which complemented macro-economic policies. Regional subsidies were seen by the UK government as simply an alternative (and a less acceptable one) to the freer operation of the market (Jones 1986). The retention of regional policy was attributed to political expendiency and to the fact that designated status was a prerequisite qualification to receive European Regional Development Fund (ERDF) assistance.

Further changes in regional policy came about early in 1988 (DTI 1988). The White Paper abolished automatic grants totally and made all assistance available only on a selective basis. Explicit technology policy was also downgraded from government policy to government procurement. The whole tenor of policy has changed. The basis for this legislation was that 'sensible economic decisions are best taken by those competing in the market place. The responsibility of government is to create the right climate so that markets work better and to encourage enterprise' (DTI, 1988 iii). Criticisms of the increased emphasis on selective assistance had come even before these changes. These stressed the unpredictable nature of selective aid, the greater complication involved for applicants, and the necessity of a more decentralized and responsive delivery system than has existed to date (Pettigrew and Dann 1986; Begg and McDowall 1987). The gradual withdrawal of central government from regional assistance, coupled with rising unemployment and economic decline, led many local authorities in the UK to become increasingly involved in economic policy making. This not only gave rise to several new policy initiatives, but also created central-local tensions, particularly as a reflection of the different political composition of central and local government.

The rise and fall of local authority policy making

Despite an earlier history of involvement in economic policy making (Mills and Young 1986), local authorities in the UK played little part in post-Second World War industrial development up until the early 1970s. The general consensus was that regional disparities were the province of central government, the local authority's role was the efficient provision of services. With rising unemployment and economic decline, local authorities began to take a more active interest in the economic fate of their areas. Much of the early response was, and still is in some areas, of a certain kind; local authorities engage in promotion, land assembly, site provision, information dissemination, etc. To several radical local authorities elected in 1981, subsidizing private capital appeared to be only a partial approach in that it retained control with those whose sole consideration may be profit accumulation, and whose interests in the local area may prove negligible. Inevitably, therefore, urban local governments sought out various alternative approaches to industrial ownership such as community and co-operative enterprise (Lawless 1986). These 'interventionist' local authorities recognized that, given their limited resources and the context of the national and international economy, they could have only a marginal impact upon the problems facing their areas. However, their involvement in policy making is intended to show that it is possible to develop cost effective initiatives at the local level (see, for example, Campbell *et al.* 1987). These also have an exemplary purpose to suggest that similar policies at the national level, allied to different macroeconomic policies, can offer a solution to economic decline (Mawson and Miller 1986). Local authority involvement was based partly on enabling legislation, such as the Urban Programme of the late 1970s, but increasing involvement can also be seen as a product of central government's abnegation of its responsibility for regional and local development. Thus as regional policy aid was reduced, local authorities' economic development policies stepped in to take their place.

Not surprisingly, perhaps, local authority involvement in economic policy making led to reaction from central government. Not only has central government attempted to negate some of what it sees as the wilder excesses of local authority policy, but also it has introduced new policy instruments in order both to outflank and reduce the significance of local authorities. Indeed, it has been argued that many of the more innovatory ideas in policy making in recent years have arisen from this tension between central and local authorities (Lawless 1986). Local authorities have expanded the range of economic activities in which they engage. There has been a movement away from promoting locational advantages and site/premises provision. These 'property-led' activities, a natural development from an authority's planning function, still form the mainstay of most local administrations. The growth areas, however, have been in financial assistance to firms, the provision of direct or indirect subsidies, and 'community economic development' (Mills and Young 1986). The more radical local authorities start from the assumption that the economic domain is not simply about job creation and investment, but also involves questions about the quality of work, industrial democracy, access to opportunities, the distribution of incomes and, ultimately, living standards (Mawson and Miller 1986). In order to achieve these social and economic aims, interventionist authorities developed a series of initiatives explicitly targeted at particular types of firm and groups within the labour market, such as co-operatives and community businesses (Whyatt 1983).

The expansion of local authorities' activities in this manner led to tension with central government. Central government and the private sector argue that extensive activity in economic planning is expensive, can in any case be undertaken by the private sector and is being attempted by local authorities inexperienced in the necessary financial and investment skills. 'Inevitably, therefore, central government has resisted any expansion of powers and finance available to local authority economic and employment planning. Indeed it has largely curtailed existing powers' (Lawless 1986: 213). In particular the abolition in 1986 of the Metropolitan counties, which were at the forefront of many of these radical initiatives, reflected central government's determination to impose its own version of economic development at the local level. Despite a valiant rearguard action by some local authorities, local authority policy-making has gone into decline. This lack of confidence in the ability of local government to tackle the complex problems of urban renewal and economic decline is reflected in the manner in which attempts have been made to regulate the activities of Partnership and Programme authorities and the decision to establish Urban Development Corporations (UDCs). The UDCs (established under the Local Government, Planning and Land Act (1980)) resemble the earlier New Town Corporations in their powers, but are 'consciously slimline organizations' (Morison 1987). They are accountable not to the local community, but directly to the Secretary of State and through that office to Parliament. UDCs thus represent in acute form the problem of the relationship between central and local government.

Indeed, UDCs represent one of the most interventionist policy initiatives since the mid-1970s. Somewhat perversely, the policy was introduced by one of the most avowedly anti-interventionist UK governments for many years. This apparent anomaly can, to some extent, be explained by seeing this as part of the restructuring of public expenditure by the state to assist transition to a new regime of accumulation by establishing a new regulatory framework. Indeed, UDCs are intended to act as catalysts, stimulating the attraction of private investment. This emphasis on private investment by central government, compared with the prominence given to the public sector as a motive force by local authorities, lies at the heart of much central-local tension (Hausner 1986). This raises the issue of how central-local relations are perceived. One view is that increasing control from the centre represents attempts to realign social relations in order that accumulation can continue (Duncan and Goodwin 1982). However, even this view allows little discretion on the part of local authorities and does not reflect the complexity of relations in government (Rhodes 1980). Saunders (1981) argues that the tension has come about through local government intruding upon areas that central government sees as its prerogative – economic and employment planning.

The European community and policy making

At the same time as national government in the UK has been under attack from below, as local authorities attempted to extend their powers, the emergence of European-level policy making has come as a challenge to national initiatives in all EEC member countries. Indeed, the European Commission has argued that regional assistance by member states distorts competition (Marshall and Bachtler 1987). Arguments for a Community industrial policy propound that it is easier for the EC as a whole to decrease external vulnerability than for each of the member countries. Thus firms may have a greater chance to become competitive at the international level if offered a significant share of the EEC market. Moreover, national policies are seen as a threat to the continued existence and eventual political integration of the Community (Lesourne 1984). The focus of EC policy making has been integration of the domestic market, the promotion of industrial investment and the development of high technology activities (Wilkinson 1984). Indeed, these are interrelated in that it is argued that only the creation of Community scale markets can support the leading edge and economies of scale that producers in high technology industries need. Market fragmentation leaves the way open for American and Japanese-based firms to dominate high technology markets (English 1984). However, there is evidence that in certain markets, such as Application Specific Integrated Circuits (ASICs), European producers are unable to compete in either the commodity, or the specialist markets (Dodsworth and Kehoe 1988). The Commission has also pioneered the concept of an indigenous development policy for the less favoured regions

(LFRs), with an early focus on small and medium sized firms (SMEs).

New policy forms

The period of the late 1970s and early 1980s therefore saw recession and the apparent emergence of a new phase of capital accumulation. The response of central government has been based upon the need for capital accumulation to continue although, following Lipietz (1986), it is obviously too simplistic to view this as an inevitable process of 'cause-and-effect'. This period certainly did involve administrations at all spatial scales in a rethink of their policy options. The limited amount of mobile industry available, the trend towards jobless or jobloss growth in manufacturing industry, and rising unemployment meant that concern was directed towards new areas of potential job growth. Four particular areas at the 'leading edge' of policy change have been the impact of new technology, small firms, the service sector, and the increase of private sector-led initiatives at the local level.

The restructuring of western economies as they have emerged from recession has been clearly associated with technological change as a means of increasing productivity, improving competitiveness, and reducing costs. Technology policy, though, has rarely been closely associated with spatial policy and has, in consequence, frequently had the effect of increasing spatial inequalities. In the USA, these unequal spatial effects have come about through the operation of government policy which is neither technologically nor regionally oriented. Thus increased spending on defence equipment and R. & D. in the USA led to indirect support for high technology industry as a consequence of decisions to increase military capabilities through modernization and improved equipment rather than by increased numbers of military personnel (O'hUallachain 1987). Indeed, it can be argued that the sectoral and geographical distribution of defence contracts within the USA form implicit industrial and regional policies (Melman 1986). This shift in favour of technological improvement has had a profound effect on the economic health of many US regions, especially 'high tech' growth in California, Texas, and some of the New England states. Conversely, it can be argued that traditional industries, like iron and steel, automobiles and machine tools have undergone reduced competitiveness through the increased concentration upon military capital formation (Melman 1986), although Rees and Weinstein (1983) point to the importance of the mid-

Western manufacturing belt as an important location for subcontract defence work.

In the UK a similar increase in defence expenditure also formed the basis for support of much high technology industry (Short 1981; Breheny *et al.* 1985). As Marshall and Bachtler (1987:474) state: 'the problem is that in countries such as the UK there is little spatial dimension in science and technology policy and no technological content to regional policy, so contradictions can arise between national policy and regional policy'. Thus national policies associated with technology increase spatial disparities, while spatial policy concentrates on limited job-related support for indigenous industry, particularly for small firms (DTI 1988).

Indeed, small firm policy forms much of the basis for recent change in the UK's industrial policy. Thus new grants have been introduced for small firms located in the Assisted Areas related to investment and product and process innovation (Duffy 1988). Assistance is also available to small and medium sized firms (SMEs) (under 500 employees) for consultancy services. The new emphasis in UK regional policy is therefore to encourage the expansion of small and medium sized companies, but at the same time to maintain selective assistance to attract large scale investment. It could be argued that aid in the UK has become polarized with a potentially large amount of assistance available for inward investment and special incentives for small firms. Indigenous UK-based firms in the peripheral regions are to be left to their own (and the market's) devices.

New policy initiatives also have grown up around the service sector. The interest in service policies is akin to that in small firms. Both seem to offer job provision at a time of 'jobless' or 'jobloss' growth in manufacturing industry. Moreover, they involve relatively little capital investment and therefore seem to provide low cost job creation which is obviously attractive to governments which are reducing levels of industrial support (Marshall 1985). Thus in West Germany, attempts have been made to encourage the creation of high grade technical and research jobs in assisted areas by providing an additional grant per job to manufacturing projects (Marshall and Bachtler 1987). In the UK, services became eligible for RDG in 1984, while regional policy changes in 1988 provided an indirect boost for services in its emphasis on support for consultancy (DTI 1983, 1988).

Finally, at the local level in the UK there has been a growth of private sector-led involvement in economic development. At its most extreme this can be seen in the form of UDCs, which circumvent local authority participation. Thus in certain cases, for example the imposition of UDCs in central Manchester and the Lower Don Valley, Sheffield, the initiative has been taken away from the local authority, even where the authority was already working closely with the private sector (*Financial Times*, 8 March 1988). Grant aid has been provided direct to developers, rather than through the local administration. It is possible to envisage a situation whereby local authorities and central government departments will only be able to participate in economic development projects in conjunction with private capital, and with private sector finance firmly in the driving seat.

The contributions of this volume address some of the issues raised in this brief survey of recent changes in the policy climate. In particular they address three broad themes; technological change, economic restructuring, and policy initiatives at the local level.

Technological change

Chapters 2 and 3 deal directly with the implications of technology policy. In particular both Williams, and Howells and Charles are concerned with the impact of technology policy at the European level. In Chapter 2 Howells and Charles outline how research and technological development (RTD) policies have been implemented at a regional level throughout Europe. They identify three basic types of policy; RTD policies with a regional dimension, regional policies with an RTD dimension and, lastly, RTD initiatives developed at the local level. They argue that RTD policies developed with a specific regional dimension (whether nationally or locally derived) are limited in extent, and that a more pro-active approach should be taken. Conversely, Williams in Chapter 3, dealing specifically with Information Technology (IT), argues that the nature of the policy-making process within Europe, plus the structural changes which surround IT have led national governments, and the EC, to develop naive policy initiatives which address problems of diminishing significance. In particular he makes the important point that rapid technological change and short product life cycles have downgraded national markets as the point of leverage for IT policy. In addition, strategic alliances by firms to respond on a Europe-wide scale and change in the nature of inter-firm linkages lead to complex questions concerning the location and nature of control within industry, which it is difficult for national administrations to address.

While Howells and Charles have, perhaps, a more optimistic

viewpoint of the potential for intervention, they point to four major problems with any policy designed to develop an RTD base in peripheral, disadvantaged regions. These are: problems arising from the extent of inward investment and external control in these regions, technological leakage, technological mismatch and, lastly, problems with small and medium sized firms. For the last they point out that supporting mechanisms other than those for technology may be needed, for example in sales and marketing (a point reiterated by Hitchens and O'Farrell in Chapter 8). In part these problems arise because of a point which Williams identifies, the conflicting nature of policy sets (for example, technology policy versus competition policy) and between policy initiatives and the behaviour of corporate actors. Indeed, Williams concludes that one of the major failings of policy responses is that they have addressed the issue of technology in isolation from the broader social and economic restructuring which have accompanied technological change.

Economic restructuring

This section contains a number of chapters which deal specifically with various aspects of the restructuring process. Moriarty and Moriarty, in Chapter 4, are concerned with the broad scale economic and social restructuring of US industry that has occurred in recent years. In particular they consider industrial decentralization in the US to be an on-going process in which factors like technological change, factor costs and corporate reorganization are related to, and influenced by, changing economic conditions and government policy. They state that US government policy has had an important indirect effect on decentralization from central cities and the manufacturing belt. Thus Federal policy in the 1970s created the infrastructure making decentralization possible. State government policies from the late 1970s took up the initiative when Federal policy was cut back by designating certain settlements to receive public service infrastructure in a form of 'growth pole strategy'.

Stafford, in Chapter 5, is also concerned with the consequences of restructuring and decentralization in the US economy, but from the point of view of those areas suffering employment decline. Thus he deals with the potential for policy measures to mitigate the impact of restructuring upon particular localities. Stafford investigates the call for plant closing legislation at both State and Federal levels as one means of providing a more orderly solution to firm movement and closure. However, while over half the

States have considered some form of legislation, only a very few States have passed even mild laws. Attempts to introduce Federal legislation in 1985 also failed. Stafford notes that while the reasons for failure were, in part, a product of the pervasive US belief in free enterprise and distrust of government regulation, there are important geographical differences. Thus no state in the 'Sunbelt' (except California) has passed legislation and party defections over the proposed 1985 Federal bill occurred on spatial lines. Thus defecting Democrats (voting against the bill) were predominantly from the South, while defecting Republicans (voting for the bill) were mainly from the North-east or Mid-West, where large numbers of closures and permanent layoffs have generated support for such laws. Those voting for such legislation argue that their main concern is over the local effects of 'capital flight'. Conversely, those against such legislation believe that regulation will reduce potential benefits to the economy as a whole. This is an area which has received more attention in the USA than in the UK and is one which warrants further attention.

Indeed, this raises the question of the extent to which governments should act to prevent industrial decline as a consequence of international competition and changing economic circumstances, or whether industries and areas should face the consequences of market forces. Harrison in Chapter 6 takes up this theme in relation to the shipbuilding industry in Northern Ireland. He argues that the reaction of the industry to changing conditions of international competition and the progressive involvement of government provides a case study of the development and delivery of industrial policy for declining industries. While significant employment and financial losses in the industry over a long period of time make it difficult to see a prima-facie case for continued aid, Harrison points to two factors that have general application in relation to industries in decline. First, social justice considerations that generate initial 'temporary' support for an industry may become permanent through astute lobbying by outside interests. In time, this may inhibit adjustment and prevent the efficient allocation of resources in the long run. Second, economic justification may be supplemented or supplanted by politico-social pressures for continued support. In the case of Harland and Wolff this became manifest through the symbolic importance of the firm as an indicator of government support for the Unionist population of Northern Ireland. However, Harrison points out that similar politico-social pressures are likely to govern the delivery of support for declining industries elsewhere, albeit in a different form.

Finally, in this section, two chapters look at the potential for assistance in two sectors which have received increasing attention from policymakers: small firms and the service sector. In Chapter 7 Bachtler and Davies look at the challenges faced by policy makers from the growth of services. They outline the ways in which services in the UK have been affected indirectly by government policy, while not subject to direct policy initiatives until recently. Although support is now available directly to the service sector, Bachtler and Davies see little evidence of co-ordinated service-oriented thinking either in the Conservative government or the opposition parties. They argue that this is due to a number of factors including a lack of information and understanding about the sector, the limited political momentum for intervention, and the lack of a national industrial policy more generally in the UK. Hitchens and O'Farrell, in Chapter 8, look at the small firm sector which has been the object of government policy in recent years, and which now forms one of the main thrusts of the Conservative government's 'enterprise culture'. Their aim is to identify regional factors inhibiting small firm growth and recommend policy initiatives. By comparing 'matched pairs' of firms in South Wales and Northern Ireland, they present evidence to suggest that inadequate design, poor quality, and lack of price competitiveness are major factors constraining the growth and threatening the survival of many small firms. Past policy has assumed that these issues are unproblematic for the small firm. This has led to the provision of grant schemes which, in the case of small firms in Northern Ireland, may have led to the introduction of technologically advanced plant and equipment but without leading to an improvement in economic performance. Hitchens and O'Farrell suggest that policy makers should provide advice on the mix of machinery and skills, increase awareness of design and quality, and help to improve quality standards. The White Paper of 1988 (DTI 1988) emphasized the need for consultancy assistance to small firms and as such is in line with some of Hitchens and O'Farrell's suggestions. However, at the same time the UK government has acted to curb intervention by local administrations which, it could be argued, are best placed to deal with small firm initiatives which need local knowledge. The next section of the volume deals with this issue of local policy initiatives.

Local policy initiatives

Lever, in Chapter 9, is concerned with the emergence of economic regeneration policies for large cities, based on a comparison of Glasgow, Turin and Cologne. In each case he looks at government intervention at the local scale by national, regional, and local administrations. Lever observes that in each city, a different level of government dominates policy making. Thus in Turin, national policies and processes have had the greatest impact, while in Cologne the city government appears as the strongest force. Finally, on Clydeside, the Scottish Development Agency operating at the regional scale has come to dominate. This powerful agency, developed on what is effectively a national scale, has led to a much less important role for local authorities in Scotland. This contrasts strongly with the rest of Britain, where the withdrawal by central government from regional assistance has led many local authorities to become much more involved with economic development measures. In Chapter 10 Sellgren outlines the range of powers and activities available to, and undertaken by, local authorities, as well as providing a summary analysis of local economic initiatives from survey material. Following Young (1985) he provides support for the concepts of 'rippling out', 'filtering down', and 'diversification'. These refer to the shift in activity from older conurbations to non-urban areas, the growing involvement of minor authorities, and the widening range of activities, respectively. In addition he identifies a fourth concept, that of 'collaboration', whereby local authorities work with other agencies to engage in economic development.

Philpott, in Chapter 11, deals with the issue of 'imbalanced development' in Stevenage New Town in terms of industrial sector, as well as size and corporate structure. He makes the point that this was a consequence of policy conflicts between national policies of industrial dispersion and the aims of the New Town Development Corporation, together with local problems of physical land policy. Philpott also makes clear the link between the New Town Development Corporations (DCs) as a means of economic development and the more recent policy initiative of Urban Development Corporations (UDCs) in the UK. However, while New Town DCs were an adjunct of planning, UDCs are intended to act as a means to override planning constraints and underpin the market. Philpott points out that while the attractiveness of UDCs lies in their ability to avoid interference from local authorities, this is the very feature that may prove least conducive to successful economic management. This is because it allows the short-term interests of both the public and private sectors to prevail over the longer term needs of both the local economy and community. Finally, he outlines two issues from the Stevenage example which may have future relevance for those local authorities which eventually 'take over' from the UDCs. First, local administrators may possess little experience of economic development after several years in the shadow of a Development Corporation. Second, this may be offset by the strength of 'localism' in an area engendered by links forged between the local authority, industrialists, trades unions, and community groups. Lowe, in the final chapter, takes up this issue of localism in relation to the development of worker co-operatives as an alternative local authority initiative by examining policies in Birmingham, Cambridge, and Leicestershire. She relates the growth of localism as a factor in several ways. Thus 'enterprise localism' refers to the climate of self-help engendered by the Conservative government since 1979, associated with the decline of regional aid measures. Conversely, local authorities have also taken 'localist' stances in response to this abnegation of responsibility by central government and the failure of past policies. Lowe documents local government policies concerning co-operatives as part of the new localist ideals and shows how differing political ideologies and local conditions affect an area's localist stance.

Policy questions

Whilst it is not the intention of this volume to provide a comprehensive analysis of policy options, the issues outlined at the start of this chapter and the work of the various authors raise a number of important policy issues. In particular:

– the switch towards assisting small firms, the service sector, and innovation by firms in the UK may require a more decentralized method of providing assistance (Armstrong 1986). While the UK government's intention is to go some way towards this, by expanding the number of regional DTI offices and through 'enterprise counsellors' linked to consultancy schemes, there must be some doubt as to the ability of delivery systems to function adequately. In addition, firm turnover will be a key issue and even a more widespread local office network will face this problem.

– following on from this, the irony is that in the UK the initiatives of those actors most likely to have a detailed knowledge of local needs have been downplayed or actively discouraged. Thus local authorities have been prevented or discouraged from taking a more active role in economic development and have been replaced, to some extent and in some areas, by non-accountable, centrally controlled initiatives such as UDCs. There must be some doubt whether development through these schemes is in the best interests of the local community and whether, contrary to declared intentions, it establishes a new form of dependency.

– the failure adequately to integrate national and regional policy can lead to contrasting effects. Thus, while local and regional policies seek to ameliorate the impact of broader scale restructuring, national policy can build up spatial inequalities for the future. This is particularly true of aspatial technology-related policies and central government policies in seemingly unrelated areas, such as defence expenditure in the USA.

– how can developments at the international scale be made compatible with national level initiatives? For example, within the European Community firms need to operate on the scale of the EC wide market in order to be competitive with Japanese and US companies, particularly in the fields of high technology. If related restructuring of companies occurs across Europe, then it seems inevitable that some countries (and some regions) will lose out in terms of investment. How can the EC market overcome problems of fragmentation yet at the same time work towards regional equity?

There can be little doubt that the present time is one of transition towards new forms of capital accumulation and regulation. While the outcome is, as yet, unclear it is inevitable that new policy forms will continue to be developed at all spatial scales. This volume attempts to indicate some of the leading edge policy areas of the late 1980s, but can do no more than to point the way for further research.

References

Aglietta, M. (1979) *A Theory of Capitalist Regulation: The US Experience*, London: Verso.

Amin, A. and Goddard, J.B. (1986) *Technological Change, Industrial Restructuring and Regional Development*, London: Allen & Unwin.

Armstrong, H. (1986) 'The assignment of regional industrial policy powers', *Regional Studies* 20:258–261.

Begg, H. and McDowall, S. (1987) 'The effect of regional investment incentives on company decisions', *Regional Studies* 21:459–470.

Boyer, R. (1979) 'Wage formation in historical perspective: The French experience', *Cambridge Journal of Economics* 3:99–118.
Boyer, R. and Mistral, M. (1978) *Accumulation, Inflation et Crise*, Paris: Presses Universitaires de France.
Breheny, M., Cheshire, P. and Langridge, R. (1985) 'The anatomy of job creation? Industrial change in Britain's M4 corridor', In P. Hall and A. Markusen (Eds) *Silicon Landscapes*, London: Allen & Unwin.
Campbell, M., Hardy, M., Healey, N., Stead, R. and Sutherland, J. (1987) *Economic Sense: Local Jobs Plans*, Manchester: Centre for Local Economic Strategies.
Castells, M. (1985) 'High technology, economic restructuring, and the urban-rural regional process in the United States', In M. Castells (Ed.) *High Technology, Space and Society*, Beverly Hills: Sage.
Department of Trade and Industry (1983) *Regional Industrial Development*, Cmnd. 9111, London: HMSO.
(1988) *DTI – The Department for Enterprise*, Cmnd. 278, London: HMSO.
Dodsworth, T. and Kehoe, L. (1988) 'Leaping ahead on a surface of silicon', *Financial Times*, 26 January.
Duffy, H. (1988) 'Regional Development', Financial Times Survey, *Financial Times*, 28 January.
Duncan, S.S. and Goodwin, M. (1982) 'The local state and restructuring social relations: Theory and practice', *International Journal of Urban and Regional Research* 6:157–185.
English, M. (1984) 'The European information technology industry', In A. Jacquemin (Ed.) *European Industry: Public Policy and Corporate Strategy*, Oxford: Clarendon Press.
Glickman, N.J. (1983) Economic policy and the cities: In Search of Reagan's real urban policy, Paper presented to North American Meeting of the Regional Science Association, Chicago.
Hausner, V.A. (1986) *Critical Issues in Urban Economic Development, vol. I*, Oxford: Clarendon Press.
Jones, J. (1986) 'An examination of the thinking behind government regional policy in the UK since 1945', *Regional Studies* 20:261–266.
Lawless, P. (1986) *The Evolution of Spatial Policy: A Case Study of Inner Urban Policy in the United Kingdom, 1968–1981*, London: Pion.
Lesourne, J. (1984) 'The changing context of industrial policy: External and internal developments', In A. Jacquemin (Ed.) *European Industry: Public Policy and Corporate Strategy*, Oxford: Clarendon Press.
Lipietz, A. (1979) *Crise et Inflation: Pourquoi*? Paris: Maspero.
(1986) 'New tendencies in the international division of labour: Regimes of accumulation and modes of regulation', In A.J. Scott and M. Storper (Eds) *Production, Work, Territory: The Geographical Anatomy of Industrial Capitalism*, Boston, Mass: Allen & Unwin.
Lovering, J. (1985) 'Defence expenditure and the regions: The case of Bristol', *Built Environment* 11:193–206.

Lovering, J. and Boddy, M. (1988) 'The geography of military industry in Britain', *Area* 20(1):41–51.
Malecki, E.J. (1987) 'Regional development – regional policy', *Environment and Planning A* 19:849–851.
Markusen, A., Hall, P. and Glasmeier, A. (1986) *High Tech America: The What, How, Where and Why of the Sunrise Industries*, Boston, Mass: Allen & Unwin.
Marshall, J.N. (1985) 'Services and regional policy in Great Britain', *Area* 17(4):303–308.
Marshall, J.N. and Bachtler, J. (1987) 'Services and Regional Policy', *Regional Studies* 21:471–475.
Martin, R. (1986) 'In what sense a "jobs boom"? Employment recovery, government policy and the regions', *Regional Studies* 20:463–472.
Mawson, J. and Miller, D. (1986) 'Interventionist approaches in local employment and economic development: The experience of Labour local authorities', In V.A. Hausner (Ed.) *Critical Issues in Urban Economic Development, vol. I*, Oxford: Clarendon Press.
Melman, S. (1986) 'Swords into ploughshares', *Technology Review, January*, 63–71.
Mills, L. and Young, K. (1986) 'Local authorities and economic development: A preliminary analysis', In V.A. Hausner (Ed.) *Critical Issues in Urban Economic Development, vol. I*, Oxford: Clarendon Press.
Morison, H. (1987) *The Regeneration of Local Economies*, Oxford: Clarendon Press.
O'hUallachain, B. (1987) 'Regional and technological implications of the recent buildup in American defence spending', *Annals of the Association of American Geographers* 77:208–223.
Pettigrew, P. and Dann, S. (1986) 'Streamlining regional industrial aid?', *Regional Studies* 20:183–184.
Quick, P.D. (1984) 'Businesses: Reagan's industrial policy', In J.L. Palmer and I.V. Sawhill (Eds) *The Reagan Record: An Assessment of America's Changing Domestic Priorities*, Cambridge, Mass: Ballinger.
Rees, J. and Weinstein, B.L. (1983) 'Government policy and industrial location', In J.W. House (Ed.) *United States Public Policy: A Geographical View*, Oxford: Clarendon Press.
Rhodes, R.A.W. (1980) 'Some myths in central-local relations', *Town Planning Review* 51:270–285.
Saunders, P. (1981) 'Community power, urban regeneration and the "local state"', In M. Harloe (Ed.) *New Perspectives in Urban Change and Conflict*, London: Heinemann.
Short, J. (1981) 'Defence spending in the UK regions', *Regional Studies* 15:101–110.
Storper, M. and Scott, A.J. (1986) 'Production, work, territory: Contemporary realities and theoretical tasks', In A.J. Scott and M. Storper (Eds) *Production, Work, Territory: The Geographical Anatomy of Industrial Capitalism*, Boston, Mass: Allen & Unwin.

Whyatt, A. (1983) 'Developments in the structure and organisation of the co-operative movement: Some policy considerations', *Regional Studies* 17:273–276.

Wilkinson, C. (1984) 'Trends in industrial policy in the European Community: Theory and practice', In A. Jacquemin (Ed.) *European Industry: Public Policy and Corporate Strategy*, Oxford: Clarendon Press.

Young, K. (1985) 'Organising for economic development', *ESRC Inner Cities Research Programme, Strengthening Local Economic Development*, London: ESRC.

Technological change

2

Research and technological development and regional policy: a European perspective

J.R. Howells and D.R. Charles

Introduction

Although there is no simple association between research and technological development and economic expansion, economic growth cannot be completely explained unless some account is taken of research and technological innovation. Studies at both the macro and microeconomic level are increasingly confirming the link between research, science, and technology, and economic growth and performance. As a consequence, policy makers at both national and local levels have increasingly moved towards science and technology policies as a way of developing national and regional economic and employment growth. It is the development and implementation of these research and technological development strategies and policies at a regional level that will be examined here. It is not the intention of this chapter to describe or specifically explain the current inequalities in research and technological development in the UK or Europe, but instead it will focus on providing a policy context and platform for more proactive research and technology strategies for the regions. In particular we will consider the applicability of research and technology policies for regions, their replicability between regions, and the overall constraints and policy contexts that impinge on the formulation and development of regional research and technology policies.

Research and technological development and regions

When looking at Research and Technological Development (RTD) and the regions at a policy level there are a number of different ways in which policies and strategies associated with research and technology on one hand and regions on the other can impact on localities. As such there are three basic dimensions of the impact of policies associated with research and technological development at the regional level. They are RTD policies with a regional dimension; regional policies with an RTD dimension; and, finally, RTD initiatives developed and implemented by regional and local administrations. However, there are other dimensions or levels associated with this; policies can influence localities both directly (intentionally) and indirectly (unintentionally) and this is an important distinction to make. However, as noted in the introduction our primary focus will be on direct policy action and its effects rather than the (considerable) indirect policy effects on RTD and regional development. Moreover, in relation to the European Community not only do we have local, regional, and national policy levels, but also a supra-national level associated with the policies and strategies of the European Commission. Therefore the policy context associated with RTD and regional policy is extremely complex within Europe and can be viewed from a number of different perspectives. The key dimensions to these policies will now be considered in turn.

Research and technological development policies with a regional dimension

In relation to RTD policies with a direct regional dimension in Europe, we are essentially discussing national RTD policies, as there are no Community RTD programmes, as yet, with a specific regional dimension, whilst RTD policies established by regional or local administrations are separately considered later.

The range between different European countries in terms of the size and extent of a regional element to a national RTD policy is immense. At one extreme there is France which has a relatively long-established and particularly comprehensive set of regionalized RTD policies (OECD 1986). The key steps involved were the establishment of Regional Science and Technology Information Centres (ARIST) in 1972, the regionalization of the National Agency for the Valorization of Research (ANVAR) in 1979, and the formation of Regional Centres for Innovation and Technology Transfer (CRITT) in 1983. At the other extreme is the UK which has little or no acknowledgement of the regional dimension in its RTD policies and associated with this (or perhaps rather as a result of this) has a marked core region concentration in most of the innovation policies it has set up (Howells and Charles 1987).

Within these two extremes there are countries like the Netherlands and Germany, which generally have detailed and sympathetic regionalization of their RTD programmes, whilst other countries, such as Portugal and Spain, have only just begun to develop regionalized strategies for their RTD programmes.

It is not possible here to go into details of the various regionalized RTD policies within the member states of the Community. Nevertheless a number of key issues are worth noting. First, it should be recognized that there are various levels or types of regionalization of RTD policy, depending on the degree of autonomy given to regional administrations (Benghozi and Matheu 1982). Thus 'regionalization' can on one hand mean that the national government still has full control over RTD policy, whilst on the other the regions can acquire full autonomy over the 'national' RTD programmes. These differences can have a marked effect on how RTD policies are regionalized and the consequent impact on the region. Second, there are a number of regionalized RTD policies throughout the Community which represent little more than token decentralization. These schemes are more likely to be those where national government still has full control. Third, it must be emphasized that there is a marked difference, particularly in the less favoured regions, between those RTD programmes which allow for regionalization, but which remain passive, demand-responsive programmes and those RTD programmes which have a strong proactive regionalization strategy. If 'regionalized' RTD programmes are actually going to have much impact on the less favoured regions they have actively to stimulate interest and the take-up of RTD schemes, because industry in such areas, almost by definition, does not see the need for research and technological development. Fourth, it should be recognized that regionalization of RTD policies does tend to increase the complexity of the whole RTD programme. This then creates problems in terms of discouraging potential participants in such schemes, particularly firms in the less favoured regions (LFRs) and small and medium sized enterprises (SMEs). It also, in some cases, produces conflicts of responsibilities between different organizations and agencies responsible for operating RTD schemes in the regions. Finally, it should be recognized that regionalized RTD programmes are becoming more common in the European Community, even if they do offer only a partial acknowledgement to the regional situation.

It has already been noted that the indirect effects of RTD policies (and indeed other sectoral and defence related policies) on the regions can be substantial and that they have been shown to favour the core regions of the Community, as has been indicated in the UK (Howells and Charles 1987). However, even in the assisted areas the economic benefits accruing to a particular locality as a result of firms, higher education institutes (HEIs) or other institutions participating in RTD programmes (such as the UK Alvey Programme) can be substantial. This is also true for Community RTD policies, such as ESPRIT (European Strategic Programme for Research and Development in Information Technology) or BRITE (Basic Research in Industrial Technologies for Europe), which although aimed at long-term strategic research, again can have important economic and employment implications for participant establishments located in less favoured regions.

Regional policies with an RTD dimension

In respect of regional policies with an RTD dimension this does involve both the Community and national policy context. Thus, although the support of technological objectives remains the prime responsibility of the Science, Research, and Development Directorate (DG XII) and the Telecommunications, Information Industries, and Innovation Directorate (DG XIII), there has been some involvement of the Regional Policy Directorate (DG XVI) in recent years where infrastructural requirements in less favoured regions have included technology related investments. This has, however, been primarily a responsive situation rather than a proactive policy and, as a result, these initiatives are more reflective of the perceived local requirements for technology, rather than the strategic technologies identified by the Framework Programme.[1] Thus, as particular regional and national authorities have identified the need for an RTD-related investment as being of importance to the structural development of an LFR, they have applied for and received European Regional Development Fund (ERDF) support for that objective.

Specific examples can be drawn, particularly from Greece and Italy, where funding has been given to regional research centres in selected high technology fields. As befitting the infrastructure orientation of the fund, expenditure has been predominantly for buildings and equipment, although this has then assisted certain facilities in achieving the technological capability to carry out European co-operative research under ESPRIT, for example. The Research Centre of Crete has had considerable success in this respect (Research Centre of Crete 1986). In the Italian case the 'Cassa per il Mezzogiorno' received funds from ERDF to help finance eleven research centres in seven LFRs covering a range of technologies (see Table 2.1; Commission of the European Communities 1986a; 1986b). The three centres in Bari are intended to form part of a new scientific centre or technopolis with the long-term aim of generating indigenous development through new technologies.

Table 2.1 European Regional Development Fund supported research centres in the Mezzogiorno, Italy

Location	*Remit*
Caserta, Campania	Electronics and Domestic Electrical Appliances
Monte Sant'Angelo Campania	Genetic Engineering
Palermo, Sicilia	Solar Energy
Catania, Sicilia	Electronics
Cosenza, Calabria	Data Processing
Alghero, Sardinia	Agrometeorology
Bernalda, Basilicata	Agri-biological research
Lazio	Telecommunications and Electronics
Bari, Puglia	Laser Technologies
Bari, Puglia	Advanced Technologies and Applications
Bari, Puglia	Agricultural Product Processing

Source: Commission of the European Communities, 1986a, 1986b.

The Mediterranean Integrated Programmes (PIMs), set up to soften the impact of the third enlargement of the Community and composed of integrated regional development strategies for particular LFRs, also support technologically oriented schemes. Thus the PIM for Crete includes programmes supporting agricultural research, immunodiagnostics (biotechnology), fish cultivation, spectrography, medical research and energy research.

Turning to national regional policy initiatives, which have an RTD dimension, it is again important to distinguish between direct RTD policy elements in a wider regional development initiative, and those that represent an indirect outcome of regional policy. The former group would include specific policies and funds in Italy for developing RTD centres and projects in the Mezzogiorno which have been established since 1976. It would also cover the French government's financial incentives for research decentralization (*prime de localisation d'activités de recherche*) which provides a series of grants for setting-up, expanding, or transferring pure and applied research activities outside the Paris region (Hull, 1980). The grants vary according to the value of investment, the number of research jobs created, and location (for example certain towns, designated '*poles de recherche*', receive higher investment allowances). In indirect terms UK regional development grants have been shown to have had a favourable influence on the level of process innovations in the LFRs of the UK (Gibbs 1984; Howells; 1986a), in addition to direct support for R. & D. investment under the Office and Service Industries Scheme.

Overall, however, national regional policies which have a specific RTD component, appear not to have spread rapidly within the Community. Instead regionalization of RTD programmes and more fundamental shifts towards providing greater regional autonomy overall, as in Spain, appear to have been more common.

Regionally and locally based RTD initiatives

There has been a steadily growing number of regional and local government initiatives designed to stimulate RTD at the local level since the late 1970s and early 1980s. In some countries, such as the UK, this has been in response to the perceived inadequacies of nationally administered RTD and regional policy. In others, however, it has been associated with the view, perceived from all sides (national, regional, and local), that something should be done on a regional basis to stimulate RTD. Above all, however, the impetus has been to develop RTD strategies which are applicable to that particular locality and, as such, has been a response or reaction away from nationally oriented RTD schemes which were seen as having little relevance to particular localities.

There are some other general points which are worth making in relation to regional and local RTD initiatives. The first is that, as noted above, local/regional RTD initiatives are still in the early stages of development. In some senses particular RTD initiatives and instruments are undergoing a diffusion process themselves between countries and regions as local and regional authorities pick up ideas, experiment with them, and then discard them or, more rarely, apply them. As yet therefore the 'best' RTD mechanisms have yet to be filtered down to many regions and localities in the Community. Related to this point is that it is going to be an even longer process before there is some clear pattern in identifying those RTD mechanisms and instruments which are best for particular sets of less favoured regions. A top ten list of best RTD mechanisms and instruments taken from all types of regions may not necessarily be the best ones for LFRs and, in particular, those regions which have little or no RTD base. Indeed, some of the major thrusts in the development of RTD mechanisms have come from core regions which have been the first to develop or adopt such initiatives.

There are also quite noticeable differences between member states in RTD mechanisms and initiatives which are most frequently adopted. Thus, in the UK, science park initiatives have developed strongly compared with the establishment of publicly funded research and technology centres, as in, for example, Denmark. In part the growth of these particular schemes is a reflection of their initial success, particularly in a 'lead' example (for example, Cambridge Science Park in the UK), and is also a reflection of the ease with which they can develop within the national/regional/local institutional context. Thus, to some extent, those schemes which have spread most rapidly within particular countries have been the ones which have met least institutional resistance. Again, this is not to suggest they are the best schemes.

It should also be noted that most of these RTD schemes have, until very recently, grown up in a government/institutional environment which has not been geared to the particular policy requirements of many RTD initiatives. Thus a high proportion of schemes have been based and funded out of infrastructure programmes because regional policy both within the Community and individual member states is still largely geared towards such schemes. As such, projects associated with the development of special industrial estates, buildings or, to a lesser extent, capital equipment have been the ones which have been able to obtain funds most easily. This, again, has meant that particular schemes have prospered at the expense of others which are just as, or even more, applicable to the RTD requirements of LFRs.

The last issue here in relation to RTD initiatives and mechanisms is that of scale both in terms of overall size of the schemes and in terms of geographical context. Thus in countries which have (e.g. Germany) or are developing (for example, Spain) a clear regional government network the main focus of regional/local government initiatives has been at a regional level. This has resulted in RTD initiatives with a large aggregate funding basis because they have been viewed in a wider regional context. By contrast, in countries such as the UK, where clear autonomous regional bodies do not exist and RTD initiatives may be pursued at the local authority level, such RTD policies are framed within a context of much smaller aggregate budgets. They are, therefore, by their nature, small scale, pay little or no attention to schemes undertaken in other areas within regions (indeed adjacent local authorities are often highly competitive), and as a consequence on an aggregate regional scale are often inefficient and simply cannot encompass the one or two large scale RTD initiatives which might provide a useful framework for the region. However, this introduces the further problem that local or even regional agencies may pursue RTD initiatives which, viewed on their own in the context of the region or locality, are based on a correct judgement, but when viewed in a wider national or even Community context may not be sensible. Nevertheless, it should be acknowledged that regional/local schemes are more likely to be applicable and relevant to local industry than more broadly based and nationally oriented central government schemes.

Wider policy and strategy issues associated with the development of RTD in less favoured regions

Regional variations and flexibility

In developing an RTD policy for a less favoured region there are a number of important issues, realities, options, and constraints that have to be recognized. Perhaps the most important is that the nature and condition of peripheral, disadvantaged regions both within the UK and Europe are varied. This is most evident in the variable levels of research and development activity in LFRs. In many regions the key obstacle to the pursuit of an RTD policy is the small or non-existent science and technology base on which local innovative activity has to be built. However, while a low RTD base is a condition found generally within less favoured regions in Europe there are peripheral, disadvantaged regions, including some within the UK, which have high levels of RTD activity but low economic prosperity relative to the rest of the Community. This is in part due to (or reflected in) technology transfer to local industry remaining weak, associated with a mismatch between the technological capacity of local firms, and poorly developed technology transfer mechanisms.

Overall, therefore, it should be recognized that peripheral regions will in some instances have quite different problems in terms of research and technology and, as such, regional RTD strategies need to be differentiated to take account of these variations. For example, in some regions it will be more of a case of building up an RTD base in the locality, whilst in other regions the focus will need to be on creating the right technology transfer mechanisms between research and technology centres and local industry. As such, the overall policy framework will have to be flexible enough to cope with these variations in the RTD situation.

The following discussion highlights some of the other key issues associated with developing a research and technology base in peripheral, disadvantaged regions.

Regional technological development, inward investment and external control

One strategy for developing research and technological development in disadvantaged regions is via inward investment, particularly in terms of attracting high technology ventures. Clearly for LFRs which have little or no science or technology base this is an attractive proposition not only in terms of its immediate impact, via job creation and prestige, but also, and perhaps more particularly, because other options may be very long term in nature. A key issue here is whether LFRs adopting this strategy will be 'locked into' a system of technology dependency or imperialism which destroys what local indigenous technology base there is and in turn become increasingly dependent on large foreign multinational companies which have little commitment to the region, particularly in terms of investing in research and technological development (Firn 1975; Britton and Gilmour 1978).

The theme of technological dependency which arises with inward investment embraces a number of sub-issues. The first is whether externally-controlled branch plants of multi-plant companies actually integrate with their local economies, particularly in relation to technology. Another is the absorption or 'creaming off' by externally controlled high technology branch plants of scarce scientific, research and technical staff in the LFRs. This makes recruitment of such key personnel even harder for smaller indigenous-based companies. More fundamental, though less tangible, is the lack of indigenous ownership, control and key decision-making which is commonly linked to a high propensity to close rather than change product lines or make large commitments to new processes (Watts 1981). A key element of the lack of local decision making is the reliance upon external sources of RTD or technical effort usually from elsewhere within the corporation (Charles 1987; Howells 1984).

Inward investment may not only take the form of greenfield developments, but also the acquisition of indigenous companies. This may lead to 'technological leakage' and the transfer of control

Table 2.2 Takeovers of UK high technology firms by foreign companies

UK high technology firm	*Activity*	*Location*	*Foreign firm*
Columbia Automation	Automatic test equipment	Berkshire, South East	Zehntel
Precima	Automated assembly equipment	Essex, South East	Emhart
Applied Research of Cambridge	Computer aided design (CAD)	Cambridge, East Anglia	McDonnell Douglas
Hoskyns	Computer systems & consultancy	London, South East	Martin Marietta Data Systems
Shape Data	CAD	Cambridge, East Anglia	Evans and Sutherland
Acorn Computers	Computer manufacture	Cambridge, East Anglia	Olivetti
General Computer Systems	Computer maintenance	London, South East	Bell Canada
Immediate Business Systems	Computer manufacture	Buckinghamshire, South East	Allied Signal
Remek	Robotics/vision systems	Bedfordshire, South East	Asea
JK Lasers	Lasers	Warwickshire, East Midlands	Lumonics
Compeda	CAD marketing/ research	Cambridge, East Anglia	Prime Computers
Computer Interactive Systems	CAD	Cambridge, East Anglia	Computer-isation
Sevcon	Microprocessor controls	Tyne and Wear North	Tech Ops Inc.

Activity	Nationality	Other comments
Automatic test equipment	US	
Electronics & engineering	US	
Aerospace/ Computer systems	US	Sold by the UK Government in 1982
Aerospace/ Computer systems	US	
Computer simulation	US	Founders moved out and formed new company Three-Space
Electronic business systems	Italy	Acorn in severe financial difficulty before Olivetti takeover
Telecommunications	Canada	Company renamed – Bell Technical Services
Computer/ Communications	US	
Automation	Sweden	Remek acquired by VS Engineering which was then acquired by Asea
Lasers	Canada	
Computers	US	Founded in 1977 by UK Government's National Research Development Corporation (now part of British Technology Group)
CAD/CAM	US	Sold by UK Government in 1981
Electronics	US	Sevcon was a division of Joyce Loebl; the division was acquired by Vickers then sold off to Tech Ops

of high technology away from the locality. This is evident on a national scale, where, for example in the UK, there have been a number of foreign takeovers of new and small UK high technology firms (Table 2.2). These then become satellite units within large corporate complexes, and the results of the research and development originating from the unit may be applied and manufactured in establishments located in other regions or continents across the globe.

Finally, inward investment may have little impact on traditional indigenous firms in less favoured regions which assume a satellite or subordinate role either in relation to more dynamic firms located outside the region or to externally controlled plants within it. Such firms make no effort to initiate technical or product change and typically they have lost all initiative in product design and possess no R. & D. facilities (Freeman 1974; see also Britton and Gilmour 1978). In the following paragraphs we examine these contentions in greater detail.

One of the problems, in relation to technological innovation, for LFRs with a high degree of external control is that of the 'technological isolation' (or 'independence effect') of branch plants (Howells 1983). This phenomenon is associated with branch plants which are not dependent on their local environment for sources of technical information and services, or on their own unit-based resources, but rather are provided with resources and information via corporate contacts and linkages (Parker 1974). Thus McDermott (1979) in a study of Scottish electronics enterprises found over 80 per cent of the externally controlled enterprises surveyed were dependent on corporate technical support and direction (see also Lever 1974). As such, branch plants, in terms of research and technological innovation, can only be considered as intrinsic elements within largely integrated corporate RTD systems. The expectation that high technology branch plants will rapidly integrate with the local and regional economy in terms of input linkages is therefore misguided. This is particularly true of high technology operations where they are likely to have much more extensive linkage patterns than less technologically sophisticated, indigenous manufacturing establishments. This arises from two main factors (Howells 1984). First, most high technology inward investment relates to products with a high value to weight ratio in which transport costs are a small proportion of total costs; this makes the location decision free from the influence of the distribution of component suppliers or markets. This has been confirmed in a recent study in Ireland by O'Farrell and O'Loughlin (1981) which found that technological status was indeed an important determinant influencing the import ratio and, to a lesser extent, degree of integration into the local economy by plants located in Ireland. The second, more important, factor is that technologically sophisticated and high value-added production requires specialized materials with more exacting technical specifications. This restricts the number of potential suppliers and produces highly geographically specific linkage patterns for each product (Erickson 1975; McDermott 1976). Thus, for example, three-quarters of the bulk pharmaceutical chemicals produced in the United States were only individually available from a single company (US International Trade Commission 1977). On the basis of this more constrained pattern of potential suppliers, input linkages are therefore likely to be more wide-ranging, with contacts being made almost regardless of the distances involved, to key input suppliers in a number of regional or national economies.

These two factors associated with the highly integrated nature of multinational manufacturing operations, and the increasing tendency of multi-plant companies to internalize their linkage contacts, all lead to a low level of technical and economic integration with their local and regional economies.

Moreover, from their technical and financial power, based on their ability to use in-house resources of the world-scale operations of the multinational, such branch plants can then capture a significant share of a particular domestic, national, or regional market through the assistance of parent-developed products or technology (Science Council of Canada 1980). This leads not only to truncated subsidiaries, with little or no export prospects, but also inhibits the entry of indigenous firms into the market.

Nevertheless, an inward investment strategy does have certain benefits for LFRs seeking to develop their science and technology base, particularly on a short-term basis, but much will be dependent on the place of the establishment in the corporate strategy. For example, the branch plant may have a world product mandate for a particular product or group of products that the multinational company manufactures. Such a situation can bring a number of benefits (Science Council of Canada 1980) including export opportunities, greater autonomy for the local management, and more involvement in long-term policy strategies, rather than in simple day-to-day operational problems. Greater autonomy may allow the management of the branch plant or subsidiary to source a greater quantity of its components from local suppliers. On a technology front such plants are more likely to have R. & D. facilities attached to them and the establishment may be involved in further development, design, and engineering activities for the product(s) concerned (Charles 1987). Notwithstanding these possibilities, it is on balance more likely that such forms of operation as world product mandates will be introduced in the core regions first, as establishments there generally have higher organizational and technical status within the company.

There are also other more general advantages associated with high technology branch plants, whether they possess a world product mandate or not. The 'technological isolation' effect as we have shown does incur a number of disadvantages and problems but it also yields certain benefits. Branch plants, associated with high technology operations, are able to operate successfully in localities which have little or no basic technology infrastructure (including personnel, support services, components supplies and HEIs) for the very reason that they can and do use their own imported corporate research and technical resources. By contrast, potential indigenous operators would encounter considerable competitive disadvantages in such places without some kind of basic technology infrastructure. Moreover multinational operations do have a fairly uniform approach when it comes to the design of plants, the processes used within them, and the quality-control standards required throughout the manufacturing operations (Howells 1984). Thus an OECD study examining technology transfer by multinational companies abroad found that production techniques in the subsidiaries were, as a general rule, entirely comparable to those which would be used in the country of origin (Germidis 1977). On a regional level, a study of capital and process technology in pharmaceutical plants found variations in technical support and sophistication on an intra-plant basis, regardless of location, were kept at a minimum (Howells 1986a).

Given the right policy stimulus, therefore, large high technology corporations may be encouraged to give more autonomy to their branch plants to allow them, for example, to purchase more products and services locally which would help stimulate firms, particularly in high technology applications. Branch plants could also be involved in the exchange of key personnel to local SMEs or education institutes. Personnel from the branch establishments could also be encouraged to take a close involvement in the community and cultural activities of the local area. All these initiatives would do much to integrate such plants more fully into their local and regional economies (Thwaites 1978). Clearly Ireland, through the Industrial Development Authority (IDA), has reaped considerable national and regional benefits from its success in attracting high technology inward investment. This is particularly evident in the growth and export performance of high technology goods. Thus taking 1980, with a base of 100, the production index of pharmaceuticals in 1986 was 176.7, and for data processing machinery was 511.6; both were high technology sectors dominated by foreign companies. By contrast, domestically oriented industries have declined significantly (for example, textiles 82.6; clothing, footwear, and leather 84.2; Carnegy 1987).

In many ways the benefits of inward investment are more quantifiable and immediate than the longer term indigenous development path, especially in terms of possible employment increase. In the case of a high technology operation, many of these jobs may also be of a scientific or technical nature, substantially increasing the local labour market for skills and possibly retaining skilled staff within the region who might otherwise have migrated. Nevertheless, the apparent benefits can be illusory. Most of the jobs created by high technology branch plants, particularly the most highly skilled and qualified, are likely to go to people from outside the region (often a sizeable number are brought in from other plants owned by the corporation). Moreover the less quantifiable negative effects on the indigenous sector (such as 'creaming off' scarce local scientific and technical staff) may in the long term more than outweigh the initial benefits. In policy terms it is the net, long-term effects of high technology inward investment which should be considered.

It should also be noted that the high technology branch plants can also do much to enhance the prestige of a region and can help to alter the perceptions that outsiders may hold of a locality. Moreover the employees of the branch plant may enhance and develop the social, educational, and cultural infrastructure of a region through their consumption patterns and community participation. Finally, in relation to policy, an inward investment strategy may be a comparatively low-cost and cost-efficient (at least based on short-term criteria) method of developing a region's research and technology base.

The availability of high technology inward investment on an extra-(mainly from US and Japan) and intra-Community basis is always going to be very small relative to the requirements of the LFRs of Europe. As such only a few regions are going to gain any sizeable numbers of mobile high technology plants and few, if any, on a sufficient scale. At most there are only going to be a few 'winners' adopting such a strategy. Indeed, successful regions are likely to create a strong 'shadow effect' on LFRs surrounding them. Thus, on a somewhat different scale, Ireland's success in attracting high technology inward investment in pharmaceuticals has had a negative impact on the UK's record in attracting foreign investment in that sector (Howells 1984). Moreover, those regions likely to benefit most are firstly those, such as Ireland and Scotland, which were amongst the first to do so, and secondly, those LFRs which have a relatively large science and technology base. Few, if any, multinationals want to be the first high technology operations in a region which is a technology desert.

Finally, although potential benefits do exist, for example in terms of components supplied by local firms, many of these will not be realized unless a very strong proactive set of policies is implemented to integrate the externally controlled establishments into the local economy and to encourage technology transfer and spin-offs from the branch plants.

New firms and SMEs: opportunities for RTD in the regions

Consideration of the potential for RTD-based growth in the regions cannot ignore the role of importance of the SMEs. They form the main element of the indigenous base of LFRs and are the most integrated sector in such economies. There is still, however, a continuing debate over how successful and efficient SMEs are in terms of generating RTD, although recent evidence suggests that small firms and very large firms have the highest levels of innovative activity and this is increasing over time (with medium-sized firms being the poorest generators, Pavitt, Robson, and Townsend 1987).

However, although small firms may be successful in generating technological innovation there is still the question of whether they are best at commercially developing and exploiting the research and technical advances they produce. Moreover there are substantial variations in entry barriers between industries (even between quite closely related sectors such as biotechnology (low/medium) and pharmaceuticals (high), with SMEs playing much less significant roles, or being totally excluded in terms of innovation in certain industrial sectors (chemicals, aerospace and mining for example; see Dasgupta and Stiglitz 1980; Pavitt 1984; Pavitt *et al.* 1987).

It should be acknowledged therefore that there may be significant entry barriers for RTD in a number of sectors and this may have implications for regions specializing or wishing to specialize in those sectors. Following on from the above, it is important to recognize that although SMEs may be successful in RTD terms this may not necessarily be followed through in a commercial and economic growth sense. The limited financial backing and sales and marketing strength of a small company are therefore likely to strongly inhibit and retard the full commercial exploitation by SMEs of a technological development generated by such a company. In policy and strategy terms, therefore, it is important to develop and incorporate parallel supporting mechanisms (for example in sales and marketing) into a wider RTD strategy for the LFRs.

Attention on SMEs as a basis for an RTD strategy in the less favoured regions must acknowledge some basic characteristics and problems associated with new and small firms in terms of economic growth and development. A whole range of studies for example have noted the very high failure rates for new firms, whilst more recently in connection with small firms a study of new manufacturing firms (1965–1981) based in the Northern region of the UK has noted 'out of every 100 manufacturing businesses which begin, 30 cease to trade within 2–3 years. A further 30 cease to trade over the next 7–8 years so that after a decade only 40 businesses will survive. Of these 40 businesses, 4 will provide half the jobs' (Storey and Johnson 1987:34). An RTD strategy based on SMEs will therefore have to acknowledge that in any set of firms it helps, a high proportion of such firms will close; this is especially true in LFRs and more high risk ventures associated with technological innovation.

A key element to survival and further growth for new and small firms is overcoming 'thresholds to development' (Taylor 1975). Hence the development of an organization can be divided into several discrete stages reflecting internal changes. Thus Moore (1959) saw a business being set up by a 'promoter or activity generator', its continued expansion requiring the expertise of a 'businessman or consolidator' and its ultimate success depending upon the skills of a 'manager or administrator', with the overall development of business requiring a progressive delegation of responsibility. Several studies have confirmed the threshold or staged nature of organizational and firm development with a study of the UK iron foundry industry finding a district break in firm size between very small and medium/large sized firms (Taylor 1975). It has been suggested that this break or threshold to growth may in part be technologically based – associated with the inability of many small firms both to be able successfully to exploit technology (due to financial barriers, lack of technical expertise and so on) and to have access to sources of new technology.

With the increasing recognition of the problems of development of new and small firms, attention has become more focused on research associated with, and measures to help, the survival and continued development of SMEs rather than simply their creation in terms of new firm formation (Taylor 1975). In turn this has been related in the UK and Europe to concern about the quality rather than the quantity of small firms (Storey and Johnson 1987).

Lastly, in relation to SME development, is the issue of small–large firm relationships. Recent studies have stressed the large firm domination of new and small firms in terms of purchasing patterns and to a lesser extent supplier relationships (Lloyd and Mason 1984). SMEs, therefore, cannot be viewed in isolation, but rather must be seen in the context of the operation of, and linkages between, large corporations. Thus, evidence that is available suggests that small firms act mainly as subcontractors and suppliers of components and specialized services to large enterprises. Indeed in many cases small firms have a very narrow customer or supplier base, comprising no more than a handful of large companies (Mason and Harrison 1985). Taylor and Thrift (1981; 1983) in developing Averitt's (1968) dual economy model, have also pointed out that most small firms depend in some way for their survival on large corporations, even if only indirectly through being left market niches which are too small for a large firm to operate in profitably.

Thus although many LFRs have an industrial structure in which the SME sector is very significant in employment terms, especially if considering only the indigenous sector, the potential for RTD-based growth in that sector is limited. Thresholds or barriers will restrict development and the high risk nature of new and small firms may lead to unfavourable success rates for specific policies. However, regions must develop existing capabilities, and policies need to be aimed at developing wider competitiveness in SMEs, within which RTD is just one element.

Two important issues arise from the implementation of existing policies for RTD in SMEs. First, the better performance of core regions in terms of new firm formation, survival rates, growth rates, and innovative capability of small firms is reflected by the better uptake of aid and greater success of initiatives. Clearly, the advantages of these regions in terms of other factors enhances assistance rather than presenting barriers to be overcome through intervention. Second, and arising from this, it is obvious that many successful initiatives are integrated with other forms of assistance. Thus innovation centres and science parks seem to work best in areas where additional financial support and, in particular, public procurement support is available.

Technological leakage and regional development

Aside from the issue of inward investment in relation to RTD expansion in the regions and comparisons with indigenous RTD strategies there is the actual problem of retaining the existing and future research and technology base of LFRs. This involves the issue of 'technological leakage'.

'Technological leakage' from LFRs can occur via a variety of ways ranging from: (i) out-migration of scarce scientific and technical personnel trained and educated in the regions; (ii) through HEIs and Public Research Establishments (PREs) in the LFRs linking-up with outside firms to provide research and technical know-how; and (iii) by HEIs and private companies in peripheral regions allowing, via licensing and patenting agreements, companies located outside the region to manufacture and develop the products and processes that have been invented in the region. Finally, it can involve (iv) the acquisition of high technology firms or the closure of existing high technology branch establishments, located in peripheral regions, through corporate restructuring. Again, dependency relations are involved in these processes.

An important problem in the expansion and development of RTD in peripheral regions is the 'brain drain' of talented scientific and technical personnel to core regions or abroad to the US or Japan. This problem has been noted not only in the UK, at a national level both on a broad basis (ACARD 1986) and a more specific sectoral basis (Pearson and Parsons 1983), but also has been identified in a broad range of other European countries notably Ireland, Spain, and Belgium. As such in both industrially declining and agriculturally based problem regions of the Community it is in many instances not the local education and training of scientific and technical manpower which is the problem but rather the subsequent out-migration of this highly qualified manpower. Thus although the long-term effects are difficult to evaluate the net export of scientific personnel from peripheral to core regions and abroad represents a serious haemorrhaging of scientific and technical opportunities which seriously constrains the whole development of a strong, indigenous technology base in such localities.

Similarly there has been a leakage of technical information and innovation from HEIs and PREs in less favoured regions to industry located in the core regions. What appears to be a common phenomenon in the less favoured regions is that the public research and technology sector in terms of HEIs and PREs often has a capability in leading edge technologies, comparable to that

Table 2.3 'Technological leakage' from UK regions

Name of HEI/PRE located in UK region which developed the innovation	*UK region*	*Sector associated with the innovation*	*Name of foreign or UK Core* Region manufacturer taking up the innovation*	*Location*
Bristol University	South West	Pharmaceuticals	Sandoz AG	Switzerland
University of Birmingham	West Midlands	Biotechnology (Diagnostics)	Amersham International	South East, UK
Royal Signals and Radar Establishment, Ministry of Defence (+ University of Sussex)	West Midlands	Chemical processing	Balzers AG and Etablissments Pième Angenieux SH (+ OCLI Optical Coatings Ltd)	Liechtenstein St Heard, France (Dunfermline, Scotland)
University of Ulster	Northern Ireland	Electronic Components	Boeing	USA
University of Leeds	Yorkshire & Humbs.	Polymers	Celanese Corporation (owned by Hoechst, W. Germany)	USA
Health and Safety Executive, Sheffield	Yorkshire & Humbs.	Gas detectors	Mine Safety Appliances	USA
Wolfson Unit (Cambridge Industrial Unit) at Cambridge University	East Anglia	Computer graphics	Control Data	USA

HEI – Higher Education Institute
PRE – Public Research Establishment

elsewhere in the world, but local industry, primarily centred on low technology manufacture, is unable to utilise such developments. What happens, therefore, is that results, and more particularly the economic benefits of publicly funded scientific research in the less favoured regions, do not remain in the region but go to private companies located in the core regions or abroad which further develop and then manufacture or use the products and processes involved.

Table 2.3 provides an illustration of this leakage from the LFRs of the UK. Of particular concern, on a Community-wide level, is that many of the ideas and innovations developed by HEIs and PREs in the less favoured regions of the UK are not even remaining within the European Community but going outside, most notably to the USA. This problem is particularly apparent in the UK where universities have traditionally sought and developed industry–academic links on a national or international rather than regional basis (Howells 1986b). It also stems from the fact that centrally funded universities in the UK are not expected specifically to tailor the types of departments they support, and the research that they undertake, to the particular characteristics and needs of local industry. This is also a reflection of the desire by universities in the UK and elsewhere in Europe to work with more prestigious, multinational companies which are most likely to have their research facilities located in the core regions, rather than with local firms which are often little known and have fewer funds to develop and implement the products and processes being generated by academic research. Above all, local industry may have had little interest in innovation and research, and therefore HEIs are naturally forced to seek collaboration and funding from outside the area.

Moreover, simply in terms of the relative size and consequent diversity of the research and technology base of the core regions *vis-à-vis* the peripheral regions, it is not surprising that product and process innovations being developed by HEIs and PREs (see next section) in the less favoured regions will lead to links with companies outside the region rather than in it. However, over and above this there is the issue of technological mismatch in the less favoured regions between the potential generators of innovations, often as we have noted in the public sector, and potential users and developers of such innovations, associated within private industry.

A final element in the process of technological leakage is that of the acquisition, restructuring or closure of high technology establishments. The acquisition of new and small high technology firms in the UK by foreign multinationals has already been noted

(Table 2.2). Of more concern is the downgrading or even outright closure of high technology establishments located in peripheral regions, with the removal or selling off of the high technology component and research base of these establishments to corporate sites located outside the region. At its most extreme it can involve what has become known as 'intellectual asset stripping'. This was highlighted in the recent case of BTRs acquisition of Dunlop. In the subsequent break up and disposal of Dunlop, BTR sold Engineering Consultants Services (ECS) to Goodyear, the US tyre company. ECS was a British research-based tyre operation which had developed a world lead in computer-controlled tyre assembly. Goodyear closed the British operations down and transferred the technology to Ohio and Luxembourg. Another slightly different example was the case of the British Ship Research Association, which was merged with a privatized PRE in London and the control of its operations on Tyneside were moved to London, along with some elements of its research.

Technological mismatch and regional development

In the light of this discussion, policies to develop research capacity in the LFRs, particularly in HEIs and PREs, must take account of potential mismatches with the needs of local industry. The issue of technological mismatch in the regions appears to be common throughout the Community and raises more fundamental issues in terms of developing a research and technology strategy for such regions. The issue of technological mismatch at a national scale has been touched upon by a recent OECD (1984) report on Greece which noted the high research and scientific potential of its universities, but the general weakness of industry in terms of research and its ability to use the research originating from the universities and public sector in Greece. Similarly, in relation to the education and training of scientific and technical personnel, there is a mismatch in the ability of local firms to use effectively the talents within their regions. In many European countries, trained scientific and technical personnel leave the LFRs, first, because of an absolute shortage of firms in specific high technology sectors and, second, because most firms in peripheral, disadvantaged regions have difficulties in incorporating such highly trained manpower because they are lower technology operations regardless of sector.

A number of questions emerge from this. How far should we expect HEIs and PREs in the less favoured regions to be involved in R. & D. activity which has direct relevance to local industry? If this were to happen, would not R. & D. in such establishments have to move away from fundamental leading edge research and become instead involved with merely mature technology, associated with applied research and development work to match the requirements of local industry (almost by definition in low technology industries)? A further set of issues are derived from this. By orienting themselves towards local industry HEIs and PREs may not necessarily be doing the best for their own internal needs and goals. They may have to forego lucrative and prestigous contracts with companies outside the region. Above all it may require a fundamental shift of research activity away from leading edge technologies. In the long term such institutions could lose the ability to generate their own ideas and innovations and become simply transfer mechanisms and adapters of technology. More fundamentally, by doing this, it could lock HEIs into technologies and markets which are in decline.

The technology orientation of less favoured regions

The preceding discussion of the problems of technological leakage and mismatch which arise in the promotion of research activity in the LFRs raises the question of what technological orientation disadvantaged regions should pursue. For example, should a regional RTD policy be based on industries and markets in which the area already specializes or should the emphasis be on a 'leapfrogging' strategy which focuses on leading-edge technologies? Similarly there are other issues associated with RTD strategy orientation (should it focus on the generation of new or diffusion of existing technologies? Should it be product or process based? and so on).

The argument that regions should build on the existing strengths of the industrial base (i.e. pursuing a vocation regionale) has much to merit it. In neo-classical terms it suggests that resource allocation should be put into those sectors which are most efficient and competitive and as such which have a comparative advantage. By building onto these industrial strengths therefore, the overall economic health of the region will be optimized. A fundamental assumption here is that regions or nations will indeed have a comparative advantage in particular sectors; however this is not necessarily the case even on a national level. For example, even in the 1950s the only sector in which Japan had a comparative advantage was in textiles (it was joined later in the decade by textile machinery; Eatwell 1982).

Of more concern in a regional sense however is the fact that those sectors in which the LFRs are likely (almost by definition) to have a competitive or comparative advantage are the very sectors which are declining in market terms or are at best stagnant. In technology terms it is suggesting that the science and technology effort of a region should be put into those sectors, such as shipbuilding, textiles, iron and steel, or mechanical engineering, which are facing declining markets and severe international competition (particularly in cost terms) from newly industrializing countries such as South Korea, Singapore, and Taiwan. Moreover, such a strategy tends to be associated with economic determinism/ imperialism and fatalism – LFRs should concentrate on those sectors which have no long-term future, leaving the core regions to concentrate on growth markets and leading edge technologies.

The arguments for 'leading edge' technologies relate to the fact that they are associated with rapid economic growth and where competition at least in cost terms, is low. Moreover, by selecting very new technologies, entry barriers are generally low and industrial and market dominance by competitors has not been established – a problem which most peripheral-based firms often find unsurmountable. However, equally there are serious problems in adopting such a strategy. It is in danger of creating high technology 'islands' (either research centres or via setting up new firms) in a region which have little or no contact or relevance to existing industry. It is also a high risk in the sense that the right markets and sectors have to be selected – not all leading edge technologies take off and, more particularly, not all research centres or firms in such sectors survive (in fact most fail). While in a competitive sense entry is much easier into these advanced technology sectors, research and development costs may be high, costs which could only be borne by the largest corporations or national governments.

Another important issue is whether a technology policy for the regions should concentrate on the generation or diffusion of technology. This issue links up with the discussion above, in terms of whether emphasis should be placed in the generation and then development of innovations by a small group of key enterprises, or whether it should be on diffusing existing technologies to industry as a whole in the region.

Moreover, it also reveals another split between product or process (capital) innovations since most inventions relate to products (since process innovations, in the form of capital equipment, sold to other firms represent a product for the firm that develops and manufactures them) whilst innovations that are diffused generally relate to process innovations which firms buy in. The exceptions here are new products which are manufactured by firms under licence, although such licensing agreements are limited usually in terms of the level of technology, geographical market, and potential for ensuing development. The main benefits tend to accrue to the firm which develops the technology.

A final dichotomy is that between the development of indigenous technology and the 'importing of technology'. Some observers in the UK (Oakey 1983) believe that the strategy of 'importing technology' has been over-emphasized to the detriment of more indigenous technology schemes. The strategy has been associated with encouraging the diffusion of process innovations in an attempt to improve the efficiency and cost competitiveness of British industry (Howells 1985), associated with such schemes as the Manufacturing Advisory Service, the Microprocessor Application Project, Low Cost Automation Centres, and Robot Advisory Services. In particular it has seen the attraction ('importation') of US and now Japanese technology and manufacturing plants as a key to the revival of 'British' industry. Set against these arguments is the view that the manufacture of existing products using new processes is an easy way to build up the technological expertise in firms in the LFRs.

In this section we have outlined some of the key issues that need to be addressed in a RTD strategy for a region. How these issues are resolved in any particular region will obviously vary according to the specific social and economic characteristics of the area. However, regional RTD initiatives are often developed with no acknowledgement of the long-term implications of their implementation. A passive, demand-led RTD funding policy is likely to reinforce the existing industrial structure of a region in comparison to a more proactive RTD strategy which has specific objectives in terms of existing and new opportunities for the region. In particular, a strategic approach is needed in order to acknowledge the future growth potential and competitive position of the markets on which the RTD resources and funding are to be focused.

Policy context for RTD and regional development

Before concluding this chapter it is important to note the policy context and tiers (European, national and, regional) within which the establishment of possible RTD strategies for disadvantaged regions have to be framed. In particular, these include the economic and institutional constraints that operate at various government and administrative levels in the formulation of RTD initiatives. These issues are briefly evaluated in the following sections at a Community, national, and regional level.

European Community context

Participation by establishments in the LFRs in both European (such as ESPRIT and BRITE) and national (such as PAFE in France and, on a smaller scale, Alvey in the UK) technology programmes brings obvious benefits to the participants. It enables local and regional establishments to be integrated in leading edge research, providing substantial spin-offs in terms of contacts with major industrial and government research institutes. It may also allow the greater utilization and take-up of research carried out in such establishments, providing greater economic returns and access to wider markets. On the other hand there is the problem already noted of technological leakage, whereby research from mainly HEIs and PREs located in the less favoured regions goes to help large corporations located in the core regions. There is also the issue of whether these Community and national research and technology programmes are the right sort of schemes in which establishments in the LFRs should be involved. Such programmes run by the European Community and national member state governments are generally of a very long-term nature and involved with pre-competitive, basic rather than applied research.

For example, the relevance of the BRITE programme to needs and problems experienced by industry may be questioned. Similarly, the other science and technology programmes of the Community can be seen as being of little relevance to industry in the LFRs of the Community, where the objectives of national and Community science and technology programmes do not tie in with the needs of firms in the peripheral, less favoured areas. Indeed, it is likely that participation by establishments in the LFRs in these programmes is actually going to have a detrimental effect on the development of the research and technology base in such localities because it commits scarce science and technology resources in the region, particularly personnel, to projects which often have very little relevance or spin-offs to the regions concerned. In some senses this discussion is 'academic', since participation and expenditure in these programmes is largely confined to the core regions of the Community member states.

National context and constraints for RTD and regional policies

Similar strictures apply to national policies, although in this respect care should be taken to acknowledge the difference between national RTD policies with a regional dimension and regional policies with a RTD dimension. Frequently national RTD policies with a regional dimension have been little more than token efforts to involve peripheral LFRs in national research and technology programmes which, as we have noted, have little direct relevance to the regions concerned.

Regional policies with a RTD dimension all too often have been associated with short-term, technology 'import' schemes in combination with property development with a high technology image. Links with national technology policy have been minimal. In part this is a reflection of the lack of consensus in terms of the need for co-ordination between national governments and local and regional authorities. This, however, can go as far as government agencies blocking initiatives by local authorities in developing industrial or technology strategies. In certain countries, such as France (OECD 1986), there have been more efforts to regionalize RTD programmes and to link with regional RTD schemes but even here there are often gaps or problems. Above all there are problems of co-ordination between national and regional and local authorities over RTD policies, which is further complicated in countries such as Germany with its intervening state-federal RTD policy initiatives.

It should be evident in some of the issues discussed in this chapter that a number of problems that the LFRs face in terms of research and technological development can often only be dealt with and resolved at a national level. Moreover it should be acknowledged that the national context for RTD has a profound influence on the research and technology environment that the LFRs have to face. The chief parameter in terms of this national framework is obviously the overall size of the national RTD base. Thus, the overall size of the RTD base in Portugal and Greece (which have RTD expenditures of below 0.5 per cent of GDP), is obviously going to have a profound effect on the relative size and nature of the RTD problem faced at the regional level. Similarly, on a dynamic basis, the decline in R. & D. employment, R. & D. expenditure in industry, the dramatic decline in university funding, and the planned cut back in total government R. & D. expenditure in the UK is obviously going to have a considerable impact on what the LFRs will experience in terms of changes in their research and technology base. Notwithstanding these changes, it is clear that national governments still exert a direct and a powerful influence on the RTD in regions through their own procurement patterns. Perhaps the best example of this is in defence expenditure, which has particular relevance to high technology operations.

There are also numerous national institutional constraints on RTD which, although they impinge on all regions, are a particular burden on the LFRs because of their low technology base. Some of the major underlying problems in developing RTD in the LFRs stem from institutional constraints and vary from country to country and from region to region. However, they often represent the most significant restraints to the development of RTD in the region and are the most difficult to deal with both from an EC and regional level. Thus in some countries HEIs are restricted in developing commercial projects and operations. In Greece, for example, universities were restricted from obtaining funds from private industry until recently (associated with reforms made in 1978, 1981 and 1982; OECD 1984). Again, in Greece, professional responsibilities are not infrequently defined by outdated laws in terms so rigid as to seriously impede the development of new disciplines and limit their potential contribution (OECD 1984).

Local and regionally based RTD initiatives

In the absence of strong support from national governments, a plethora of local initiatives has been pursued to support RTD in the LFRs of the Community. In general these 'bottom-up' initiatives have not fitted well with technology policies pursued by national governments from the 'top-down'. There has also been little co-ordination between agencies within the regions leading to an excess of initiatives of a particular type (e.g. science or technology parks) and insufficient attention to other RTD problems (e.g. technology transfer mechanisms). This has partly reflected the constraints on the types of policy that local agencies are permitted to undertake – generally property-related initiatives are approved but financial aids are disallowed.

Within any LFR there are therefore likely to be a wide variety of agencies with a stake in RTD development whose actions may be controlled by policy agenda and powers determined locally, regionally, and nationally. In very few instances are there regional authorities with the powers and resources to determine and implement a regional RTD strategy in its entirety. This is particularly the case in the field of higher education research and training, which is generally a national activity implemented within the region through autonomous non-locally funded institutions.

Conclusion

In conclusion, a final issue which needs to be raised here is that any policy proposal in relation to the research and technological development in peripheral LFRs has to recognize the constraints and limitations of implementing such a policy. Acknowledgement has to be made of the considerable variation between LFRs in terms of the availability of actors and instruments which will be able to implement the proposed research and technological development schemes. This is particularly true in the UK where three less favoured 'regions': Scotland, Wales and Northern Ireland, have regional actors which have provided effective vehicles for implementing strategies. By contrast other LFRs in England have multi-layered and poorly co-ordinated sets of actors responsible for various areas and types of regional policy. In addition, given the tendency for most regional policies in the past to be demand responsive, it is likely that the less co-ordinated and, indeed, less well-off regions in most need of aid for research and technological development will in fact lose out.

Note

1. The Framework Programme of Community Activities in the Field of Research and Technological Development (1987–1991) is the overall framework for RTD support by the European Commission. It sets out objectives, priorities, main activities to be funded, overall budgets, and detailed rules for participation. Specific technology programmes are then implemented within this context, but require additional legislation.

References

Advisory Council for Applied Research and Development (1986) *Exploitable Areas of Science*, London: HMSO.

Averitt, R.T. (1968) *The Dual Economy: The Dynamic of American Industry Structure*, New York: Norton.

Benghozi, P.J. and Matheu, M. (1982) *Regional Innovation Policy: Technology Policies or Regional Policies*, Delft: Six Countries Programme.

Technological change

Britton, J.N.H. and Gilmour, J.M. (1978) *The Weakest Link – A Technological Perspective on Canadian Industrial Development*, Background Study No. 43, Science Council of Canada.

Carnegy, H. (1987) 'Technology on the rise', *Financial Times* 18 July.

Charles, D.R. (1987) 'Technical change and the decentralised corporation in the electronics industry: regional policy implications', in K. Chapman and G. Humphrys (Eds.) *Technical Change and Industrial Policy*, Oxford: Basil Blackwell.

Commission of the European Communities (1984), *The Regions of Europe*, Brussels: CEC.

(1986(a)) *European Regional Development Fund Tenth Annual Report* (1984), Brussels: CEC.

(1986(b)) *European Regional Development Fund Eleventh Annual Report* (1985), Brussels: CEC.

Dasgupta, P. and Stiglitz, J. (1980) 'Industrial Structure and the nature of innovative activity', *Economic Journal* 90:266–93.

Eatwell, J. (1982) *Whatever Happened to Britain? The Economics of Decline*, BBC/Duckworth, London.

Erickson, R.A. (1975) 'The spatial pattern of income generation in the lead firm growth area linkage systems', *Economic Geography* 51:17–26.

Firn, J. (1975) 'External control and regional development', *Environment and Planning A* 7:393–414.

Freeman, C. (1974) *The Economics of Industrial Innovation*, Harmondsworth: Penguin.

Germidis, D. (1977) 'Transfer of technology by multinational corporations and absorptive capacity of the developing countries: a synthesis', in D. Germandis (Ed.) *Transfer of Technology by Multinational Corporations: volume I, A Synthesis and Country Case Study*, Paris: Development Centre of the Organisation for Economic Cooperation and Development.

Gibbs, D.C. (1984) 'The influence of investment incentives on technological change', *Area* 16:115–120.

Howells, J. (1983) 'Filter-down Theory: Location and Technology in the UK Pharmaceutical Industry', *Environment and Planning A*, 15:147–64.

(1984) Location, Technology and Filter-down Theory: An Analysis of the United Kingdom Pharmaceutical Industry, Unpublished Ph.D thesis, University of Cambridge.

(1985) 'Product Sophistication, Industrial Organisation and Location: The UK Pharmaceutical Industry', *Environment and Planning A*, 17:1045–1062.

(1986a) 'Capital sophistication and regional development: industrial organisation and pattern within the UK pharmaceutical industry', *Tijdschrift voor Economische en Sociale Geographie* 77:92–102.

(1986b) 'Industry-academic links in research and innovation: a national and regional development perspective', *Regional Studies* 20:472–476.

Howells, J. and Charles, D.R. (1987) 'Research and Technological Development in the Less Favoured Regions of the European Community: A UK Dimension' in K. Dyson (Ed.) *Local Authorities and New Technologies: The European Dimension*, London: Croom Helm.

Hull, C. (1980) 'Regional incentives in France' in D. Yuill, K. Allen and C. Hull (Eds), *Regional Policy in the European Community*, London: Croom Helm.

Lever, W. (1974) 'Manufacturing linkages and the search for supplies and markets', in F.E.I. Hamilton (Ed.) *Spatial Perspectives on Industrial Organisation and Decision-Making*, Chichester: John Wiley.

Lloyd, P.E. and Mason, C.M. (1984) 'Spatial variations in new firm formation in the United Kingdom. Comparative evidence from Merseyside, Greater Manchester and South Hampshire', *Regional Studies* 18:207–220.

McDermott, P.J. (1976) 'Ownership, organisation and regional dependence in the Scottish electronics industry', *Regional Studies* 10:319–35.

McDermott, P.J. (1979) 'Multinational manufacturing firms and regional development: external control in the Scottish electronics industry', *Scottish Journal of Political Economy* 26:287–306.

Mason, C.M. and Harrison, R.T. (1985) 'The geography of small firms in the UK: towards a research agenda', *Progress in Human Geography* 9, 1–37.

Moore, D.G. (1959) 'Management strategies' in W.L. Warner and N.H. Martin (Eds) *Industrial Management*, London: Harper.

O'Farrell, P.N. and O'Loughlin, B. (1981) 'New industry input linkages in Ireland', *Environment and Planning A*, 13:285–308.

Oakey, R.P. (1983) 'New technology, government policy and regional manufacturing employment', *Area* 15:61–5.

OECD (1984) *Reviews of National Science Policy: Greece,* OECD, Paris.

(1986) *Reviews of Innovation Policies: France*, OECD, Paris.

Parker, J.E.S. (1974) *The Economics of Innovation: The National and Multinational Enterprise in Technological Change*, London: Longman.

Pavitt, K. (1984) 'Sectoral patterns of technical change: towards a taxonomy and a theory' *Research Policy* 13:343–73.

Pavitt, K., Robson, M. and Townsend, J. (1987) 'The size distribution of innovating firms in the UK:1945–1983', *The Journal of Industrial Economics* 35:297–316.

Pearson, R. and Parsons, D. (1983) *The Biotechnology Brain Drain* Swindon/Brighton: SERC/IMS.

Research Centre of Crete (1986) *The Research Centre of Crete*, University of Crete, Iraklion.

Science Council of Canada (1980) '*Multinationals and industrial strategy: the role of world product mandates*', Working Group on Industrial Policies, Science Council of Canada, Ottawa.

Storey, D.J. and Johnson, S. (1987) *Are Small Firms the Answer to Unemployment*? London: Employment Institute.

Taylor, M.J. (1975) 'Organisational growth, spatial interaction and decision making', *Regional Studies* 9:313–323.
Taylor, M.J. and Thrift, N.J. (1981) Organisation, Location and Political Economy: Towards a Geography of Business Organisation, *CURDS Discussion Paper* No. 38, University of Newcastle upon Tyne.
(1983) 'Business Organisations, Segmentation and Location', *Regional Studies* 17:445–65.
Thwaites, A.T. (1978) 'Technological change, mobile plants and regional development', *Regional Studies* 12:445–462.
United States International Trade Commission (1977) *Synthetic Organic Chemicals: United States Production and Sales 1975*, Washington DC: Government Printing Office.
Watts, H.D. (1981) *The Branch Plant Economy: A Study of External Control*, London: Longman.

3

Industrial dynamics and policy debate in the information technology production industries

H. Williams, A.E. Gillespie and A.T. Thwaites

Introduction

The theoretical foundations that underpin this paper are Schumpeterian. It is argued that the Schumpeterian theory of technological change and economic development, and recent extensions of this (e.g. Freeman 1982, 1984; Dosi 1984; Perez 1983), are the most pertinent to the study of new information technology (NIT) because of the emphasis upon the process of technological change. This emphasis on technological change and economic development not only embraces those firms that are the carriers of a new technological paradigm, but also the consequent transformation of existing products and processes. The 'creative gales of destruction' that surround the emergence of a new technology paradigm reconfigure the existing sources of value-added and thus patterns of employment and capital investment. In a geographical context these changes lead to a new and different set of issues that confront regional economic development (e.g. Thwaites 1978).

In the late 1970s and early 1980s there have been a growing number of authors (e.g. Freeman 1986; Rada 1984) who have argued that digital electronic technology, specifically new information technology, is rightly classified as a new technology paradigm with profound economic consequences. The significance of this technology lies in its ability to capture, manipulate, communicate, and store information. Such characteristics offer the potential for the commodification of, and trade in, information and are omnipotent in that the impacts pervade all aspects of economic activity, blurring traditionally defined boundaries between sectors, firms and occupations.

Thus from a policy perspective the Schumpeterian framework not only exposes the importance of the carriers of the new paradigm, but also the process of transformation of existing economic activities. Respectively, in the case of NIT the specific concerns are with both those firms, organizations and institutions that cohere around the technology, and the realization of a myriad of new economic opportunities in which 'tradeable' information is of central importance.

Following this distinction of two fundamental policy domains is the necessity to define the nature and scope of the NIT industry. Here, it is argued that the traditional boundaries of industrial sectors provided by standard industrial classifications and trade figures are inadequate. Such taxonomies fail to recognize the complex and dynamic interactions between large and small firms, often across national boundaries, and the interweaving of such inter-firm relationships across a wide range of technologies, 'high and low tech'.

The working definition that was used in the empirical research upon which this paper is based was derived from a 'delphi' type process in that industry itself suggested the definition (Williams *et al.* 1985). What emerged is that there is a kernel of NIT which in its most reductionist sense consists of the products and technologies of semiconductors and software. The telecommunications equipment and the data processing equipment industries are perhaps best defined as major markets for semiconductors and software, yet the actual structure of the NIT industry suggests this reductionist perception is ill considered. In consequence the NIT industry can be defined as software, semiconductors, telecommunications equipment and data processing hardware. It is important to recognize that this definition encompasses a wide range of activities from advanced molecular physics, epitaxial ion implementation methodologies and tools, through to the writing and printing of manuals and low-tech 'metal bashing' activities. It is a composite of these activities focused upon the core technologies and processes that constitute the NIT sector. In the collection, classification, and analysis of data such a definition may create more problems than it solves, but in the formulation of policy such a definition is axiomatic to any attempt to 'direct' or engage in discussion with the industry.

Within a European context the emergence of a new technology paradigm coincided with a period of continuing recession and the 'end-game' in the erosion of the international competitiveness of some of the traditional industries which had fuelled European economic development over the decades. Moreover, this loss in international competitiveness threatened to inhibit the development of a NIT sector within Europe and thereby circumscribe future economic opportunities. This latter concern was dramatically illustrated in the McKinsey report (1983) to the European Commission which identified potential job loss in excess of two million if the Community failed to develop an internationally competitive NIT sector.

It is against this general background and within a Schumpeterian theoretical framework that this paper attempts to consider the policy domains of NIT. The central thesis is that the nature of the policy-making process within Europe, and particularly within the European Commission, conjoined with the structural changes that surround the NIT industries, results in naive policy initiatives, addressing problems that are of diminishing significance. To expose these issues the paper first dwells on the nature of change within the NIT sector and, second on the nature of the policy-making process by a preliminary review of actors, agendas, and policy instruments.

Change and the new information technology sector

The purpose of this section is to outline briefly the pressures for change within the NIT industrial sector and to point up some of the impacts in terms of employment, industrial structure, and the location of production. The growth of the NIT industrial sector has been both rapid and turbulent, particularly as a consequence of a seemingly endless improvement in the functional capability of the technology at decreasing costs (see for example Moore's Law, which states that the number of components on a semiconductor doubles every five years). This phenomenon, however, masks a number of different but interrelated trends, some of which are discussed below.

1. Research and development

The rapid pace of technological change necessarily commits firms to relatively high levels of R. & D. activity, but with the need to make complex choices between research targets in the technology, processes or products, and a choice between different product/ market segments. These choices are particularly acute in terms of semiconductor and software design and development, two product areas that permeate all aspects of the NIT industry. The rapid process of change has excluded all but a few organizations from pursuing on their own account a major R. & D. portfolio across a very broad range of NIT interests. Significantly, the inherent complexities of the technology and the associated products and processes, are beginning to imply an absolute level of investment to maintain a leading technological presence. Thus for relatively small companies, including many major European manufacturers, the costs of R. & D. act as a significant barrier to entry. For example, neither Phillips nor Siemens felt able in the early 1980s to enter the one-megabit semiconductor market and consequently entered a joint research and development and production agreement which was further supported by the Dutch and West German governments, yet ultimately licensing agreements with Japan were required to sustain the project. The consequence of an ever-tightening tourniquet of increased R. & D. costs and market uncertainty has led to the recent (March 1988) designs for a Joint European Semi-Conductor Silicon Initiative (JESSI).

One of the consequences of the uncertainties created by rapid technological change has been upon the nature of inter-firm linkages (a theme developed more fully below). At the 'fundamental' or 'basic' research level much has been made of university/industry links as a model of both local economic development and improved competitiveness of firms (Segal Quince, 1985). Within the NIT sector these linkages at a research level can be seen as the externalization of risk and, given the relative price differentials between the university and industrial sector, the maximization of research options.

2. *Product life cycles*

Related to the processes of rapid technological change are the relatively short product life cycles of NIT products and services, especially that period in the market place where premium prices can be sustained on increasing volumes. The effect of technological change does not just manifest itself in the technical obsolescence of products but also reflects in customer expectations and specifications.

The challenge of short product life cycles forces companies to adopt a dual strategy. First, companies attempt to seek large homogeneous markets for their products in order to maximize volumes in the immediate post launch period. This necessarily involves international markets, and for European manufacturers in effect global markets. One of the consequences of this need to achieve high volumes in international markets immediately the product is launched is the increased risk, for example, in terms of the delivery and guarantee of product functionality, quality, and manufacturing systems with the benefit of time to move along the 'learning curve'. Failure to achieve global volumes will force individual companies into 'peripheral' but related markets (e.g. Honeywell into control systems).

The second strategy pursued by manufacturers is to attempt to stabilize markets by agreeing non-proprietorial standards. This is a complex process of international negotiation and bargaining which is taking place against a background of established market shares and therefore *de facto*, proprietorial standards. The debate at one level is currently characterized in terms of OSI (Open Standard Interconnection) versus SNA (System Network Architecture). As the name suggests OSI is a non-proprietorial standard and is broadly supported by a number of manufacturers; SNA is the IBM standard. The process of negotiation is further complicated in that OSI is a seven-layer model spanning the physical elements of the technology through to applications, but detailed and agreed OSI standards do not exist for each of the seven layers.

Within Europe the impact of rapid technological change and short product life cycles is to downgrade national markets as the point of leverage for NIT policy. Protecting national markets for the 'national champion' is becoming a barren strategy in an increasing number of NIT markets. This is exposing European manufacturers to new and different threats to their growth, both in terms of the breadth of their product ranges and in the geographical scope of their activities.

3. *Economies of scale and scope*

One of the corporate responses emerging as a consequence of the impacts of rapid technological change and relatively short product life cycles is to exploit economies of scale and scope. The purpose here is to reduce the cost base of the company. In terms of economies of scale this is resulting in the reorganization of production on a global scale exploiting an international division of labour. This method of production organization is resulting in the adoption of single (or limited) product production sites supplying numerous national markets. For established producers, the result has been, at worst, a decline in the numbers of production establishments, creating the ironic position of a sunrise industry grappling with the problems of a sunset industry, at best, the ability to sustain increased volumes within existing production complexes and levels of employment, for example Olivetti's personal computer production facility at Ivrea (data given at interview with Olivetti). Recent evidence suggests that the prospect of single global production sites are becoming a reality in terms of technical and economic criteria (e.g. IBM memory devices at the Winchester production site in the UK) although political and security factors may force at least dual sourcing.

The impact of technological change upon products and processes is beginning to challenge the international division of labour exploited by the NIT industry during the 1970s with low-cost labour being a forceful inducement to investment in, for example, South East Asia. This was particularly true for the semiconductor industry. The increasingly sophisticated nature of both products and processes is resulting in the transfer back to HQ (core areas) of certain functions, if not entire operations. For example, Plessey in the UK have substantially withdrawn from overseas, Far East, production as the nature of the technology and production processes have changed. Furthermore, the increasing risk associated with some of the new production processes is forcing companies to exploit novel methods of production organization using advanced telecommunication facilities to transmit machine instruction, mask patterns, and production schedules to off-shore production sites daily. This separation of functions raises the interesting question of what value can be placed on any production establishment if the information that controls the site is held entirely off-shore. A common thread through these different changes designed to exploit economies of scale is the reaffirmation by corporate headquarters of their control over production activity over and above that of national subsidiaries.

For the larger companies the rate of technological change, and with it technological convergence and substitution, is creating new opportunities to diversify product ranges. The opportunities are most commonly realized by using the same core sub-assemblies across a broad range of products. Significantly this allows global volumes to be achieved for technologically innovative products through the aggregation of the demand of numerous sub-assemblies. For example, office automation has brought about the integration of traditional office equipment, data processing, and communications, which allows many of the same components and sub-assemblies to be used in different products.

4. Inter firm linkages

The increasingly complex and turbulent environment in which NIT firms find themselves is bringing about profound changes in the organization of individual firms and their relationships with others. There are two different phenomena at work, 'strategic alliances', and changing manufacturing systems, particularly the adoption of just-in-time (JIT).

'Strategic alliances', that is the confederation of corporate interests as opposed to conglomerates, are increasingly becoming the preferred strategy for survival in turbulent NIT markets (English 1984; Gorbis 1985). The change in consumer sophistication and the convergence and substitution of NIT technologies is forcing suppliers to operate more broadly and provide integrated solutions. However, the often perceived simple convergence on the level of technology, often characterized as IBM versus ATT, does not result in the smooth transition of a complex organization from one strategy to another. As a result some firms are expanding the breadth of their product range by providing products from other manufacturers. This exchange within a strategic alliance is beyond that of simple marketing or distribution agreements and involves the development of mutual interest, for example the exchange of product and research plans. This necessarily commits firms to greater inter-dependencies upon each other and the actions of one firm begin to influence the individual development of other firms within a confederation.

The role of manufacturing strategies as a key element in competitive advantage is becoming increasingly significant. Manufacturing strategies, particularly the adoption of just-in-time (JIT), are becoming one of the major mechanisms used by firms to adjust to the volatility in the market place. JIT is a method of production organization that allows the delivery of products directly to the customer from the production system (including distribution) and not from a stock of pre-made (anticipated orders) products. Thus the rate of production is determined by current levels of sales and in so doing production is more closely integrated with consumption. For individual firms this poses major questions of organizational change.

On a cursory view the most obvious effect of JIT is its impact on stocks which can lead to substantial cost savings (Mortimer 1986). Some authors have commented on the locational impacts of JIT upon suppliers, arguing that JIT means within-the-locality (Estall 1985). It is argued here, however, that JIT poses far more fundamental changes within firms and upon their linkage structure, reflecting the consequences of turbulence within markets and technologies.

Concomitant with the introduction of JIT, companies redefine their in-house manufacturing and (re-)allocate resources only to those activities which are perceived to be the major sources of sustained value-added and capable of growth. Activities which fall outside these criteria are externalized, creating opportunities for new, small, independent firms, some of which will be 'spin-offs'. For example, when ICL reorganized its activities in Scotland in the early 1980s several product areas were abandoned, which subsequently became the core activity of a number of independent new firms run by ex-ICL employees.

This analysis of competitiveness in manufacturing is extended to suppliers so that each enterprise in the system is responsible for that element in which it can singly achieve greatest competitive advantage. The result of this process is that through complex linkage structures competitive advantage is aggregated and formalized into the total production system. These decisions are made in an international comparative context, although the actual linkage structure may articulate itself within a particular locality, e.g. Silicon Valley.

One of the axioms upon which JIT rests is the notion of 'total quality'. This is expressed in various terms such as 'ship-to-stock', zero defect rates. In effect each enterprise in the chain has to provide 'fault-free' products. This results in detailed inter-firm discussions of production strategies, process automation, quality standards, and therefore work-organization. The objective is not to 'catch' faults in the process which is implicit in setting quality targets, of say 90 per cent pass rate, but to eliminate faults by design, production, organization, and changing corporation organization and culture. In the semiconductor industry the standards for quality are commonly expressed in parts per million and the objective is fault-free product. The focus upon quality also poses difficult problems for some smaller independent companies as the failure to achieve quality standards results in the loss of entire contracts, not just reduced orders. For some firms the risk of this is too great, especially if their other customers are prepared to accept existing standards. The difficulty of finding suitable suppliers in terms of quality was a major problem facing Brother in establishing its production facility in South Wales.

These changes in the distribution of manufacturing activity and the nature of inter-firm linkages, coupled with the growth of strategic alliances, raises complex questions of control. Historic measures of capital ownership do not necessarily equate to control in the NIT sector. What is clear, however, is that key 'nodes' in these alliances and manufacturing systems can be identified and most commonly these are the final product manufacturers. The effect of changing corporate linkage is to vest 'arms' length' control in these final product manufacturers which is not necessarily reflected in traditional measures of control and concentration.

Several significant issues of control are implicit in the development of interfirm dependencies at the international level, namely extraterritoriality, temporal lags, partial supply, and even non-supply. The assumption that individual enterprises enter these linkage structures on equal footings is fallacious. Moreover, the external political environment can and does impose upon the nature of these linkages from both military security (e.g. Comecon) and trade perspectives (e.g. semiconductor trade dispute between US and Japan). Thus the role of national governments and supranational agencies is significant in shaping the nature of linkages between firms and the extent to which firms are able to share their technology and resources in exchange for access to other benefits, for example, markets.

5. *Employment*

The productivity improvements made possible by process automation and product changes have resulted in what Sayer and Morgan (1984, 1986) have described as '*jobless* growth' which in some regions is expressed as '*jobloss* growth' (Williams and Charles 1986). In the telecommunications equipment industry the transition from electro-mechanical to digital-based products has had a severe impact on labour demand, with major European producers – such as STC, Plessey, Siemens, and Italtel – all reducing their labour force requirements. Indeed, Alcatel have suggested that their labour force requirements for telecommunications production are only 25 per cent of ten years ago. In parallel with labour shedding, the extent of over-capacity has led to a major restructuring of production locations. The extent of the problem is suggested by Italtel, who have stated that the optimum yearly output from a plant manufacturing digital technology network products was in the order of one million lines. The total European demand, however, is in the order of 7–10 m lines; Italtel alone have six plants in Italy. Further plant closures are thus inevitable as over-capacity is reduced.

Furthermore, the shift within individual firms towards high value-added activities is reflected in the very distinctive set of labour force requirements in most of the IT industries. These requirements can be characterized as bifurcation or polarization, between on the one hand a relatively small but rapidly growing segment of a highly qualified labour group (scientists, technicians and managers) and, on the other hand, a relatively large but rapidly decreasing unskilled or semi-skilled workforce engaged in assembly. The concept of a bifurcated workforce, however, disguises the extent to which highly qualified scientific and technical staff are becoming increasingly integrated into the production process itself as a result of extensive investment in process automation and the need to achieve extremely high standards of quality. This trend is particularly important in the production of semiconductors, where employees are a major source of contaminants that reduce the yield of the production process. Here the solution is the adoption of process automation in specialist environments (clean rooms), a straight substitution of capital for labour. Within this process of substitution there is another in which one pattern of work organization is supplemented with a bifurcated work force in which scientific and managerial staff are increasingly and intimately involved in the production process.

Within the software sector the pattern of labour recruitment is heavily biased towards graduates. One of the explanations of this is the nature of software production in that there is no clearly defined or understood production function in which a given output can be achieved by different combinations of inputs. The preferred solution to this problem is the recruitment of educated and motivated individuals capable of exploring issues that surround a particular problem.

The policy debate

Information technology has been identified as a focal point of various policy initiatives in recent years. However, the complexities of the sector, some of which have been outlined above, in terms of its composition and the forces of change which are buffeting it, have, at their minimum, led to the questioning of the efficacy of policy initiatives, for example the debate which raged in the UK over the after-Alvey programme.

The purpose of this section is to expose this policy community by consideration of key actors, the policy agenda, and policy instruments. The objective is to illustrate the often conflicting nature not only of the various facets of the policy sets, for example technology policy versus competition policy, but also between the policy initiatives and the behaviour of the IT corporate sector, for example technology policy versus strategic alliances.

The entry point into this analysis is, first, to define the key actors and, second, to identify the agenda around which each of these actors wishes to negotiate. There are four key groups of actors. The first are governments which can be sub-divided by both their jurisdictional authority, e.g. supra-national, national, regional, and local, and by their functions, for example, trade, industry, defence. The second industrial actors can be simplistically divided between the transnational corporations, national champions, particularly important in Europe, and the small to medium sized enterprises (SMEs). Also included here are some summit organizations, most notably the various trade associations. A key group of actors which link both governments and industries are the international and national standard setting organizations. These organizations have quasi-governmental status yet their technical committees are invariably staffed by industrialists. The third group of actors are consumers. Here governments feature as a major group both directly and indirectly in terms of the nationalized industries, including in many countries the national telephone administrations. As a consumer the government has both a straightforward commercial interest in its dealings as well as broader political and bureaucratic interests. Another group of consumers is the corporate sector, and finally there is the household sector. The fourth set of actors are the labour groups. First there are the trade unions which have a tendency to represent those groups of employees that are bearing the brunt of changing sources of value-added and jobloss growth. The second group are the professional associations. Here various attempts are taking place to 'professionalize' the technical and administrative grades within the information technology industries. For example, the British Computer Society is adopting the attributes of the engineering sector professions and is moving towards the position where it not only validates degrees but can bestow chartered engineer status, the fulcrum of many technical professional societies in the UK.

Each of these groups wish to develop their own agenda and prioritize items within that agenda. This inevitably leads to conflicts, for example between competitiveness and competition, between technological leadership and technological collaboration, between the nature of work organization, the level of employment, the skill profile of the workforce and the rights of that workforce, and regionally between the disparities in the actual presence of the industry and in terms of income, capital formation, and employment. Moreover the actual process of setting the agenda creates opportunities for conflict in that the interchange of personnel results in some individuals being key actors within different interest groups.

Surrounding each of the items on the policy agenda are options of supply- and demand-side initiatives. For example, government procurement and industrial targeting provide both demand based stimulation to the industry, whilst education and training is more concerned with the supply side. Another source of conflict is the division between those industries which can be classified as the carriers of the new paradigm and those industries which are experiencing a restructuring or transformation of their products and processes as a result of the new technological paradigm.

There are essentially six types of policy instruments that are available. There is regulatory policy, that is the rules that determine what can or cannot be done and the legal structures that legitimate activity. There is fiscal policy, which is essentially the taxation of industries, or the tax relief that is provided for industries and is a policy instrument that can be used differentially across sectors or individual firms to achieve a desired result. There are financial instruments, essentially the provision of grants and loans to subsidise certain activities. There is also procurement policy, whereby government agencies purchase equipment and supplies specifically from firms which they have targeted, either because of their technological profile or the employment that they provide. There is also promotional policy which is primarily concerned with changing the appreciative setting; for example the UK's IT year in 1982 was designed to make people aware of the opportunities and threats that information technology offers rather than directly to fund or encourage activity in a targeted manner as is possible with some of the other policy instruments. The final set of policy instruments are about prohibition and coercion. These are policy instruments which are finding less favour in the industrial policy debate but have been used extensively through time across a wide range of countries.

The intersection of the key actors, the agenda and policy instruments, raises an inevitable set of conflicts; a set of conflicts that are compounded by the ever-changing nature of the 'pitch' in which policy negotiation and formulation is being constructed. Recently, in the UK, a major conflict has arisen over the funding of the technology *per se* in the form of the Alvey programme and proposals for an after-Alvey programme and the use and applications of the technology. The current UK government position is that the technology is not worth funding unless applications which lead to competitive advantage can be identified and used to determine the nature of the technological development. This is a marked shift in policy from the debates that existed in the early 1980s where in response to the Japanese fifth-generation project the ESPRIT project was announced in Europe, 'Plan Filiere Electronique' in France, Alvey in the UK, and the VLSI in the USA. The primary focus of all these initiatives was the development of novel technologies. The research was not located in a broader perspective of applications and markets.

Another major debate is between international competitiveness and the need for competition. The nature of the information technology industry and the increasing concentration of market power and technology into the hands of very few companies runs into conflict with the desired goals of competition policy. For example at the European Community level ESPRIT, which was sponsored by the Information Technology and Telecommunications Task Force, now DGXIII, ran into conflict with the established policy objectives which were determining detailed policy and policy instruments for regional policy (DGXVI) and DGV and DGIII.

Another area of concern and conflict is between technology policy and regional development. Inevitably a technology policy expedites the processes by which changing sources of value-added are converted into economic opportunities and the consequences of this in terms of the changing skill balance required by the industry and the supply of labour from local labour markets. In the UK the changing sources of value-added have led to significant job losses in some of the peripheral regions.

Another area of conflict is between the trade objectives articulated under GATT and within the European Community for the free trade of goods and services in Europe, the opening up of the internal market, and the desire to protect national champions as repositories of skills and technology.

In short the information technology policy debate is complex, with numerous conflicting and cross-cutting issues. Moreover, it is a policy debate which is being constructed in a rapidly changing environment in which the relative strength and power bases of individual actors and constituencies, which cohere around key issues, are continually being reshaped. It can be argued, however, that the underlying tension that has emerged in the policy debate has resulted from the historical dominance of a technologist paradigm which has underpinned the development of NIT policy and its almost exclusive orientation towards technology, a process aided by the strength of corporatist policy making in western

Europe, and within this process the role of actual companies. As a result of these conflicts the IT sector is surrounded by abject failure defined by most measures, for example in terms of technological leadership in the research environment and in the market, employment opportunities, and international competitiveness. The fundamental failure of the policy debate has been to avoid grappling with the key issue of the new paradigm which is information and the consequent need to develop coherent policy initiatives which address not only the technology, but also the social, economic, and legal structures which surround information. To date information technology policy has been myopic in its focus upon technology.

References

Dosi, G. (1984) *Technical Change and Industrial Transformation: The Theory and an Application to the Semiconductor Industry*, London: Macmillan Press.

English, M. (1984) 'The European Information Technology Industry' in Jacquemin, A. (Ed.) *European Industry: Public Policy and Corporate Strategy*, Clarendon.

Estall, R.C. (1985) 'Stock control in Manufacturing: The Just-In-Time System and its Locational Implications' *Area* 17, 2:129–33.

Freeman, C. (1982) *The Economics of Industrial Innovation*, second edition, Cambridge, Mass: MIT Press.

(1984) *Long Waves in the World Economy*, London: Butterworth.

(1986) 'The role of technical change in national economic development' in Amin, A. and Goddard, J.B. (Eds) *Technological Change, Industrial Restructuring and Regional Development*, London: Allen & Unwin.

Gorbis, M. (1985) *Conglomerates to Confederation*, SRI International, Mimeo.

McKinsey (1983) *A Call for Action*, Report to the European Commission.

Mortimer, J. (1986) *Just in Time: An Executive Briefing*, Institute of Fiscal Studies, London.

Perez, C. (1983) 'Structural Change and the Assimilation of New Technologies in the Economic and Social System', *Futures* 15:357–75.

Rada, J.F. (1984) 'Development, Telecommunciations and the Emerging Service Economy', Conference Paper, Second World Conference on Transborder Data Flow Policies, Rome 26/29 June.

Sayer, A. and Morgan, K. (1984) 'A modern industry in a declining region: links between method, theory and policy' in Massey, D. and Meegan, R. (Eds) *Politics and Method*, Methuen, London, 147–68.

(1986) 'The Electronics Industry and Regional Development in Britain' in A. Amin and J.B. Goddard (Eds) *Technical Change,*

Industrial Restructuring and Regional Development, London: Allen & Unwin.
Segal Quince and Partners (1985) *The Cambridge Phenomenon*, Cambridge.
Thwaites, A.T. (1978) 'Technological Change, Mobile Plants and Regional Development', *Regional Studies* 21:445–61.
Williams, H. and Charles, D. (1986) 'The Electronics Industry in the NE: Growth or Decline?', *Northern Economic Review, Summer* 13:29–38.
Williams, H., Thwaites, A.T., Gillespie, A.E. and Howells, J.H. (1985) *The Location of New Information Technology Production in the UK*, Centre for Urban and Regional Development Studies, University of Newcastle upon Tyne.

Economic restructuring

4

Capital restructuring, government policy and the decentralization of US manufacturing

B.M. and L.R. Moriarty

Introduction

Industrial production in many countries has been undergoing a geographic redistribution at both inter-regional and intra-regional scales for several decades. In the USA manufacturing has been decentralizing from the North-east and North Central regions to the South and West and from metropolitan centres to suburban sites, small cities, towns, and rural areas (Berry and Kasarda 1977; Cromley and Leinbach 1981; Erickson 1976a, 1976b, 1981; Erickson and Leinbach 1979; Erickson and Wasylenko 1980; Fuguitt and Beale 1984; Garnick 1983, 1985; Hansen 1979; Heaton and Fuguitt 1978; McCarthy and Morrison 1977; Moriarty 1980, 1981, 1983, 1986; Norton and Rees 1979; Park and Wheeler 1983; Rees 1979; Schmenner 1982; Struyk and James 1975; Till 1973; Zelinsky 1962). Decentralization has been observed in other countries as well (Barta 1984; Dennis 1978; Dicken and Lloyd 1978; Holmes 1983; Keeble 1978, 1980; Lever 1975; Massey 1982; Massey and Meegan 1978; Schroder *et al.* 1984; Watts 1982). While there is general agreement that significant decentralization of industrial production has taken place, there is disagreement concerning the relative importance of the different factors responsible for the decentralization. Some researchers stress the state of technological progress in different industrial sectors. Others stress the reduction of factor costs, particularly labour costs. Still others stress firm reorganization to improve or maintain market share under conditions of growing international competition and uncertainty. A way of dealing with the problem is to consider industrial decentralization in the context of an ongoing process in which all three forces are not only related, but, in turn, are influenced by changing economic conditions and government policy.

The first section of this chapter will review the inter-regional and intra-regional shifts in the location of US manufacturing employment. The next section will examine capital investment trends involved in the restructuring of manufacturing firms' functional operations and the adoption of new process technology. The following section will review government policies that have contributed to the decentralization of manufacturing. The final section of the paper will present a conceptual model interrelating manufacturing locational shifts, firm functional restructuring and technology adoption.

Manufacturing locational trends

Inter-regional and intra-regional locational trends

The geographic distribution of manufacturing employment in the US by 1980 could be characterized as being fairly equally distributed between the Manufacturing Belt (New England, Middle Atlantic, and East North Central regions) and the more peripheral southern and western regions (Table 4.1).[1] The dominance of the Manufacturing Belt has been on the wane for

Table 4.1 Manufacturing employment in US regions: 1930–1980

Region	*1930 (000s)*	*1940 (000s)*	*1950 (000s)*	*1960 (000s)*	*1970 (000s)*	*1980 (000s)*
New England	1,099	1,158	1,381	1,479	1,541	1,606
Middle Atlantic	2,950	2,995	3,902	4,235	4,274	3,814
East North Central	2,682	2,909	4,167	4,664	5,361	5,120
Manufacturing Belt	6,731	7,062	9,450	10,378	11,176	10,540
South Atlantic	1,087	1,248	1,623	2,134	2,789	3,222
East South Central	470	489	685	930	1,277	1,437
West North Central	745	550	818	1,035	1,250	1,450
West South Central	566	399	644	915	1,286	1,770
Mountain	187	101	161	295	385	597
Pacific	692	586	1,019	1,788	2,172	2,722
Other US	3,747	3,373	4,950	7,097	9,159	11,198
Total Mfg. Employ.	10,478	10,435	14,400	17,475	20,335	21,738
Total US Employ.	47,402	49,625	60,203	64,374	76,581	96,947

Source: Compiled by author from US *Census of Population*.
Note: Data are for the continental US only.

decades as new industrial growth has dispersed more equitably throughout the country. Whereas 64 per cent of the nation's manufacturing labour force was located there a half century ago, it contained 49 per cent in 1980, representing a decline of 15 percentage points.

Throughout the past fifty years the number of manufacturing workers has fluctuated between 21 and 28 per cent of the country's total labour force (Figure 4.1). The Manufacturing Belt in comparison with the southern and western regions, however, always has had a greater share of its workers employed in manufacturing than the rest of the country: 28 per cent in the Manufacturing Belt and 16 per cent in the rest of the country in 1930, for example. While this gap has also been narrowing over the decades, 27 per cent of the Manufacturing Belt's total workforce was still engaged in manufacturing activities in 1980 compared to 19 per cent in the rest of the country.

When manufacturing employment changes are compared to population changes in each census region of the country, the

Figure 4.1 Percentage of US labour force in manufacturing by major economic areas, 1870–1980.

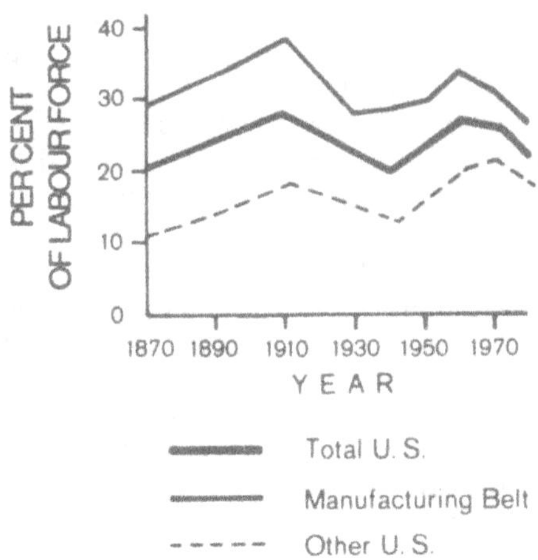

Source: Compiled from *Census of Population*

Table 4.2 Change in SMSA manufacturing labour force: 1947–1967 (Constant SMSA boundaries adjusted for annexation)

Region	*No of cities*	*Change in manufacturing employment in 000s* *Total SMSAs*	*Central cities*	*Suburban rings*
Manufacturing Belt[(a)]	110	1,236	−809	2,045
Other US	135	2,373	516	1,857
Total US	245	3,609	–293	3,902

Source: Compiled by author from Berry and Kasarda 1977, p. 234.
Note: (a) Includes the West North Central Census division.

relative declines in manufacturing employment in the Manufacturing Belt census regions have been considerably greater than the declines in their populations. The most important trend shown by this comparison is the equalization of manufacturing employment and population in every region of the country. The relationship suggests a growing tendency for industrialists to locate their plants close to their markets. Such a conclusion may be correct for some industries and firms but premature in the case of others.

Not only has the dispersement of manufacturing occurred between regions of the country, but it has occurred within regions as well (Table 4.2). In 1947, 11.5 million manufacturing workers were employed in the 245 metropolitan centres of the country existing in 1980 (75 per cent of the total number of manufacturing workers). Of the total number of manufacturing workers in the country, 7.4 million (48 per cent) were employed in metropolitan central cities while 4.1 million (27 per cent) were employed in suburban locations. In 1967, 7.1 million workers (36 per cent) were employed in the central cities and 8 million workers (41 per cent) were employed in the suburbs. The remaining workers were employed in smaller urban centres and rural communities. While the central cities declined slightly in their total amount of manufacturing employment, the suburban areas nearly doubled their number of workers to overtake central cities as the main source area for manufacturing jobs. The Manufacturing Belt and remainder of the country differed considerably in the employment shifts that took place between their central cities and suburbs. While metropolitan areas in both regions grew considerably in their number of manufacturing jobs, the 110 central cities in the Manufacturing Belt declined by a total of 809,000 workers, and the 135 central cities in the rest of the country grew by a total of 516,000 workers. The suburbs grew by 2,045,000 workers in the

Manufacturing Belt and 1,857,000 in the rest of the country. Between 1967 and 1977, the central cities of the Manufacturing Belt lost an additional 1,300,000 manufacturing workers while those in the peripheral regions gained 222,000. Over 80 per cent of the job losses occurred in the thirty-three metropolitan areas of the country with 1970 populations in excess of one million people. The data reveal that manufacturing, at one time, was primarily a metropolitan central city function but that it has been dispersing outward into the suburbs for some time, more so in the Manufacturing Belt than in the rest of the country.

The average percentage of the total labour force residing in nonmetropolitan areas that were employed in manufacturing has been increasing for some time also – from an average of 13.7 per cent in 1950 to 20.6 per cent in 1970 (Table 4.3). The portion of the labour force residing in non-metropolitan areas employed in industrial sectors paying above average wage rates for the nation as a whole nearly doubled between 1950 and 1970 (from 5.9 per cent to 11.5 per cent) while the proportion working in sectors characterized by low wage rates (food processing, textiles, apparel, lumber, and furniture) increased only slightly (from 7.9 per cent to 9.1 per cent). Manufacturing employment increased by 4.4 per cent in metropolitan areas of the country during the decade of the 1960s whereas non-metropolitan counties increased by 23.8

Table 4.3 Average percentage of labour force in US non-metropolitan areas employed in manufacturing, 1950–1970 (Number of counties adjusted for change in Settlement Type)

	Type of County						
	Total United States	*Adjacent to SMSA*		*Nonadjacent to SMSA*		*Region*	
		Urban	*Rural*	*Urban*	*Rural*	*Frostbelt*	*Sunbelt*
Total manufacturing employment							
1950	13.7	20.1	13.4	14.2	9.1	13.1	14.6
1970	20.6	25.1	21.4	19.8	14.8	17.0	24.8
Low-wage manufacturing employment[(a)]							
1950	7.9	8.9	8.6	8.0	6.7	5.5	10.6
1970	9.1	9.5	10.4	9.0	8.1	5.3	13.7
High-wage manufacturing employment							
1950	5.9	11.2	4.8	6.2	2.4	7.6	4.0
1970	11.5	15.6	11.0	10.8	6.7	11.7	11.1

Source: Heaton and Fuguitt 1979.
Note: (a) Low-wage industries are food processing, textile, apparel, lumber, and furniture.

per cent. In the decade of the 1970s, metropolitan areas increased by 7.3 per cent and non-metropolitan counties by 20.3 per cent (Fugitt and Beale 1984).

Non-metropolitan areas in the 'Sunbelt' had a larger proportion of their resident labour force employed in manufacturing by 1970 than did similar areas in the 'Frostbelt', which includes states in the northern Pacific, Mountain, and Central regions along with the Manufacturing Belt states (24.8 per cent compared to 17 per cent). Thus, non-metropolitan areas of the 'Sunbelt' contained a higher proportion of manufacturing workers in their labour forces than did the southern and western region as a whole, while non-metropolitan areas in the 'Frostbelt' had a lower proportion than the Manufacturing Belt did as a whole. The data indicate that manufacturing was more dispersed in small towns and rural areas of the 'Sunbelt' but continued to maintain an attraction for metropolitan (suburban) areas of the 'Frostbelt'. The proportion of low-wage industry workers residing in non-metropolitan areas of the 'Frostbelt' throughout the 1950s and 1960s was relatively small and tended to remain stable at 5.5 per cent. The low wage proportion in the 'Sunbelt' was twice as large and grew from 10.6 to 13.7 per cent. A sizeable increase occurred in the proportion of high wage industry workers residing in 'Sunbelt' non-metropolitan areas; the proportion nearly tripled from 4.0 to 11.1 per cent of the labour force. In 'Frostbelt' non-metropolitan areas high wage industry workers increased from 7.6 to 11.7 per cent of the total labour force. Evidence indicates the intra-regional decentralization trends slackened in the 1980s (Garnick 1985).

Production and non-production worker locational trends

During the three and a half decades following the Second World War (1947–1982) manufacturing employment in the United States grew by 4.73 million jobs (Table 4.4). The Manufacturing Belt experienced a net loss of 0.78 million jobs while the rest of the country experienced a net gain of 5.51 million workers. For the country as a whole, 90 per cent of the entire net growth in manufacturing employment was in non-production workers, mostly salaried workers engaged in management, supervision, sales, R. & D. and other support activities. Only 10 per cent of the net jobs were gained in wage earners directly involved in production. Non-production workers accounted for 17 per cent of manufacturing employment in 1947, 28 per cent in 1967 and 35 per cent in 1982.

Table 4.4 Changes in US manufacturing employment by type and region: 1947–1982

	1947–1967			*1967–1982*			*1947–1982*		
Region	*Total employment change (000s)*	*Production worker change (000s)*	*Nonproduction worker change (000s)*	*Total employment change (000s)*	*Production worker change (000s)*	*Nonproduction worker change (000s)*	*Total employment change (000s)*	*Production worker change (000s)*	*Nonproduction worker change (000s)*
Manufacturing Belt	1,396.0	−144.3	1,540.3	−2,175.7	−2,323.4	146.7	−779.7	−2,467.7	1,687.0
Other US	3,535.2	2,155.9	1,379.3	1,973.9	778.9	1,195.0	5,509.1	2,934.8	2,574.3
Total	4,931.2	2,011.6	2,919.6	−201.8	−1,544.5	1,341.7	4,729.4	467.1	4,261.3

Source: Compiled by author from US *Census of Manufacturers*.

An important difference, however, occurred throughout the period in the growth of production and non-production workers between the nation's two major regions. While the Manufacturing Belt registered a total employment loss of 0.78 million workers, the loss represented a decline of nearly 2.5 million production workers but a gain of 1.7 million non-production jobs. The Manufacturing Belt for some time up until the 1981–1982 recession had been more than compensating for net losses in production workers by net gains in non-production workers. Data also reveal the total net substitution of durable goods manufacturing employment for nondurable goods employment in the Northeast (New England and Middle-Atlantic states) between 1950 and 1980: durable goods employment increased by 656,200 workers while nondurable goods employment declined by 544,053 jobs. The 5.5 million worker gain realized by the rest of the country over the 1947–1982 period was nearly evenly divided, with a slightly greater increase in production workers compared to non-production workers. During the first two decades of the period production jobs accounted for 61 per cent of the growth in the country outside the Manufacturing Belt. During the more recent decade and a half, production jobs accounted for 40 per cent of the net growth. By 1982 approximately 10 per cent of the Manufacturing Belt's total workforce was employed in non-production manufacturing jobs compared to 6 per cent of the workforce in the rest of the country.

The data reveal that since 1947 production workers have become more evenly distributed throughout the country whereas non-production workers, while increasing in numbers throughout the country, became more concentrated in the Manufacturing Belt. The data further reveal that, within each region, non-production employment grew more steadily in large urban centres while production employment tended to grow more in smaller settlements.

The principal theme of industrial development in the US for some time has been decentralization from and within established manufacturing districts to more peripheral locations. Formerly, low wage industry dominated the pattern of dispersal. More recently, traditional high-wage industries have taken part in the decentralization. The empirical trends are evidence of the capital restructuring of different industrial sectors as manufacturing firms trade-off the comparative advantages of different size settlements in different regions of the country for different manufacturing operations to maintain a competitive stance in national and global markets.

Capital investment trends

Restructuring trends

While manufacturing has been decentralizing, industry has been undergoing a change from having a significant proportion of employment in single-plant establishments operated by production-oriented proprietors and managers to having multinational-

Figure 4.2 Multiplant firms' share of US manufacturing 1947–1982.

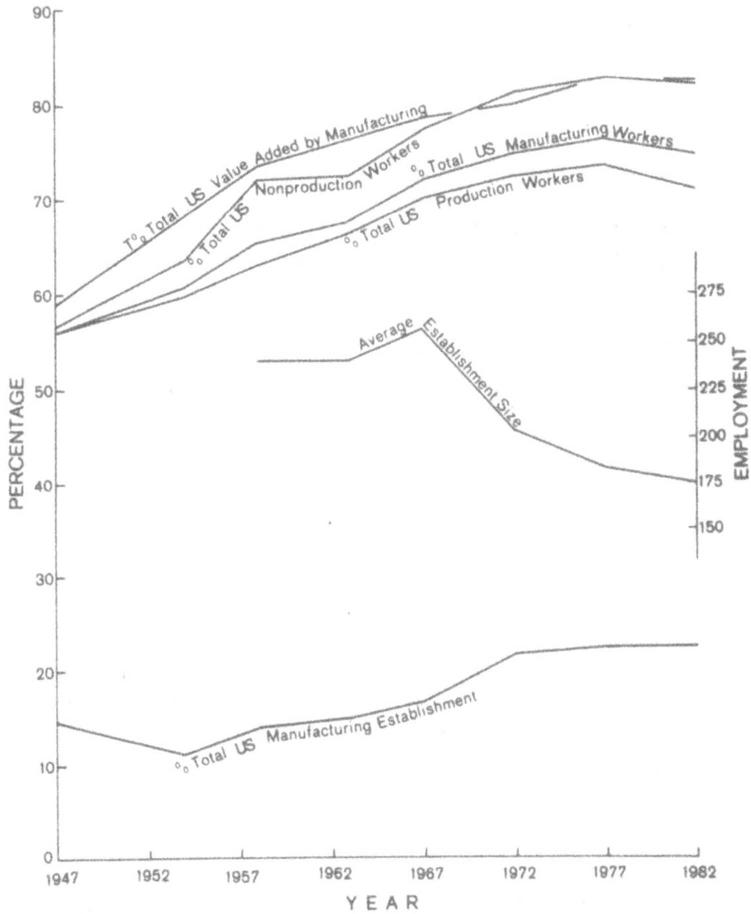

Source: Compiled from *Census of Manufacturers*

multiplant firms operated by financially-oriented managers as the main generators of manufacturing employment (Figure 4.2). Multiplant firms employed 76 per cent of the country's manufacturing workforce in 1982, up 20 per cent from 1947. A much greater share of this increase in employment was in non-production jobs compared to the share of similar jobs in single plant firms. By 1982 an average of 67.2 employees in each multi-plant facility (38 per cent) were non-production workers, almost double the 1947 average. In single plant facilities only 4.4 employees (26 per cent), on the average, were non-production workers, nearly one less than in 1947. Multi-plant firms, on the other hand, accounted for only 23 per cent of the total number of manufacturing facilities in the country in 1982, up from their 15 per cent share in 1947. Thus, the growth of a relatively small number of large corporations was at the expense of a large number of small firms.

A survey of plants newly opened between 1972 and 1978 by 410 *Fortune* 500 companies revealed 58 per cent produced a single product only for distribution to all the firms' markets and 9 per cent were process plants producing components for distribution to other plants belonging to the firms (Schmenner 1982). Only 31 per cent manufactured multiple products for a specific market only. Between 1972 and 1978, 535 major mergers took place among US manufacturing firms (mergers in which the acquired assets were greater than $10 m, Federal Trade Commission 1981). Conglomerate mergers, involving the diversification into new product lines to spread risk and even-out profit cycles, accounted for the largest number of acquisitions (69 per cent). Horizontal mergers between firms producing the same products, to improve market share while simultaneously eliminating competition, involved 23 per cent of the total. Eight per cent were vertical mergers to increase control over more sources of supply, or over the distribution of allied product lines.

During the same period American firms were establishing production facilities abroad. In 1950 total US direct investment in manufacturing in offshore locations amounted to only 3.9 per cent of the fixed capital investment in domestic locations. By 1977 the ratio had reached 9.4 per cent, and 1,841 US multinational corporations owned a majority share in 9,702 offshore affiliates with half owning two or more separate facilities (Bureau of Economic Analysis 1981). American parent firms employed 17.1 million workers overall: 11.8 million in the US (59.4 per cent of the nation's manufacturing workers) and 5.3 million abroad, or nearly one-third of their total workers. The largest investments were in Canada, followed by the UK and West Germany. Between 1972 and 1979 a sample of 1900 joint venture agreements between US firms and firms from other countries resulted in the creation of 322 new facilities (Federal Trade Commission 1972–1979). The data reveal that the majority of ventures resulting in new facilities were with western European firms (25 per cent) followed by Japan (20 per cent). Australia and New Zealand accounted for the location of 34 per cent of the new facilities established by the ventures, followed by western Europe (26 per cent) and Japan (22 per cent). Only 15 per cent of the ventures resulted in new facilities being established in the US, suggesting that American firms were largely responsible for promoting the agreements.

The empirical findings reveal the dynamic growth of a relatively small number of large firms that occurs through a process of adoption of new product lines (along with the expansion, contraction or divestiture of existing lines) and the geographic expansion of the firms into new markets. As a consequence, such firms are constantly restructuring their functional operations affecting linkages among their facilities, customers, suppliers and subcontractors. The restructuring has manifested itself geographically by a redistribution of labour in which the Manufacturing Belt has spun off lower income production jobs to other regions of the country while growing in higher income external control and support functions and higher value manufacturing.

Productivity and technology trends

Important internal relations exist within firms among labour, production technology, investment decisions and location. New capital investments often embody new technologies that are an important ingredient in plant staffing patterns, productivity, and employment growth. During the 1970s US expenditures for new plants and equipment (measured by value of investments to value of output) were lower than any major industrial country. This was an important factor contributing to the nation's poor productivity performance (National Science Board 1981).

Manufacturing productivity during the decade (measured by value of output per worker hour) increased 28 per cent in the US compared to 102 per cent in Japan, 60 per cent in West Germany and 26 per cent in the UK. The US, in the 1980s, continued its weak productivity growth rate compared to other industrialized nations, including the UK. The loss of over 1.5 million production jobs in the country between 1967–1982 compared to an increase of over 1.3 million non-production jobs is one reason for the nation's poor productivity performance.

The tradition of American capital investment in manufacturing innovations has been different from that of other countries and may be another factor underlying the poor performance. A study of 1,866 product and process innovations developed between 1945–1974 revealed that 40 per cent of US innovations were labour-saving compared to 13 per cent in Western Europe and 6 per cent in Japan (Davidson 1976). Material-saving innovations were more important in other countries: 47 per cent of Western European innovations and 34 per cent of Japanese innovations compared to 21 per cent of US innovations. Capital-saving reasons accounted for 7 per cent of the innovations in both the US and Japan and 11 per cent in Europe. While the US was improving productivity by reducing labour costs, other countries were doing so by reducing material costs. The concentration of US investment in labour-saving innovations helps to account for some of the low net increase in the number of production workers in the country.

Still another factor that underlies low productivity is the growing dominance of large, multi-national-multi-plant firms in the country. Medium-sized firms were found to spend four times the amount of investment in R. & D. per dollar of sales as large firms, while small firms spent twenty-four times the amount (National Science Board 1976). Certainly, the acquisitions of some firms were to acquire other firm's advanced technology and factor mixes as well.

Technological innovations, productivity increases, capital investment, plant staffing patterns and employment growth tend to be related to each other and have affected the rate of change in manufacturing employment among the nation's regions. As production facilities age, severe production problems result from the lack of adequate space, from poor plant layout and materials flow, or from obsolete equipment and process technology. The capital costs associated with the modernization of such vintage plants are more excessive than the cost of establishing modern facilities, especially when the locational advantages underlying the original site choices have been lost. As many of the products manufactured in the Manufacturing Belt neared the end of their life cycles, firms either closed facilities or adopted labour-saving process technology, both of which resulted in employment declines. On the other hand, changes in: (1) transportation, communication, process and material technology, (2) capital, utility and labour force availability, and (3) firm organization and management practices, have allowed manufacturing facilities to locate on formerly inaccessible and unsuitable sites in small towns and rural areas in all regions of the country.

Government regional policy

The impact of government policy on industrial decentralization

The inter-regional and intra-regional decentralization of industry has occurred more in response to private economic forces which affect the cost and efficiency of production than from government policies directed at spreading social and economic benefits more equitably to backward, underprivileged, and problem areas of the country. Nonetheless, government policies that had an effect on the geographic expansion of manufacturing were those associated with the development of local and regional infrastructure. The policies that exerted the greatest influence were those which resulted in the construction of the national highway, waterway, and airway networks. Such policies increased the accessibility of many formerly inaccessible areas and helped lower transport costs in addition to promoting faster service between locations. Regulations that eliminated discriminatory rail freight-rates after the Second World War also helped to accelerate decentralization. If the discriminatory rates had not existed in the first place, industry may not have become as concentrated in the Manufacturing Belt as it did.

Government policies that promoted the development of utilities in small towns and rural areas also influenced industrial decentralization. Until the Rural Electrification Act, small towns could not afford the costs of electric service, and industries were constrained to locate in built-up urban settlements. Waste disposal services and especially water service have long been proclaimed the harbingers of industry. Until government funds became more readily available in the 1960s and 1970s, few small communities were able to finance public works projects. Whereas in the 1960s the government programmes provided assistance, with the decisions as to the use of the funds made at the federal level, in the 1970s the funds were provided by the federal government, but the decisions as to where they would be spent were made at the state and local level. During the 1970s a significant increase also occurred in the number of programmes created by state governments to improve local infrastructure. In addition, a number of states established regional technical college systems to train workers either in specialized trades or in skills required by existing or new manufacturing establishments. The overall effect was that within a short period of time, small towns in non-metropolitan areas grew remarkably in their ability to provide the basic external urbanization economies required by industry.

The factors that influence the location of industry are of two types: critical factors and trade-off factors. Critical factors are necessary criteria or conditions that must exist in a place before it can be considered for a plant location: easy access, sufficient utility capacity, available labour skills, for example. Critical factors differ from one industry to another and from one plant to another in the same industry or firm depending upon the functional responsibilities of the different plants. Trade-off factors are criteria that can be substituted one for another in the site selection decision: for example, the substitution of lower cost labour, land, utilities, and taxes to more than offset higher transportation costs or the added costs of internalizing necessary external economies as firms locate in less accessible areas. A substantial amount of the geographical decentralization of industry occurred because the large number of critical factors determining plant locations in the past have been reduced to a relatively few today. Conversely, the number of trade-off factors has increased. This is because many smaller settlements are now able to provide the required criteria whereas, in the past, the criteria were likely to be found only in larger urban centres. The changes occurred largely as a result of government policies.

Government spatial policy

With the realization by the federal government that most of their regional development policies – those providing guaranteed loans and grants to industry – primarily aided existing industrial firms to shift their facilities more easily from one region to another rather than creating the development of new industry, a cutback in federal programmes occurred in the late 1970s. This spurred some states to develop policies that concentrated funds only in designated places to establish public services rather than dispersing the limited funds among all places in the state (Committee on Balanced Growth and Economic Development 1978). In essence, the policies were modified growth-pole strategies that attempted to balance job opportunities, public service availability, and resident populations in different size settlements within different regions of the states. The policies served to reinforce the urban hierarchical diffusion of economic development.

Multi-county regions, each with its own regional council of government (COG), were established in each state. Within each region some states assigned settlements the responsibility to provide different public service functions in somewhat the same manner that central place theory allocates commercial functions to different size settlements. In order of descending population size in each region, the largest place was designated as the regional centre, the next largest two or three places were designated as district centres, while the approximately six to nine next largest places provided the functions of area centres. Eighteen to twenty-seven smaller places would serve as community centres while the large number of lowest order settlements were designated as support centres. Seasonal centres that provided jobs during different periods of the year, such as those associated with tourist areas, were assigned public service functions on a place by place basis. Thus, a hierarchical system of services was established in which each type of centre was to provide all the services found in the next lowest order centre as well as other services that were particular to its own centre's designation. Each higher-order centre was responsible for providing its particular services to all lower-order centres in its service area. A typical region contained approximately 81 to 121 centres.

While population size was an important criterion in determining a settlement's service designation, an equally important criterion was the settlement's central location within its assigned service area so as to minimize the distance people would have to travel to obtain the required service. Settlements' service designations were initially assigned by state government officials with the provision that any settlement could petition the government for a change in its designation. Several settlements were not interested in growth and, after public hearings, chose to be assigned a lower order designation. Many settlements wanted to be assigned a higher order designation, some a few orders higher than their initial assignment. Settlements petitioning for an increase in their designation had to substantiate their request and agree to provide most of the funds to establish the higher order services. Alternative competing project-proposals submitted by local governments for funding were judged on their correspondence with an overall multi-county regional plan. Project authorization was determined by the Office of Management and Budget's (OMB) A95 review process vested in the local regional councils.

Faced with the realization of declining employment in the nation's manufacturing workforce, except for industrial sectors investing heavily in research and development and employing a high percentage of scientists and engineers, nearly all states became involved in the development of research or science parks by the 1980s. The evidence of economic prosperity in areas where high-tech industry was concentrated (route 128 in Massachusetts, Silicon Valley in California, Research Triangle Park in North Carolina, and the Austin–San Antonio corridor in Texas, for example) provided testimony of the link between major research universities, entrepreneurship, and new business formation. This, coupled with the evidence that small businesses were the major generators of employment in the country, particularly those engaged in providing business and producer services, prompted the adoption of entirely new development strategies by state governments in the 1980s. Rather than the single focus on industrial recruiting, the strategies dealt with business assistance programmes, including the establishment of new-business incubator facilities, venture capital loan programmes, high-tech research facilities, and technology transfer fairs. While such strategies were relatively new, the evidence from the few states that were involved early in developing research facilities and universities in conjunction with science parks suggests that it leads to a new, higher-order urban centre designated a technopolis (Kawashima and Taketoshi 1986).

Government policies to decentralize manufacturing after the Second World War, initially for the purpose of national security but later to stem the tide of rural-urban migration and to spread social benefits to backward, underprivileged, and problem areas, were responsible for the more equitable distribution of public services throughout the country. This allowed industry to take advantage of the various levels of external economies offered by the nation's hierarchical system of cities. The development of the technopolis is a manifestation of the influence of a special external economy on the location of high-tech industrial development. Many high-tech industries need to be close to major research universities that produce new scientists and engineers, maintain the latest scientific equipment for teaching and research, offer continuing education and reciprocal internships for personnel, and possess a faculty involved in the development of new theories and techniques to replace outmoded ideas and obsolete practices.

Interrelationships among technology adoption, firm functional-restructuring, and locational adjustment

While a substantial portion of the decentralization of manufacturing in the US can be attributed to the growth of markets in peripheral regions of the country compared to the stagnating growth trends in the traditional Manufacturing Belt, a significant portion can also be attributed to the growing dominance of multi-plant, multi-functional, multi-regional firms in the country. Faced with growing competition, uncertain economic conditions, and rapidly changing technology advances, such firms have adopted both location and technology investment strategies for different functional operations, or have substituted one strategy for another.

In the past, location strategies were not as readily available to firms, since individual plants were more multi-functional in their operations and required greater accessibility to subcontractors, suppliers and markets (such as do many single plant firms today) in addition to necessary public services (utilities, police, and fire protection, etc.) and a labour force with a wide range of skills. With the more recent emergence of the single-function plant, linked to other plants in the same firm, coupled with the growing availability of public services in small towns and rural areas within easy access of a large commuting labour pool, made available by the widespread use of the automobile, firms were more able to adopt location strategies to lower the overall marginal costs of production.

It is the thesis of this chapter that the principal spatial mechanism underlying a substantial amount of the geographic decentralization of manufacturing can be found in the direct relationships that exist among settlement size, external economies, and worker compensation for identical jobs, regardless of the region in which they are performed (Fuchs 1967; Goldfarb and Yezer 1976; Hock 1972; Johnson 1983; Moriarty 1978). This mechanism is reinforced by inter-regional differences that exist among urban size, external economies, and worker compensation. Since wage levels (and worker benefits) tend to increase automatically with the growth of urban centres (and with plant size), the higher wage bills either price the less competitive plants out of the larger centres or cause them to become more capital intensive in their operations by the adoption of labour-saving process technology (Rees, Briggs, and Oakey 1986). The aspatial aspects of firms that interact with the city-size mechanism are the direct relationship that exists between plant size and worker compensation, and the degree to which advanced production technology is applied to individual functional operations to improve internal economies regardless of location. Plants in large centres that fail to adopt advanced production technology become less competitive and tend to go through a process of vertical disintegration either by ridding themselves entirely of the unproductive operations and relying upon subcontractors for their completion, or by locating the operations in branch facilities in smaller settlements some distance away. The least competitive labour-intensive industries or operations locate in the smaller towns and rural areas in even more peripheral areas or offshore countries having lower than average wage compensation, worker skills, and external economies. Consequently, different size urban centres in different regions provide different comparative advantages for different functional operations so that settlement size is an important consideration in firms' location strategies, including vertical and horizontal integration and disintegration decisions. To remain competitive, firms can adopt both location and technology investment strategies for different functional operations or substitute one strategy for another. The poor productivity performance and low level of capital investment in new technology, along with the growth of industry in non-metropolitan areas, suggest that US firms have opted more for the location strategy.

The settlement-size industrial-sorting process can most readily be linked to the product life-cycle model in which different inputs and scales of production are required during the different stages of new, mature and standardized product manufacturing (Moriarty 1983; Vernon 1966, 1979). While, in recent years, multi-plant firms have taken advantage of the marginal returns that can be derived from different size urban centres, regardless of the life-cycle stage of their products, in general the manufacture of new products is a small-scale operation involving short production runs that are highly dependent upon conventional production techniques using high-cost engineers, technicians, and skilled craftsmen, normally found in the larger urban centres of the core regions where specialized inputs and services (external to the firm) can also be found (Malecki 1979). Administrative and marketing personnel are readily available to monitor and decide changes in product design to improve market share. Thus, small plants with average wage bills lower than those of large plants are more marginally cost-efficient in larger metropolitan centres with their overall higher labour costs. In the manufacture of standardized components or products, production processes become routinized and labour-skill requirements are reduced so that low-cost labour sites, many with ready access to markets, become important for plant facilities utilizing specialized mass-production techniques (Clark 1981; Erickson 1976a, 1976b; Erickson and Leinbach 1979; Moriarty 1983; Park and Wheeler 1983; Norton and Rees 1979).

Such facilities require little in the way of administrative, sales and R. & D. personnel or local inputs and services other than low-cost land, labour and utilities. Thus, large plants with higher average wage bills than small plants are more marginally cost-efficient in small settlements (or offshore sites) with their overall lower labour costs. Multi-plant firms more recently have moved beyond this simple relationship between location and product stage evident in the two decades following the Second World War by realizing that small settlements can provide greater marginal cost-advantages for a variety of functional operations regardless of a product's stage. It should be emphasized that this proposition does not imply a strict inverse city-size, plant-size relationship. A plant's location is also contingent upon its particular function(s) and its requirements for external localization economies.

While the direct relationships between city size and labour cost and plant size and labour cost are established empirical regularities within the USA, it is unclear how evident they are in other countries. Those with high levels of unionization, and nationwide collective bargaining, and benefit packages, are unlikely to have wage bills that differ in a systematic manner with plant size and city size. Consequently, in those countries the urban hierarchy may have less influence on the location of a firm's different functional operations, resulting in greater technology adoption or subcontracting to remain competitive.

Note

1. The values among the different tables do not necessarily correspond for similar periods, partly as a result of business-cycle fluctuations and partly because some tables (4.2 and 4.4) are based upon employment data collected at establishment locations, and other tables (4.1 and 4.3) are based upon occupation data collected at residence locations.

References

Barta, G. (1984) 'Spatial impacts of organizational changes of industrial enterprises', paper presented at the IGU Symposium on Industrial Systems, Nebian, France.

Berry, B.J.L. and Kasarda, J.D. (1977) *Contemporary Urban Ecology*, New York: MacMillan Publishing Co.

Bureau of Economic Analysis (1981) *US Direct Investments Abroad 1977*, Washington, DC: Government Printing Office.

Clark, G. (1981) 'The employment relation and spatial division of labor', *Annals of the Association of American Geographers* 71:412–24.

Committee on Balanced Growth and Economic Development (1978) *A Balanced Growth Policy for North Carolina*, State Goals and Policy Board, North Carolina Department of Administration, Raleigh, NC.

Cromley, R. and Leinbach, T.R. (1981) 'The pattern and impact of the filter-down process in nonmetropolitan Kentucky', *Economic Geography* 57:108–224.

Davidson, W.H. (1976) 'Patterns of factor-saving innovations for the industrialized world', *European Economic Review* 8:207–217.

Dennis, R. (1978) 'The decline of manufacturing employment in central London, 1960–1974', *Urban Studies* 15:63–74.

Dicken, P. and Lloyd, P.E. (1978) 'Inner metropolitan industrial change, enterprise structures and policy issues: case studies of Manchester and Merseyside', *Regional Studies* 12:181–97.

Erickson, R.A. (1976a) 'The filtering-down process: industrial location in a nonmetropolitan area', *Professional Geographer* 28:254–60.

(1976b) 'Nonmetropolitan industrial expansion: emerging implications for regional development', *Review of Regional Studies* 6:35–48.

(1981) 'Corporations, branch plants and employment stability in nonmetropolitan areas', in J. Rees, G. Hewings and H. Stafford (Eds) *Industrial Location and Regional Systems*, New York: J.F. Bergin Publishers.

Erickson, R.A. and Leinbach, T.R. (1979) 'Characteristics of branch plants attracted to nonmetropolitan areas', in R.E. Londsdale and H.L. Seyler (Eds) *Nonmetropolitan Industrialization*, Washington DC: V.H. Winston and Sons.

Erickson, R.A. and Wasylenko, M. (1980) 'Firm relocation and site selection in suburban municipalities', *Journal of Urban Economics* 8:69–85.

Federal Trade Commission (1972–1979, 1981) *Statistical Report on Mergers and Acquisitions*, Washington, DC: Bureau of Economics.

Fuchs, V.R. (1967) 'Hourly earnings differentials by region and size of city' *Monthly Labor Review* 90:22–26.

Fuguitt, G.V. and Beale C.L. (1984) 'Changes in population, employment and industrial composition in nonmetropolitan America', University of Wisconsin Center for Demography and Ecology, Madison, Wis.

Garnick, D.H. (1983) 'Shifting patterns in the growth of metropolitan and nonmetropolitan areas', *Survey of Current Business* 63:37–44.

(1985) 'Patterns of growth in metropolitan and nonmetropolitan areas: an update', *Survey of Current Business* 65:33–38.

Goldfarb, R.S. and Yezer, A.M.J. (1976) 'Evaluating alternative theories of intercity and interregional wage differentials', *Journal of Regional Science* 16:345–63.

Hansen, Niles (1979) 'The new international division of labor and manufacturing decentralization in the United States', *Review of Regional Studies* 9:1–11.

Heaton, T.B. and Fuguitt, G.V. (1978) 'Metropolitan industrial growth and population change', Paper presented at the annual meeting of the Association of American Geographers, New Orleans, Louisiana.

Hoch, I. (1972) 'Income and city size', *Urban Studies* 9:299–328.

Holmes, J., (1983) 'Industrial reorganization, capital restructuring and locational change: an analysis of the Canadian automobile industry in the 1960s', *Economic Geography* 59:251–72.

Johnson, G.E. (1983) 'Intermetropolitan wage differentials in the United States' in J. Triplett (Ed.) *The Measurement of Labor Cost*, Chicago: University of Chicago Press.

Kawashima, T. and Taketoshi, M. (1986) 'Spatial Agglomeration Economies in Technology Development: National and Local Implications of Tsukuba Science City and Technopolis Development Plan in Japan', paper presented at the 33rd annual meeting of the Regional Science Association, Columbus, Ohio.

Keeble, D. (1978) 'Industrial decline in the inner city and conurbation', *Transactions: Institute of British Geographers* 3:101–114.

(1980) 'Industrial decline, regional policy and the urban-rural manufacturing shift in the United Kingdom', *Environment and Planning A* 12:945–62.

Lever, W.F. (1975) 'Manufacturing decentralization and shifts in factor costs and external economies', in L. Collins and D.F. Walker (Eds) *Locational Dynamics of Manufacturing Activity*, New York: John Wiley and Sons.

Malecki, E.J. (1979) 'Agglomeration and intra-firm linkages in R. & D. location in the United States', *Tijdschrift voor Econ en Soc Geografie* 70:322–32.

Massey, D. (1982) *The Anatomy of Job Loss: The How and Where of Industrial Decline*, London: Methuen.

Massey, D. and Meegan, R.A. (1978) 'The geography of industrial reorganization: the spatial effects of the restructuring of the electrical engineering sector under the IRC, *Progress in Planning* 10:155–237.

McCarthy, K.F. and Morrison, P.A. (1977) 'The changing demographic and economic structure of nonmetropolitan areas in the United States', *International Regional Science Review* 2:123–42.

Moriarty, B.M. (1978) 'A note on unexplained residuals in north-south wage differential models', *Journal of Regional Science* 18:105–108.

(1980) *Industrial Location and Community Development*, Chapel Hill, NC, The University of North Carolina Press.

(1981) 'Spread and diffusion processes in regional industrial employment growth', in W. Buhr and P. Friedrich (Eds) *Regional Development Under Stagnation*, Baden-Baden, Germany: Nomos-Verlag.

(1983) 'Hierarchies of cities and the spatial filtering of industrial development', *Papers of the Regional Science Association* 52:59–82.

(1986) 'Productivity, industrial restructuring and the deglomeration of American manufacturing', in J. Rees (Ed.) *Technology, Regions and Policy* Totowa, NJ: Rowman and Littlefield.

National Science Board (1976) *Science Indicators 1975*, Washington DC: Government Printing Office.

(1981) *Science Indicators 1980*, Washington DC: Government Printing Office.

Norton, R.D. and Rees, J. (1979) 'The product cycle and the spatial decentralization of American manufacturing', *Regional Studies* 13:141–51.

Park, S.O. and Wheeler, J.O. (1983) 'The filtering down process in Georgia: the third stage of the product life cycle', *Professional Geographer* 35:18–31.

Rees, J. (1979) 'Technological change and regional shifts in American manufacturing', *Professional Geographer* 31:45–54.

Rees, J., Briggs, R., and Oakey, R. (1986) 'The adoption of new technology in the American machinery industry', in J. Rees (Ed.), *Technology, Regions, and Policy* Totowa, NJ: Rowman and Littlefield.

Schmenner, R.W. (1982) *Making Business Location Decisions*, Englewood Cliffs, NJ: Prentice-Hall Inc.

Schroder, M., deSmidt, M., and Staring, W. (1984) 'Corporate growth, foreign investment and locational choice', in M. deSmidt and E. Wever (Eds) *A Profile of Dutch Economic Geography*, Assen: Van Gorcum & Co.

Struyk, R.J. and James, F.J. Jr. (1975) *Intrametropolitan Industrial Location*, Lexington, Mass: D.C. Heath and Co.

Till, T. (1973) 'The extent of industrialization in southern nonmetro labor markets in the 1960s', *Journal of Regional Science* 13:453–61.

United States Department of Commerce (1947, 1954, 1958, 1963, 1967, 1972, 1977, 1982) *Census of Manufacturers*, Bureau of the Census, Washington, DC.

(1950, 1960, 1970, 1980) *Census of Population*, Bureau of the Census, Washington, DC.

Vernon, R. (1966) 'International investment and international trade in the product cycle', *Quarterly Journal of Economics* 80:190–207.

(1979) 'The product cycle hypothesis in a new international environment', *Oxford Bulletin of Economics and Statistics* 41:255–67.

Watts, H.D. (1982) 'The interregional distribution of West German multinationals in the United Kingdom', in M. Taylor and N. Thrift (Eds) *The Geography of Multinationals*, New York: St Martin's Press.

Zelinsky, W. (1962) 'Has American industry been decentralizing: the evidence for the 1930–1954 period', *Economic Geography* 38:251–289.

5

Geographic implications of plant closure legislation in the USA

H.A. Stafford

Manufacturers are constantly adjusting to change in their environments. Among these adjustments are investments and disinvestments which are place specific. For manufacturing plants, these may be incremental, with increases to capital in place and additions to the labour-force, or reductions in capital and/or labour. On this continuum the building of a new facility is one end, and the closing of a plant the other. For the places (localities, regions) involved, a new plant is usually deemed a positive economic development, while the closure of a plant produces human and economic dislocation and hardship. It is contended by some that in competitive societies capital, as represented by corporate management (and typically with pressure from shareholders), has a disproportionate degree of power relative to labour and to the communities affected by management decisions. This imbalance is not generally perceived as a problem in the case of positive investment, in part because communities do have some real power over new investment through land use controls, permits and taxation policies, but mainly because communities usually welcome the economic benefits of new manufacturing activity. In the situation of plant closure, however, communities often see themselves as weak victims of the excessive mobility of capital (Bluestone and Harrison 1982). In order partially to redress this imbalance, communities (and larger political units) may turn to legislative remedies which allow for more orderly adjustments to the negative impacts of plant closure and/or to impose some additional closure costs on capital. There are intense debates over the merits of plant closure legislation, and there are geographic implications.

The provisions and incidence of plant closure legislation

Although a number of African and Asian countries have elements of plant closure legislation, and Mexico has procedures for government review of collective dismissals of employees, among the free market countries legislation is most common, and enforced, in those most industrialized (Office of Technology Assessment, September 1986:5). An overview of programmes to assist displaced workers in the USA, Canada, Sweden, France, West Germany, the UK, Japan and Australia is presented in Table 5.1.

Table 5.1 Features of programmes to assist displaced workers by selected countries

	Feature			
Country	*Extent of programme coordination*[(a)]	*Extent of target population*[(b)]	*Wage subsidies*	*Relocation assistance*
United States	Low	Broad	None	Yes
Canada	High	Narrow	Growth firms	Yes
Sweden	High	Broad	Firms which provide training instead of layoffs	Yes
France	High	Narrow	Employers who hire the difficult to employ	Yes
West Germany	High	Broad	Same as France plus OUT and settling-in allowance	Yes
United Kingdom	Medium	Broad	Employers who split a FT job into two PT ones	Yes
Japan	Medium	Narrow	Growth and declining firms; ranges from ¼ to ¾ of wages	Yes
Australia	Medium	Narrow	Declining firms	Yes, (Special programme)

Notes: (a) Subjective rank based on an active and visible agency, such as the Canadian Manpower Consultative Service and the German Federal Employment Institute, which has responsibility for overall co-ordination of employment and training policy.
(b) Subjective rank based on whether a country designates specific industries and/or geographical areas for assistance; those that do, received a 'narrow' ranking.

Table 5.1 continued

Country	*UI benefits*	*Feature* *Income maintenance beyond UI*[c]	*Training: how provided*
United States	26–39 weeks, amount varies by state; 35–40% of previous wage	Yes, Supplementary Unemployment Benefits (SUB) and/or Trade Adjustment Assistance	Publicly funded in public and private training institutions; OUT in firms
Canada	Usually 12 months, longer if in training; 50% of previous wage	Workers 55–64 years on permanent layoff with 10 years tenure	Use both public and private institutions
Sweden	300 days if under 55 yrs of age, 450 days if 55+; 80% of previous wage	Agreements may be negotiated in special circumstances	Public compulsory job vacancy requirement
France	Usually 12 months, 70% of previous wage	Workers in training or designated industries	Government financed training agreements between firm and National Vocational Association, 1.1% of firm's wage bill must be spent on training
West Germany	312 days at 68% of previous wage; drops to 50% for unlimited time	Workers in designated industries or dismissed unwarrantably	Government incentives to firms to provide training; emphasize occupational mobility training
United Kingdom	312 days at $38/wk if single, $61/wk if married; amount based on need after 1 yr.	Lump sum, based on tenure and wage; 30 wks pay maximum or full salary if in training	Use both public and private institutions; emphasis on training youth
Japan	Ranges from 300 days if 55+ yrs and 10 yrs. of tenure to 90 days if under 30 yrs; and 1 yr or less of tenure; 60–80% of previous wage	90 days for workers 40 yrs + in designated industries	Wage subsidy to firm that conducts training

Table 5.1 continued

Country	UI benefits	*Feature* Income maintenance beyond UI[(c)]	Training: how provided
Australia	In 1980: $48.50 wk if single, $96.50 if married; rec'd while on active job search	No	Training allowances to workers

Note: (c) European Economic Community (EEC) countries also receive money for dislocated workers from EEC funds from levies on steel and coal production.

Table 5.1 (continued)

Country	Tripartite co-ordination	Timing of programme implementation	*Feature* National advanced notification requirement	Job creation[(d)]
United States	No, but Public Industry Councils under JTPA	Post	No	No
Canada	Yes	Prior	Yes, industries under Federal jurisdiction and in 7 of 12 Provinces; 1 wk to 16 wks	Government sponsored public or private sector employment
Sweden	Yes	Prior	Yes, notice rises as number affected rises	Temporary public relief work
France	Yes	Post	Yes, 2–14 wks depending upon reason and scale of dismissal	$3,420 from general revenues to unemployed to start own firm
West Germany	Yes	Post	Yes, 30 days after notifying government	Government funded jobs in-the-public-interest for the long term unemployed
United Kingdom	Yes	Prior	Yes, rises as number affected rises; up to 90 days	$56/wk from UI plus $1,400 of your own to start new firm

Table 5.1 (continued)

Country	*Feature* *Tripartite co-ordination*	*Timing of programme implementation*	*National advanced notification requirement*	*Job creation*[d]
Japan	Yes	Prior	Yes, 'sufficient' time must be given for workers to comprehend problem	Wage subsidy to firms that hire displaced workers
Australia	Yes	Post	No	Temporary public service and pilot programme to help unemployed to start own firm

Note: (d) A number of countries also offer regional development assistance (loans and other incentives) to attract and/or develop jobs in certain localities.

Table 5.1 (continued)

Country	*Feature* *Government supported early retirement*	*Work-time reduction schemes*
United States	No	No
Canada	Yes	No
Sweden	Yes	No
France	Yes	Yes
West Germany	Yes	Yes
United Kingdom	Yes	Yes
Japan	Yes	No
Australia	Yes (Compulsory at age 60)	No

Source: Secretary of Labor's Task Force on Economic Adjustment and Worker Dislocation, December, 1986, Appendix A, 29–33.

Note that (1) most of the programmes are government rather than private industry, sponsored, (2) tripartite co-ordination between management, labour and the public sector is required in seven of the eight countries listed, the exception being the USA, and (3) advance notification of an impending mass layoff or plant closing is required in many industrialized nations, but there was no national requirement in the USA (Office of Technology Assessment, September 1986, 5). The implication that the USA may be the 'odd man out' among the industrialized nations regarding worker and community adjustment provisions to plant closure is consistent with observations regarding the basic approaches to assisting displaced workers:

> Simplifying the matter considerably, there are three *general approaches*. In the first approach, certain societies accept that workers whose skills are no longer in demand should take the initiative in equipping themselves with new skills or re-integrating into stable employment, perhaps at a new location with the assistance of traditional labor market programs. The role of the employer may be limited to strict compliance with his contractual obligations. In the second approach, the state may be seen as having its main role to play in providing income support and encouraging local communities to provide training for alternative jobs. Other societies consider that the whole community should be involved in implementing a plan to safeguard the local community's economic base. A third view stresses the need to contain the impact of structural adjustment within the enterprise so that workers may be reallocated to new functions without recourse to the external labor market. The US perhaps falls into the first camp, Europe the second and Japan the last.
>
> (Secretary of Labor's Task Force, December, 1986, Appendix A, 3)

Within the USA, there is intense debate over whether or not plant closing legislation is in the ultimate best interests of the workers, regions, and businesses involved. The current situation is that (1) national (Federal) legislation was not made law until August 1988, amidst intense political confrontation, (2) the legislation which existed prior to this was only at the state or community scale, and (3) both existing and proposed legislation tends to be at the most basic level, that of advance notice. It is instructive to look at these elements, in reverse order.

The three major possible components of plant closure legislation are advance notice, income guarantees, and worker retraining. Although some companies voluntarily engage in some of these activities, and others are bound to do so by virtue of collective bargaining agreements with unions, in most cases income protection, via unemployment benefits, and retraining and job search services are state governmental functions.

Regarding plant closing and relocation obligations under the National Labor Relations Act, it is clear that:

> while under current case law management has the obligation to negotiate over effects, any obligation to provide the union with effective notice or input into the decision itself is much less certain or, in the case of a total plant closing, nonexistent. Thus, if a union desires certain rights – such as notice about closings, the potential to influence the decision itself, or the ability to block mid-contract relocations – and these rights are not assured by a collective bargaining agreement, they can be assured only through various forms of plant closing legislation.
> (Greenfield, 1984:27)

Clark contends 'that current labor relations policies of the Reagan Administration, and especially of the National Labor Relations Board (NLRB), are essentially unjust' (1986:290). The NLRB has narrowed the scope of collective bargaining by holding that firms are not required to bargain with unions over plant

Table 5.2 Typical provisions of plant-closing laws

Provisions	*Number of plant-closing laws with provision*
Prior notice of closing	20
Firm-paid severance benefits	14
'Good-faith' sale efforts, incentives for employee ownership and firm reimbursements for employee retraining	11
Continuation of health-insurance coverage for specified period after termination	10
Effects bargaining, or requirement for employer to discuss effects of plant-closing with workers	10
Employer payments to State of specified proportion of annual wage bill	9
Firm reimbursement for employee relocation expenses	8
Paid leave time for workers prior to shutdown	7
Preferential transfer rights for affected workers	6
Decision bargaining, or requirement for employer to discuss decision to close with workers	2

Source: Littman, D. A. and Myung-Hoon Lee, 'Plant Closings and Worker Dislocation: An Analysis of Proposed Policy Remedies', *Economic Review of the Federal Reserve Bank of Cleveland*, Fall 1983:3.
Note: Provisions of existing and proposed plant-closing laws are listed in order of descending frequency.

closings and production consolidation in another plant, even if a contract is still in force, and thus the legitimate interests of labour are restricted to issues of compensation, and 'as a consequence organized labor is drastically limited in their attempts to bargain over the changing economic environment' (Clark 1986:297). The impotence of collective bargaining within the USA helps explain the push by organized labour, and by pro-labour legislators, for national plant closing legislation.

The major thrust of closure legislation is for advance notice, as indicated in Table 5.2. It is argued that advance notice of a major layoff or plant closure is not only fair, but necessary for other programmes to be effective, e.g., time for retraining prior to job loss. Perhaps even more important is that while any regulation which decreases corporate managerial control tends to be resisted, advance notice has the least onerous financial implications for businesses.

At the present time, over half the fifty states have considered some form of plant closure legislation. Such legislation typically would apply to all businesses over some specified size, e.g., 100 employees, but the primary concern is with manufacturing plants since 'worker dislocation and closure-layoff rates are dominated by events in the manufacturing sector' (General Accounting Office, July 1986:15). However, only a handful of states so far have passed closure legislation. These include Maine, Wisconsin, Massachusetts, Michigan, Maryland, California, New Jersey, Rhode Island, and Illinois. Note that not represented by these states are the south-eastern and south-western portions (excepting California) of the nation – the 'Sunbelt' – nor are prairie, Rocky Mountain, or Pacific north-west regions covered. With the exception of California, which is now the nation's leading manufacturing state, the state-level closure legislation activity has been earliest in the northeastern quadrant of the nation. This might seem reasonable since this encompasses the 'Snowbelt'/'Rustbelt' which had been losing ground (relatively) to the 'Sunbelt' for the past decades, and especially during the 1970s. The 1970s were also a decade of extraordinary mobility. It is no accident that state-level plant closing laws date from 1975. However, it is possible to make too much of this pattern. Note that three core states of the Manufacturing Belt, Pennsylvania, Ohio, and Indiana have not been among the leaders in passing legislation. Ironically, the lead was taken by the Ohio Public Interest Campaign, and a bill was introduced into the Ohio Legislature; the bill set the pattern for most other state and federal attempts that followed, but plant closure legislation has yet to be enacted in Ohio (Harrison 1985, in Staudohar and Brown 1987). Conversely, two states early to act were Maine and Wisconsin; Wisconsin is on the edge of the old Manufacturing Belt, and Maine is definitely peripheral.

Though many are considering legislation, most states do not have regulations currently in place, and even those that do have very mild laws. For example, the Maine law, which applies only to establishments that employed 100 or more workers in the prior 12 months, provides for 60 days advance notice of closure or relocation and severance pay, under specified conditions, equivalent to one week's wage for each year an employee worked at the establishment. To enforce the severance pay provisions the state can bring court action to recover unpaid amounts. However,

> the law does not explicitly provide the state government with the power to enforce the sixty-day notice provision. Aside from a possible judgement of $500 for failing to provide notice to a municipality or the employees when moving an establishment outside the State, no other penalties are specified in the law
> (Office of Technology Assessment, September 1986:57)

The penalty for not complying with the sixty-day advance notice requirement in Wisconsin is a minimal $50 per employee. In Massachusetts, the state 'expects' a 'good faith effort' to provide at least ninety-day notice, but no minimum period is prescribed. In Maryland there are voluntary guidelines for advance notice and continuation of benefits, and Michigan also has a voluntary notice provision which is part of an act to encourage the formation of employee-owned corporations (Office of Technology Assessment, September 1986:56–59).

Why is plant closing legislation either absent or weak at the state and local scales within the USA, relative to other industrialized countries? As already suggested, it is part cultural ethos, the North American belief in free enterprise and distrust of governmental regulation. North Americans tend to be suspicious of any form of industrial policy, and even of planning in general. Regarding Rhode Island's Greenhouse Compact, Goldstein notes that although it was 'considered by many a model of what state industrial policy should be, the ambitious, comprehensive, highly detailed plan was rejected soundly in an "all-or-nothing" statewide referendum in June 1984, despite the strong backing of most of the state's business, labor, and political leaders' which may be interpreted 'as a rejection of the process of comprehensive planning, not of the substantive contents of the plan' (1986:263). It is partly a consequence of the business communities' natural reluctance to be regulated, and the relatively weak position of American labour unions. And this may be related to the relative mobility of labour within the USA as compared, for example, to Europe where 'the lack of mobility . . . due to national boundaries and cultural values' may be a factor in the evolution of 'the European approach which gives employed workers more employment stability than most American workers get' (Office of Technology Assessment, September 1986:35). Indeed, 'a major objection to the adoption of such job security legislation in the US is that it is largely responsible for Europe's low job growth and high unemployment', even though 'this conclusion is *not* supported by the evidence available to date. Macroeconomic policy, residual inter-country barriers, more nationalized industries and a lower spirit of entrepreneurialism all seem to contribute significantly more than employment security legislation to this problem' (Secretary of Labor's Task Force, December 1986, Appendix A, 8). Another critical element is that regional economic development efforts are primarily concerned with expanding employment and attracting new industry. There is the fear that any jurisdiction that enacts strong plant closure legislation while other areas do not significantly weakens its competitive position for new investment.

In 1974 Senator Mondale and Congressman Ford introduced the first national plant closing bill into Congress. The National Employment Priorities Act called for mandatory prenotification of intended closures; it failed to gain sufficient support. Congressional supporters of labour have continued to work in conjunction with labour unions (especially the United Auto Workers and the AFL-CIO) and introduced several subsequent bills (Harrison 1985, in Staudohar and Brown 1987). In 1987, Senator Metzenbaum (and others) proposed legislation (S 538, HR 1122), which was added to the Omnibus Trade Bill (S 1420), 'to aid dislocated workers, including a requirement that companies give employees minimum periods of notice of plant closings' (*Wall Street Journal*, 19 February 1987:20). Debate continues, but any passage will be the result of 'watered-down' plant closing provisions by the sponsors in view of the opposition of the business community and the Reagan administration (*Congressional Quarterly*, 1987:1384). The 1987 proposal is almost identical to the 1985 legislation proposed by Congressman Ford, a bill which began as a more comprehensive approach on how businesses conduct closures, relocations, and major work force reductions, but which became more narrow and with less political impact, reflecting a 'more politically viable approach' in the face of strong opposition from business and Republicans (Ford 1985, in Staudohar and Brown 1987:307). Since the record is complete, it is instructive to examine the fate of the 1985 proposed national legislation more closely.

The proposed Labor-Management Notification and Consultation Act of 1985 (HR 1616)) had three major provisions. The first was a ninety-day advance notice requirement, so to give employees and communities time for adjustment and retraining, and, hopefully, even find a buyer for the facility to be closed. The second provision was that employers consult with employees during the notice period about alternatives to a closure or layoff. Third, the act called for the establishment of a National Commission on Plant Closings and Worker Dislocation, to study such things as health insurance for displaced workers, retraining, severance pay, transfer rights, and pension protections, and recommend administration or legislative action (Ford 1985, in Staudohar and Brown, 1987:307–311).

Even this mild bill was rejected by the US House of Representatives in 1985.

> The House Nov. 21 narrowly rejected watered-down legislation intended to cushion the impact of mass layoffs and plant closings. The labor-backed bill (HR 1616) fell victim to well-organized opposition from business and deep philosophical differences among members. On the final 203–208 vote, 54 Democrats – 49 from the South – joined 154 Republicans in opposing the revised measure, which would have required employers to give advance notice when they intended to close a plant or lay off a large number of workers. Twenty Republicans and 183 Democrats voted for the bill.
>
> (*Congressional Quarterly Almanac*, 1985:469)

Although the final House vote largely followed party lines, with the typically more liberal and labour-oriented Democrats voting for, and the traditionally more conservative and business-oriented Republicans voting against national plant closing legislation, the pattern of defections is of interest. Of the 54 defecting Democrats, 49 are from the south; of the 20 Republicans who voted 'yes', contrary to the party line, all are from the North-east and Mid-West regions of the country, with the exception of the affirmative vote from Alaska's lone Representative. The state level pattern of the majority of votes is shown in Figure 5.1. With the exceptions of North Dakota, South Dakota (whose lone Representative did not vote), and Minnesota in the upper Midwest, New Mexico in the South-west, Washington in the North-west, and California, Alaska,

Figure 5.1 Voting by representatives on Labor-Management Notification Consultation Act of 1985.

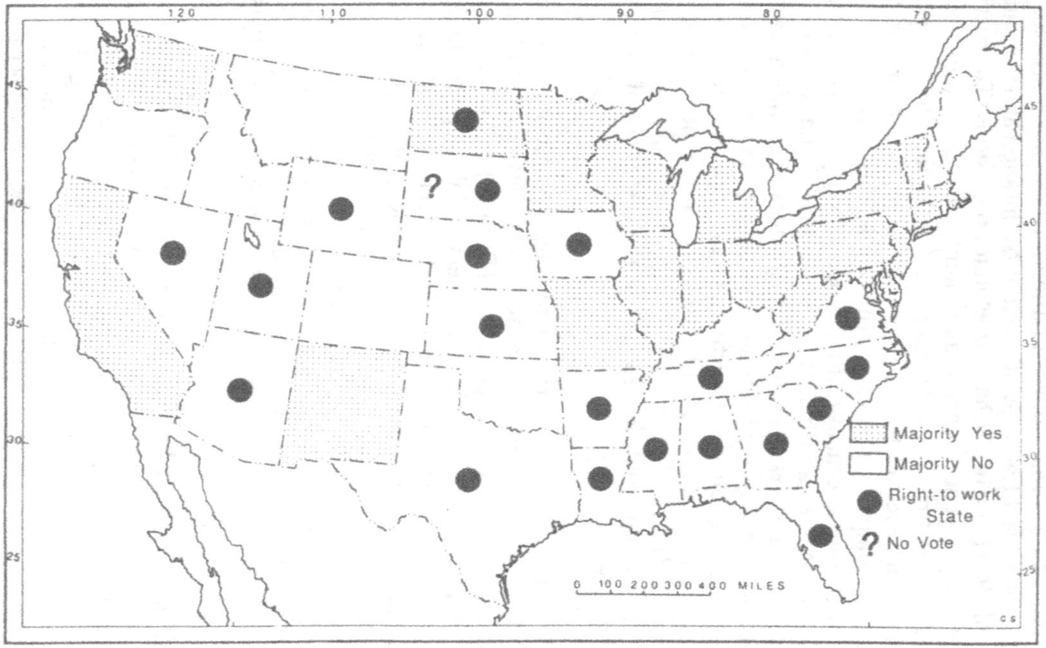

Sources: *1985 Congressional Quarterly Almanac*, p. 120–21 H.; *Site Selection Handbook*, September 1984

and Hawaii, support for plant closing legislation is shown on Figure 5.1 to be concentrated in the north-eastern quadrant of the country, and especially in the old Manufacturing Belt. This pattern is generally consistent with historic trends. Of the twenty states with a Right to Work Law (which may be seen as a rough indication of a pro-business legislature and public) all but North Dakota had a majority voting 'no' (and North Dakota has only one Representative in the House, in contrast to California's 45, Illinois' 22, or Texas' 27 Representatives).

While opposition to plant closure legislation appears to conform to traditional pro-business attitudes, support for such laws seems more closely linked to experiences with large numbers of closures and permanent layoffs. Table 5.3 reports aggregate estimated data for 1983–84 by the nine census regions for all business establishments (manufacturing, wholesale-retail trade, services, and other). The General Accounting Office report estimates that 'over half of the establishment closures and layoffs in the USA occurred in the

Table 5.3 Regional differences in closures and layoffs in the USA, 1983–84

Region	*Number of establishments*[(a)]	*Percent of total*	*Rate of occurrence*[(b)]	*Number of employees*	*Percent of total*
Total	7,790	100	7.8	1,049,000	100
Northeast	1,880	24	7.6	227,000	22
New England	640	8	9.3	80,000	8
Mid Atlantic	1,240	16	6.9	147,000	14
Midwest	2,190	28	9.0	312,000	29
East North Central	1,690	22	9.6	227,000	21
West North Central	500	6	7.4	85,000	8
South	2,460	32	7.4	299,000	29
South Atlantic	850	11	5.2	76,000	7
East South Central	310	4	5.5	48,000	5
West South Central	1,300	17	12.0	175,000	17
West	1,260	16	7.0	211,000	20
Mountain	320	4	7.2	36,000	3
Pacific	940	12	6.9	175,000	17

Source: General Accounting Office 1986, p. 12.
Notes: (a) Establishments with 100 or more employees experiencing closure, or permanent layoff (of 20 per cent or more of the workforce, or over 199 employees).
(b) Percentage of all establishments per region with 100 or more employees experiencing closure or permanent layoff.

Northeast and Mid-West regions. This is not surprising since about half of the business establishments with 100 or more employees are located in these two regions. However, the South and West regions also experienced significant numbers of establishment closures and layoff' (July 1986:13). It may be significant that the Northeast and Mid-West closures and layoffs are concentrated in the eight states of the Mid-Atlantic and East North Central sub-regions, while those in the South and West are spread over twenty-eight states. Support for, or opposition to plant closing legislation however, does not correlate well with regional rates of closure and layoffs. While the East North Central and New England region experienced high rates, the Mid-Atlantic region shows a relatively low rate but this area tends to support closure laws, and the West South Central region had the highest rate of occurrence but tends not to support legislation.

Table 5.4 and Figure 5.2 present the 1983–84 General Accounting Office data for the manufacturing sector alone. 'Regions that had the highest closure-layoff rates for the manufacturing sector had the highest overall closure-rates . . . thus, our findings reinforce the perception that worker dislocation and closure-layoff rates are dominated by events in the manufacturing sector' (July

Table 5.4 Manufacturing sector impact of closures and layoffs by region in the USA, 1983–84

	Closures and permanent layoffs		
Region	*Number of establishments*[(a)]	*Percentage of total*	*Rate of occurrence*[(b)]
New England	530	11	19.4
Mid Atlantic	780	17	12.9
East North Central	1,140	24	15.9
West North Central	245	5	10.7
South Atlantic	540	12	8.9
East South Central	180	4	6.5
West South Central	590	13	19.4
Mountain	125	3	13.7
Pacific	520	11	12.4
Total Manufacturing	4,650	100	13.2

Source: General Accounting Office 1986, p. 14.
Notes: (a) Establishments with 100 or more employees experiencing closure, or permanent layoff (of 20 per cent of more of work force, or over 199 employees)
(b) Percentage of all establishments per region with 100 or more employees experiencing closure or permanent layoff.

Figure 5.2 Closure and layoff rates, all industries and manufacturing sector, by region, 1983–84.

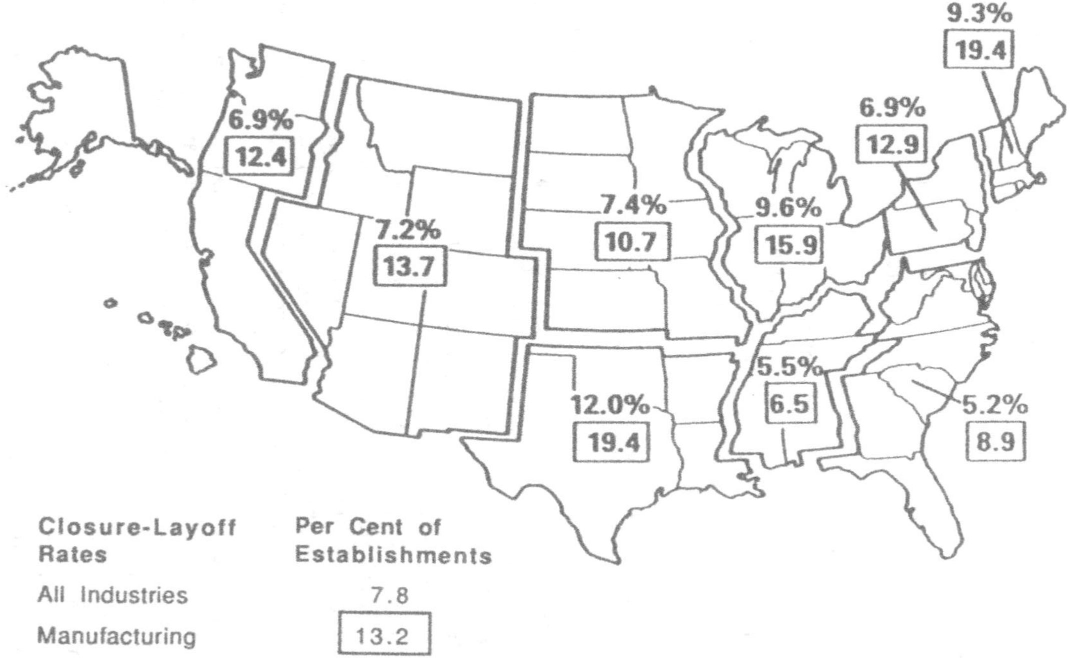

Source: General Accounting Office 1986, p. 14.

1986:15). Again, it appears that support for plant closing legislation is more a function of the absolute magnitude of closure and layoffs than a function of the relative importance of these to state and regional economies. This, of course, does not obviate the earlier observation that voting on national plant-closing legislation in the USA has largely followed political party lines. In 1988 the Republican–Democrat split was clearly evident. In May, 1988, President Reagan vetoed the massive, and otherwise unrelated, trade bill because it contained an advance notification of plant closing provision. Sensing widespread citizen support, Democrats quickly reintroduced a separate plant closing bill. Mr Reagan allowed this advance plant closing notification bill to become law in August, 1988, so as not to jeopardize the political campaign of the then Vice-President George Bush for the Presidency (*The Wall Street Journal*, 30 September, 1988:42).

Potential geographic impacts

Proponents of plant closing legislation argue that 'capital flight' from communities and relatively immobile workers is excessive, 'even out of control' (Bluestone and Harrison 1982:35). In many, perhaps most, cases multiplant firms are not closing unprofitable plants, but rather shifting production and/or investments to locations and facilities which produce an (anticipated) even higher (or acceptable) rate of return on capital. Critics contend that accounting from the narrow and short-run perspective of the firm is incomplete, inadequate, and socially unacceptable; the 'social costs' of the mobility of capital are omitted from the equation. The relocation of production creates immediate economic hardship on the community left behind. The direct wages formerly paid, plus the multiplier effects, are lost; purchasing power declines, impacting the demand for and ability to pay for goods and services, both public and private. The social costs to newly unemployed workers include the deterioration of mental and physical health, and increases in homicides, suicides, child abuse, alcoholism, and crime (Bluestone and Harrison 1982). The closing of a viable plant is particularly galling to communities and states which have provided substantial economic inducements to attract or retain the firm's operation. While communities and workers can, and should, adjust to economic change, it is argued that the pace and magnitude of capital mobility is too rapid, even unconscionable. Note that the crux of the concern for 'capital flight' is geographic; at issue are those communities and workers left behind, without sufficient time to react properly to changed economic circumstances. Understandably the most common and basic component of plant closing legislation is for prenotification.

Those against plant closing legislation have a more macroeconomic viewpoint, argue that capital should not be restricted in its (necessarily) trial and error search for the best combinations of production arrangements and location, and that the absence of regulation will produce benefits to the economy as a whole which will exceed the combined social and economic costs to individual communities and to workers. It is further argued that 'since these laws amount to exit penalties or taxes they deter the entrance of new firms into the state because new firms will be reluctant to locate under these potentially punitive conditions and higher taxes. The legislation, therefore, in addition to being unnecessary, is counterproductive in that the state will lose rather than maintain or gain jobs in the long run' (Leary 1985:115). Again, note the explicitly spatial context, and the reason for the push for national legislation by proponents so that no domestic community is at risk by unilaterally imposing plant closing laws.

Both the proponents and opponents of plant closure legislation are cognizant of the spatial dimensions. However, the polarized nature of the arguments – with opponents basically arguing economic efficiency and proponents grounding their positions in social justice – tends to obscure the full range of possible spatial implications of legislation, even within the more narrow economic context. A series of questions may be raised: (1) will plant-closing legislation deter or impede capital shifts? (2) Will such legislation improve managerial perceptions of place, and their creative abilities to utilize places more effectively, including alternative uses? (3) (a) Will/does state level legislation really make a state less attractive for general business investment? (b) Might it make a state more attractive? (c) Or, might the influences be so minor relative to other locational factors that the effects are spatially neutral? (4) If there is national legislation, will there be no regional or state level impacts? (5) If there is national legislation, what are the implications for international competitiveness?

Regarding the first question, if the costs of exit were sufficiently high, then legislation would impede plant closings. However, if the requirements were for little more than 60 or 90 days' advance notice, then it is not likely that there would be much impact on decisions to close and/or relocate. Even though managements may not often now provide advance notice, they in fact know of their intentions much longer than two or three months prior to actual closings. Thus, advance notice of a real closing amounts to little more than letting workers and the public know of decisions already taken. Exit penalties so high as to create major financial barriers to closure would represent a substantial alteration to a free-market economy and will not be enacted in the USA. Even laws in Western Europe, which are the most stringent in the world, do not contain penalties sufficient to prevent closings, and 'surveys show that employers' objections to the legislation tend to focus not on the central provisions of the law, like advance notice, but on subsidiary aspects like the administrative complexity, protection for special groups like white-collar workers, and legal coverage of newly hired workers and small firms,' the latter being provisions which are 'unlikely to be incorporated into any U.S. legislation' (Secretary of Labor's Task Force 1986, Appendix A, 13).

Advance notice, however, may be expected to increase pressure on managements to explain and reconsider closure decisions prior to implementation. To the extent that the motivation for closure is

Table 5.5 Reasons for closure or layoff: results of survey of 355 establishments

Factors	*Percentage of establishments*[(a)] *citing factor as significant*
Reduced product demand	70
Increased competition	69
High labour costs	57
Inflated value of US dollar	32
Low productivity	29
Consolidation of product line or service	27
State and/or local regulations	27
Poor management	26
Federal regulations	24
Facility obsolescence	23
Limited access to foreign markets	18
Production automation	16
Product obsolescence	14
Industry deregulation	9

Source: General Accounting Office 1986, p. 16.
Note: (a) Establishments with 100 or more employees, all industries, experiencing closure or permanent layoff (of 20 per cent or more of the workforce, or over 199 employees).

In general, businesses indicated that the major reasons for closure or layoff were related to the problems of competition in the market-place. About 70 per cent indicated that reduced product demand and/or increased competition were major factors influencing their decision to close or lay off workers. High labour costs were also cited by 57 per cent of the establishments as a major factor in their decision.

Such factors as product obsolescence, facility obsolescence, and production automation were cited relatively infrequently as being major reasons for the closure or layoff. In addition, only 7 per cent of the establishments studied indicated that they had experienced a bankruptcy or financial reorganization before closure or layoff.

Table 5.6 Industrial location: ten most important location factors at four spatial scales, for the interviewed firms (N = 54)

Rank	*National*		*Regional*		*Subregional*		*Local*	
1	Markets	102	Markets	170	Markets	91	Labour availability	161
2	Transport costs	55	Materials	54	Environmental regulations	65	Utilities	158
3	Geography of the firm	44	Transport costs	35	Materials	58	Transport availability	156
4	Materials	38	Geography of the firm	31	Labour unions	55	Site characteristics	148
5	Environmental regulations	27	Labour costs	23	Utilities	55	Quality of life	134
6	Labour costs	26	Utilities	18	Developmental organizations	51	Environmental regulations	104
7	Quality of life	24	Developmental organizations	16	Labour costs	43	Transport costs	100
8	Utilities	22	Transport availability	15	Transport availability	43	Markets	90
9	Transport availability	20	Environmental regulations	14	Labour availability	42	Labour costs	87
10	Labour availability	20	Labour availability	14	Business climate	42	Materials	83
	Total counts	378	Total counts	390	Total counts	545	Total counts	1,221

Source: Stafford 1985.

related to attributes of the area, as distinct from more general market-place pressures, then advance notice may allow for negotiation and reconsideration. Instructive are the results of the General Accounting Office survey relative to the reasons for closure or layoff (Table 5.5). The most important community/region factor cited is high labour costs; related to this may be low productivity. It is possible that labour issues may be renegotiated. Conversely, if in the process of preparing a public defence of contemplated action, managements more clearly recognize that their difficulties stem from reduced product demand and/or increased competition, then there may be the realization that relocation probably is not a solution. Of course, this would not apply to situations where the motive is to reduce, rather than relocate, productive capacity, but in any event it behoves management explicitly to distinguish between plant related (e.g. facility obsolescence), firm related (e.g. consolidation of product or service, poor management), area, and market-place factors. Plant closing legislation might induce more creative thinking about the modified use of facilities in areas in which the firm already has a presence, to the potential benefit of both the firm and the area.

As previously indicated, one argument against plant closing legislation being enacted by a state or community is that the area with legislation will become less attractive to new business because investors will direct capital to unregulated places. The same argument could be extended to countries at the level of international competition. Is this a real danger? Might it be that closure legislation would be of such minor importance in location decisions that it would be of little significance? Is it possible that closure legislation could even be a positive force for the location of new investment? To speculate on these questions, the focus must be shifted from disinvestment to investment. The factors most influencing the location of new manufacturing plants within the United States are given in Table 5.6.

Studies of the location of new manufacturing investment repeatedly show that the primary factors are labour and markets. If plant closing legislation would have the same impact on location decisions as taxes then it is unlikely that it would exert very much influence on new investment placement. Taxes are not among the ten most important location factors for most firms, at any geographic scale (Table 5.6). If the analogy is correct, it is not probable that relatively weak plant closing legislation, e.g., advance notification, would override the more critical location forces. Another possibility does exist. The enactment of closure laws may be seen by decision makers as an indication of a poor regional 'business climate,' and this may work against a region's attractiveness. Business climate is a very subjective factor and its influence is difficult to gauge. The available evidence, however, indicates that it, too, is a relatively minor influence and that it rarely is sufficient to steer investments away from places which make economic sense on other grounds. Perhaps the best analogy is with marriage. Perhaps firms, like couples, are willing to make commitments when sufficient benefits are perceived, in spite of exit penalties.

It is even possible that regional closure legislation could have a positive effect on future new business investment. Although the management of the closing plant may not wish to provide it, advance notification should be welcomed by other firms in the area, both those who provide the plant to be closed with goods and services, and those who rely on the incomes produced. Firms might be more prone to invest in areas in which advance notification was the norm, thus allowing them more time to adjust to economic change. This, in turn, might promote regional economic stability, and the more stable and predictable a region the more attractive it is for business investment. Both of these may have a positive effect on an area's 'quality-of-life,' a subjective variable, but one which has been shown to be relatively important in location decisions, especially at the local scale (Table 5.6). Thus, it may be that those legislators who perceive their 'no' votes on plant closing legislation to be pro-business votes are, in fact, producing the opposite effect.

The enactment of national plant closing laws presumably would provide a level playing field for all sub-regions of the nation. Experience with national environment protection legislation, however, suggests that this may not be so. Although the technical aspects of environmental protection measures are relatively uniform across the USA, decision makers perceive spatial variations in their administration, so the favoured areas are those in which compliance is less complex, more certain, and less of an administrative headache for the firm (Stafford 1985). This is in accord with European experience which indicates that a major objection to plant closing laws is not the laws themselves, but rather the administrative complexities entailed (Secretary of Labor's Task Force, Appendix A, 13). At the international scale, variations in the scope and complexities of national plant closing legislations might have some impact on location decisions when other factors are essentially equal but like the intra-national situation, it is unlikely that such laws will have much impact on the placement of new business investments.

References

Bluestone, B., and Harrison, B. (1982) *The Deindustrialization of America*, New York: Basic Books.

Clark, G.L. (1986) 'Restructuring the US Economy: The NLRB, the Saturn Project, and Economic Justice.' *Economic Geography* 62(4):289–306.

Congressional Quarterly (1987).

Congressional Quarterly Almanac (1985).

Ford, W.D. (1987) 'Coping with Plant Closings,' *Labor Law Journal*, June 1985:323–326, in P.D. Staudohar and H.E. Brown (Eds), *Deindustrialization and Plant Closure*, Lexington, MA: Lexington Books.

General Accounting Office, United States, July (1986) *Dislocated Workers: Extent of Business Closures, Layoffs, and the Public and Private Response*, Washington, D.C. (GAO/HRD-86-116 BR).

Goldstein, H.A. (1986) 'The State and Local Industrial Policy Question,' *American Planning Association Journal*:262–64.

Greenfield, P.A. (1984) 'Plant Closing Obligations Under The National Labor Relations Act', in A. Aboud (Ed.) *Plant Closing Legislation*, Ithaca, NY: ILR Press, Cornell University.

Harrison, B. (1987) 'The International Movement for Prenotification of Plant Closures,' *Industrial Relations* (Fall, 1985, 400–7), in P.D. Staudohar and H.E. Brown (Eds) *Deindustrialization and Plant Closure*, Lexington, MA: Lexington Books.

Leary, T.J. (1985) 'Deindustrialization, Plant Closing Laws, and the States', *State Government* 58:3, 113–18.

Littman, D.A.and Lee, M-H (1984) 'Plant Closings and Worker Dislocation,' *Economic Review of the Federal Reserve Bank of Cleveland*, Fall 1983:2–18, in McKenzie, R.B. *Plant Closings: Public or Private Choices*? Washington, DC: Cato Institute.

Office of Technology Assessment, US Congress, September (1986) *Plant Closing: Advance Notice and Rapid Response – Special Report*, OTA-ITE-321, Washington, DC: US Government Printing Office.

Secretary of Labor's Task Force on Economic Adjustment and Worker Dislocation, December (1986) *Economic Adjustment and Worker Dislocation in a Competitive Society*, Washington, DC.

Site Selection Handbook, September (1984) Atlanta: Conway Data.

Stafford, H.A. (1985) 'Environmental Protection and Industrial Location', *Annals of the Association of American Geographers* 75(2):227–40.

Wall Street Journal, 19 February 1987; 30 September 1988.

6

The politics of industrial decline and restructuring in the Northern Ireland shipbuilding industry

R.T. Harrison

Introduction

On the basis of recent discussions of the post-1945 development of the UK shipbuilding industry in its international context (Harrison 1983; Thomas 1983; Todd 1986) and the analysis of the regional economic impact of the industry in Northern Ireland (Harrison 1985, 1986a, 1988), two conclusions can be drawn. First, the shipbuilding industry in Northern Ireland, as in other regions, has contracted sharply as the competitiveness of the UK shipbuilding industry has been eroded by the rise of Japanese and Third World competition (Peck and Townsend 1984). Second, the impact of this decline on the wider regional economy, through both the labour market and inter-industry multiplier effects, has been less substantial in recent years than in the past, and is not as significant as many local commentators and politicians feel it to be (Harrison 1988). Nevertheless, the injection into the regional economy of some £40 m (gross) spending power annually in the form of wage and salary payments is not insignificant, and represents around 6 per cent of total wage and salary payments to employees in the production industries.

Despite these changes in the relative importance of the industry, its historic actual importance to the regional economy and its current symbolic importance (particularly in the context of the polarized pattern of employment in Northern Ireland) has, as in other parts of the UK, been a factor underlying the provision of government financial assistance to the industry (Hogwood 1979; Todd 1983). Both the symbolic and actual importance of the industry have been summed up in the recent official history of Harland and Wolff:

> it would be misleading to see aid from Government as being an entirely one-way transaction. The Company has been a

> demonstrably peaceable symbol of British commitment to Northern Ireland, generating a significant proportion of all employment in the Province's manufacturing sector. It has also been a leader in United Kingdom shipbuilding, producing, in the largest construction yard in Europe, the biggest, the best and the most technically advanced products. Queen's Island has been a training ground not only for first-class shipbuilders and marine engineers but also for skilled workers and managers for the whole of Northern Ireland. The Company's purchases of materials and components – amounting to almost two-thirds of the price of a ship – provide a market for hundreds of United Kingdom suppliers. The purchasing power of Harland & Wolff employees is of vital importance to the city of Belfast and to Northern Ireland as a whole
>
> (Moss and Hume 1986:492)

The reaction of the Northern Ireland shipbuilding industry to the changing conditions of international competition, and the progressive involvement of government as a significant influence in the external environment of the industry, therefore, provides a useful case study of the development and delivery of industrial policy for declining industries (Pinder 1982; Gillis 1980; Flam *et al.* 1983; Hillman 1982; Strange and Tooze 1981; Forster and Rees 1983). Furthermore, the still important, albeit declining, role of the industry as an employer in a regional economy which has experienced a significant erosion of its manufacturing base through plant closures and restructuring (Northern Ireland Economic Council 1983b; Harrison 1986b; Rowthorn 1987; Teague 1987), suggests that its performance, and the policy response, may be indicative both of the problems of older industries in the region and of the difficulties inherent in designing and delivering an appropriate policy response.

Against the background of these wider changes, this chapter examines the recent performance of the shipbuilding industry in Northern Ireland (which is, by definition, an examination of the performance of a single company – Harland and Wolff plc), reviews the response of the company to changes in the pattern of market demand and international competitiveness, and summarizes the nature and magnitude of the policy response to the decline of the industry since the early 1960s.

Financial performance

The anticipation (yet to be confirmed in the published accounts

Figure 6.1 Harland and Wolff plc: profit and loss account 1960–1985/86.

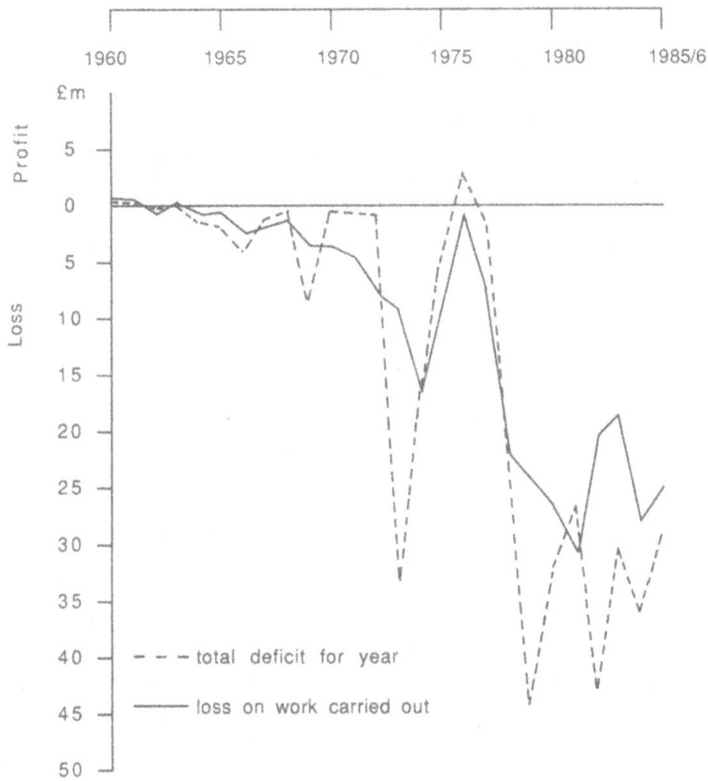

Source: Harland and Wolff Annual Reports; Harrison 1988:199.

which are not available at the time of writing) that Harland and Wolff in Belfast made record losses of over £60 m in the financial year 1986/87 underlines the parlous state of the industry in Northern Ireland. However, although these losses are historically high, Harland and Wolff's slide into unprofitability and financial crisis is a long-standing phenomenon (Figure 6.1). Losses in the early and mid-1960s, which were generally under £2 m per annum, initially reflected changes in competitive conditions in the world shipbuilding industry, particularly the shift from a sellers' to a buyers' market, in which profit margins were reduced or eliminated altogether, and the rise of significant competition from the rapidly expanding Japanese shipbuilding industry (Thomas 1983). The slight dip in performance in 1966, considered significant at the time but relatively insignificant in the light of events in the following two decades, reflected the company's own diagnosis of untidy management, lack of effective budgetary control, and poor marketing (Harland and Wolff Annual Report 1966). It also coincided with the sharp contraction of the industry in Belfast (employment fell by almost 50 per cent between 1960 and 1966) following the cessation of labour-intensive passenger liner and naval construction in the early 1960s (Harrison 1985). As will become clear later in this chapter, this dip in the performance of the company took on a wider, and long-term, significance as it prompted the first formal intervention of government in the financial management of the industry in the region.

During the 1960s and early 1970s Harland and Wolff engaged in a series of major investment programmes in an attempt to create and maintain an important niche for the company in the then most rapidly growing market sector, that for tankers, and in particular for very large crude carriers (VLCC). The scale of this investment was considerable. In 1968 and 1969 the shipbuilding industry accounted for around 11 per cent of total capital expenditure in the manufacturing sector in Northern Ireland, and for around 30 per cent of capital expenditure on new building and works. In the period 1973 to 1975 these proportions rose to almost 14 per cent and over 40 per cent respectively (Harrison 1988).

Despite this investment, most significantly in new building dock facilities to replicate Japanese techniques of block construction and prefabrication in the construction of VLCCs, there was a sharp escalation in the company's losses as production costs continued to outstrip the estimates underlying ship contract prices: losses on work carried out rose from £1 m in 1968 to £4.5 m (14 per cent of turnover) in 1971 and to £16.5 m (41 per cent of turnover) in 1974. After making provision for additional anticipated losses on contracts in progress, the total deficit for 1973 rose to over £33 m, equivalent to 108 per cent of turnover (Figure 6.1).

The situation in the mid-1970s represented something of a turnaround in the fortunes of the company. Between 1974 and 1976 turnover almost doubled from £40.3 m to £79.4 m, and losses on work carried out decreased sharply: indeed the company reported in 1976 that had it not been necessary to renegotiate the price of steel for certain ship contracts there would have been a small profit on work carried out during the year (Harland and Wolff Annual Report 1976). After taking account of the release from provision for future losses there was, nevertheless, a small overall surplus for the year: the first and only such surplus since 1963. This improvement in performance reflects the contribution made by a series of investment programmes: by 1976 the building dock and associated steel handling facilities were finally and fully brought into commission. The company was consequently able to record significant improvements in productivity which were facilitated by a full order book and the full utilization of production facilities which that allowed.

However, the improvement in financial performance was short-lived. World shipbuilding output peaked in 1975 and remained high in 1976, and Harland and Wolff's output of almost 0.5 m gross tons of shipping in 1975 was at an all time high. Nevertheless, the effect of the 1973/74 oil crisis, and the consequent dislocation of the world economy, were beginning to show. In 1974 and 1975 Harland and Wolff announced no new ship orders, and three VLCCs (each of 333,000 dwt) ordered by Maritime Fruit Carriers in 1972, as part of a £300 m package of orders placed with Harland and Wolff, Scott Lithgow, and Swan Hunter, were cancelled in 1974 to avoid heavy losses on fixed price contracts (Thomas 1983). Faced with the almost complete disappearance of the VLCC market in which Harland and Wolff had made more strenuous efforts to concentrate than any other UK shipbuilder, and with the emergence of severe excess capacity in the shipbuilding industry world-wide as new facilities, particularly in the newly industrializing countries, came on stream, Harland and Wolff was forced into both a series of rationalizations of its activities and a major re-examination of its market strategy and orientation.

Rationalization and retrenchment

The rationalization of the activities of Harland and Wolff, the corporate response to the financial crisis which has been characteristic of the company in one form or another since 1963, has proceeded in a number of phases. Four main stages in the process can be identified and will be discussed briefly here. More detail on the context, process, and impact of change during the last two decades is given elsewhere (Moss and Hume 1986; Harrison 1988).

Diversification or rationalization?

In the early 1960s Harland and Wolff, in common with many other shipyards in the UK, had diversified into the field of industrialized housing where, it was felt, there were prospects for the profitable use of existing skills and productive capacity (Ministry of Public Buildings and Works 1963). Further diversification in the local economy was facilitated by the rapid expansion of public investment in infrastructure and on industrial development in the early 1960s (Northern Ireland Economic Council 1983a), which generated considerable structural steelwork activity for the company. However, following the onset of financial problems in the mid-1960s the continuing importance of this activity was being questioned by the company:

> The true basis of the company is shipbuilding at the Queen's Island yard at Belfast. While of importance in another context, our other activities, such as Ship Repairing, Marine Engine Building, Electrical Engineering, General Engineering, Structural Steelwork, Industrial Housing, etc., are of secondary importance to the main issue. Either the company will survive because it succeeds in building good ships at acceptable prices at Queen's Island or it will go out of existence. It cannot be saved by diversification or ancillary activities in themselves
>
> (Harland and Wolff Annual Report, Statement by the Chairman, 1966, 1)

As a consequence of this decision the company progressively closed divisions and concentrated on marine-related activities on the Belfast site. During the 1960s, therefore, the industrial building division in Belfast, and shipbuilding, foundry, and engineering divisions on Clydeside were closed. The company's ship repair facilities in London, Liverpool, and Southampton were closed between 1971 and 1973, with the loss of around 2,000 jobs (Moss and Hume 1986). In parallel with this process of rationalization and concentration, the company began planning the construction of a building dock to capitalize on its reputation for the construction of large bulk carriers and tankers which, in the late 1960s, appeared to offer the best future prospects for the company (Moss and Hume 1986). Indeed, by 1975 the company's order book consisted of six VLCCs, three large bulk carriers, and two products tankers. In addition to engine construction for these contracts, the engineering department had orders for eleven main diesel engines, ten for the Hyundai yard in South Korea, and one for an Indian shipyard (Harland and Wolff Annual Report 1975).

Diversification out of shipbuilding

As already indicated above, the boom in the VLCC market did not survive the 1973/74 oil crisis, and the concentration strategy developed in the mid- and late-1960s had to be rethought in the light of market collapse, lack of new orders and rapidly escalating losses after 1975. Between 1978 and 1985/86 losses on work carried out by Harland and Wolff ranged between £20 m and £30 m annually, equivalent to between 23 per cent and 47 per cent of turnover (Figure 6.1). This deterioration in performance, and the continued absence of orders for the types of vessel which the company was best equipped to build, encouraged a fundamental re-examination of the need for, and desirability of, diversification. In 1975, therefore, the company reported that 'every effort is being made to attract new work including the possibility of diversification into new products which could utilise the unique and extensive facilities at Queen's Island' (Harland and Wolff Annual Report 1975, 14). This position was taken a stage further the following year as the company reported that:

> with the rundown of traditional markets we are exploring possibilities for using our resources of skilled labour and facilities in other fields . . . foundations are being laid on which it is hoped we can build an organisation which is not so dependent on the highly sensitive shipbuilding industry, and which will bring benefit not only to the Company but Northern Ireland as a whole
>
> (Harland and Wolff Annual Report 1976, 11)

These plans did bear some fruit. Nevertheless, diversification out of marine activity remained peripheral: between 1971 and 1982/83, the last year for which data are available in this form, the shipbuilding division of the company accounted for 78 per cent of total turnover (only falling below 70 per cent in 1970), and the engineering division accounted for a further 18 per cent, comprising for the most part marine engine construction for the company's shipbuilding division and for external customers. The viability of Harland and Wolff, it became clear, lay in its viability as a shipbuilder and marine engineer. Diversification into non-marine related structural steelwork and engineering was increasingly limited in the 1970s as both competition and capacity increased as other UK shipbuilders attempted to follow the same route. Furthermore, the scope for such diversification by Harland and Wolff was severely constrained by the size and nature of the Northern Ireland economy. In the early 1960s Harland and Wolff had benefited from public expenditure on infrastructure (e.g. bridges, power stations) and on industrial development. By 1971, however, only 2 per cent by value of the company's sales were to customers within Northern Ireland, and although the figure increased to a peak of 6 per cent in 1981/82, over the period as a whole it averaged only 3 per cent (Harrison 1988). By the end of the 1970s it was becoming clear that diversification into non-marine related activities was a relatively marginal, although welcome, means of using spare productive capacity on an *ad hoc* basis rather than the sustained basis for future profitability.

Product market diversity

Given that diversification into non-marine work could only have a marginal impact on the overall financial performance of the company, a strategy of enforced diversification into other sectors of the shipbuilding market had to be adopted in the late 1970s. Accordingly since 1976 Harland and Wolff has been awarded contracts for the construction of liquefied natural gas carriers, bulk carriers, oil tankers, roll-on roll-off passenger/vehicle ferries, refrigerated cargo vessels, and North Sea barges. In the 1980s the company has further diversified into the quasi-naval and off-shore markets. Defence-related contracts include the construction of a floating harbour installation for the Falkland Islands, conversion of a large container vessel to an aviation training ship (ATS) for the Ministry of Defence, and the design and build contract for the first in a proposed series of auxiliary oiler replenishment (AOR) vessels for the Royal Navy. Offshore-related work centres on the high-technology Single Well Oil Production System (SWOPS) vessel currently being built for British Petroleum.

While these diverse orders have provided sufficient work to keep the company going, if not to ensure full efficient use of the production facilities, the mix and, increasingly, complexity of ship types in the order book has placed considerable demands on the company's key management and technical resources. Major changes in management structure and work practice have followed. This has been seen most recently in the adoption of full project management techniques to maintain control and co-ordination in contract administration for these more sophisticated contracts, notably the ATS and AOR contracts for the Ministry of Defence, and the SWOPS project for BP. Given the strict penalty clauses attaching to the AOR contract in particular (a 10 per cent cost overrun will prompt an immediate Ministerial review of alternative arrangements for completing the contract elsewhere and a review of the future of Harland and Wolff itself), the future of the company may well depend on the absorption of new techniques (project management and the widespread application of CAD/CAM and computerized planning systems) being more straightforward than in the past. The diagnosis of conservative, inward-looking management and poor financial control as key problems in 1966, and the appointment of John Mallabar as chairman and 'company doctor', did not lead to any immediate cure. It soon became clear that 'a large company producing one-off products was quite different from a firm engaged in series manufacture of relatively small items' (Moss and Hume 1986:424), and losses continued to rise (Figure 6.1). Similarly, the building dock, originally conceived in 1966/67, only came into full effective operation after eight years and two separate investment programmes in which revisions to the flow of steelwork through the shipyard and, significantly, to the managerial organization of production, lagged behind construction of the facility itself (Harrison 1988). If success in winning AOR contract was vital to the future prospects of Harland and Wolff (Grunback 1986), success in adopting and adapting to new management techniques at all levels is equally vital to its survival.

Rationalization and retrenchment

The cumulative effect of the company's performance in the late 1970s and early 1980s was to encourage further rationalization of productive capacity within the Belfast complex, which parallels the earlier rationalization onto the Belfast site. Two major areas were identified as requiring attention (Harland and Wolff Annual Report 1981/82). The first was a reduction in overheads: for the conditions and requirements of the contemporary market Harland

and Wolff was recognized to be grossly over-facilitized with little or no prospect of the recovery of the net book value of the tangible fixed assets over their useful lives. The second area requiring action was the improvement of productivity, through effective work programming, well organized supervision, workforce commitment and well-trained, well-directed management.

The importance of reducing operating costs was emphasized as a condition for the continued provision of government financial assistance in a number of Ministerial announcements. The most striking comments came from Adam Butler MP, then Minister of State at the Northern Ireland Office, during the debate on the draft shipbuilding (Redundancy Payments Scheme) (Northern Ireland) (Amendment) Order 1982:

> There is plenty of room for cost-cutting and improvements in delivery. The company's costs are far higher than they should be, and all too frequently it delivers ships late. That also contributes to major losses, which have to be added to the losses arising from the maintenance of production capacity far in excess of demand . . . The Company must, therefore, strive towards two targets: first, it must lower its costs; and secondly, it must improve its delivery performance . . . That is critical if employment in a more efficient company is to be secured, and I assure the House that cost-saving measures will have the Government's full support. Savings must be made if the company is to survive. The company – workforce and management – has a simple but very stark choice – cut costs or go under.
>
> (House of Commons Debates, 26 July 1982, Col. 864).

Similar comments were made by Dr Vivian Wadsworth, then Chairman of Harland and Wolff, at a naming ceremony in May 1982:

> We are going to have a go at making this a viable shipyard. This could mean a lot of major reorganisation. If we do not get this, we will not survive. We cannot go on using Government money. I do not think we will ever again be asking Government for the kind of money we have in the past
>
> (Quoted in *Belfast News Letter*, 20 May 1982)

As subsequent experience was to show all too clearly, the aim of financial viability within eighteen months rested on an enormously

Figure 6.2 Employment in Harland and Wolff's Belfast facilities, 1962–1987/88.

Source: Moss and Hume 1986; Harland and Wolff Annual Reports.

optimistic view of the short-term future of the merchant shipbuilding market.

This physical rationalization of the Company's facilities was significant: in 1985 the Company occupied 45 per cent less area than it did in 1982, generating anticipated savings on overheads of £6.5 m annually. This reduction was achieved at a cost of almost £5 m over the period 1982 and 1984 (Harland and Wolff Annual Report 1984/85). One consequence has been a further reduction in employment in the company and the consequent declaration of major redundancies in the 1980s (Harrison 1986a). Throughout the period since 1962 rationalization and restructuring, whatever the precise form it has taken, has involved considerable job loss: the profile of the company's financial performance is matched by a profile of its employment (Figure 6.2). By 1962 the first major post-war shake-out of labour from the shipbuilding industry in Northern Ireland had already taken place in response to a major change in product mix following delivery of the last major labour intensive passenger liner contract in May 1961 (Steed 1968; Harrison 1985). Between 1962 and 1966 employment in Harland and Wolff in Belfast fluctuated around 12,000 before falling sharply to around 9,000 by 1968. Despite relatively stable employment between 1968 and 1974, there have been a series of further sharp falls in employment since. From a peak of almost 10,000 employees in 1974, shipbuilding employment in Belfast fell by almost 50 per cent by early 1985; between early 1985 and the end of 1987 employment fell by a further 25 per cent to less than 4,000. This has involved the company in considerable expense: between 1981 and 1984/85 manpower reduction costs incurred by the company amounted to £5.6 m, and between 1978 and 1985/86 the Government incurred total costs of £19.3 m under the Shipbuilding Redundancy Payments Scheme in Northern Ireland.

This significant contraction of employment in shipbuilding and marine engineering in Belfast over the last decade reflects the disfunctional relationship between the company's production facilities and optimum product range and the state of the world shipbuilding market. The financial performance of the company mirrors this trend: since 1978, and despite fluctuations in the level of losses (Figure 6.1), the financial situation of the company has remained precarious. Between 1978 and 1985/86, for example, losses on work carried out as a percentage of turnover averaged 35 per cent; the equivalent figure for the total deficit for the year averages out at 48 per cent for this period. Even if it is accepted that globally the shipbuilding industry is in crisis, this level of losses sustained over a period of almost a decade make it difficult to develop a prima-facie case for continued support to the industry in its present form in Northern Ireland. The possible reasons for continued Government support in the face of this financial history will be discussed below. Furthermore, the very sharp deterioration, in absolute terms, in the financial position of Harland and Wolff after 1978 occurred at a time both of rapid inflation in the UK and of considerable labour shedding by the company. Accordingly, the real (constant price) level of losses per employee in Harland and Wolff has remained fairly steady between 1978 and 1985/86 at around £5,400 per employee per annum (1984 prices).

The British shipbuilders' experience

Although critical, this level of losses in Harland and Wolff is not unique. Using data from the Report and Accounts for British Shipbuilders it is possible to compare the performance of the non-privatized segment of the UK shipbuilding industry with that of Harland and Wolff. Consistent data on turnover, trading losses and employment in British Shipbuilders' 'continuing business' are available for the period 1981/82 to 1985/86. 'Continuing businesses' are defined as those activities remaining the responsibility of the Corporation following completion of the privatization of the warshipbuilding and shiprepairing sectors, and include companies engaged in merchant shipbuilding, enginebuilding and related activities (British Shipbuilders Report and Accounts 1985/86). All turnover, profits/losses and employment attributable to activities previously part of the Corporation have been excluded from the comparison with Harland and Wolff, as have additional provisions in connection with the disposal of Scott Lithgow in 1984 to Trafalgar House plc.

Trading losses as a percentage of annual turnover for British Shipbuilders' continuing business and for Harland and Wolff (where the figures relate to the total loss for the year on ordinary activities rather than just to the loss on work carried out to ensure as nearly as is possible given differences in accounting conventions and detail a comparison of like with like) are shown in Figure 6.3. Total losses in Harland and Wolff have fluctuated between 35 per cent and 60 per cent of turnover during the five-year period, around an approximately horizontal trend. In British Shipbuilders, however, relatively low losses in 1981/82 and 1982/83 have rapidly given way to high and accelerating losses which represented 40 per cent of turnover in 1983/84 and 1984/85 and over 80 per cent of turnover in 1985/86. These figures are also reflected in the pattern of losses per employee in each company over the period (Figure 6.4). In Harland and Wolff, total losses per employee have fluctuated around £6,000 per employee per annum (current prices) since 1982/83. In British Shipbuilders, which has experienced considerable job loss and rationalization in the early 1980s, (Peck and Townsend 1984), annual trading losses have risen from less than £2,000 per employee in 1981/82 to over £13,000 per employee

Figure 6.3 Trading loss as a percentage of turnover in Harland and Wolff and British Shipbuilders (continuing activities only) 1981/82–1985/86.

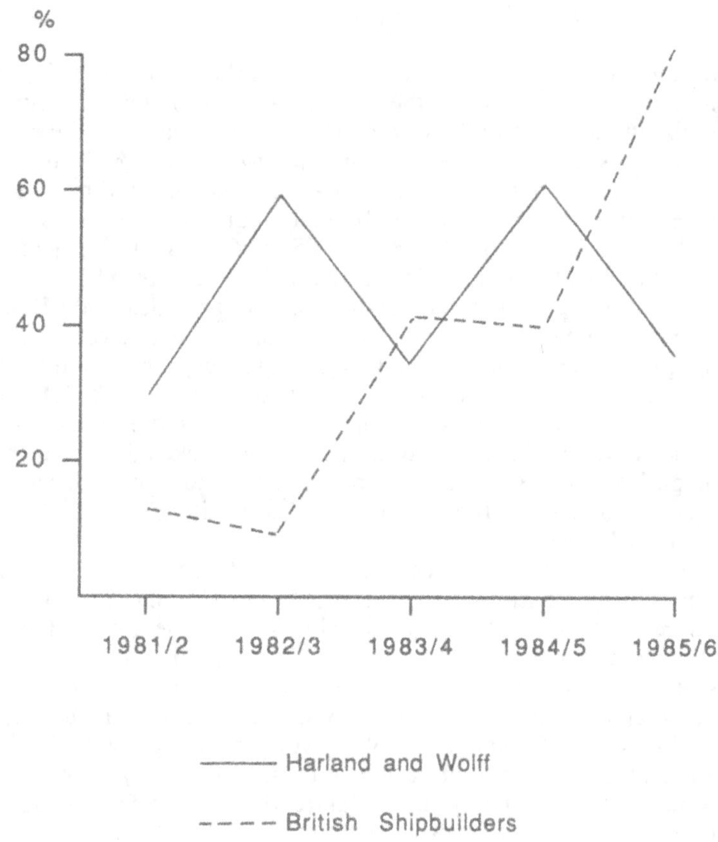

Source: Harland and Wolff Annual Reports, British Shipbuilders Report and Accounts 1985/86.

Figure 6.4 Trading loss per employee in Harland and Wolff and British Shipbuilders (continuing activities only) 1981/82–1985/86

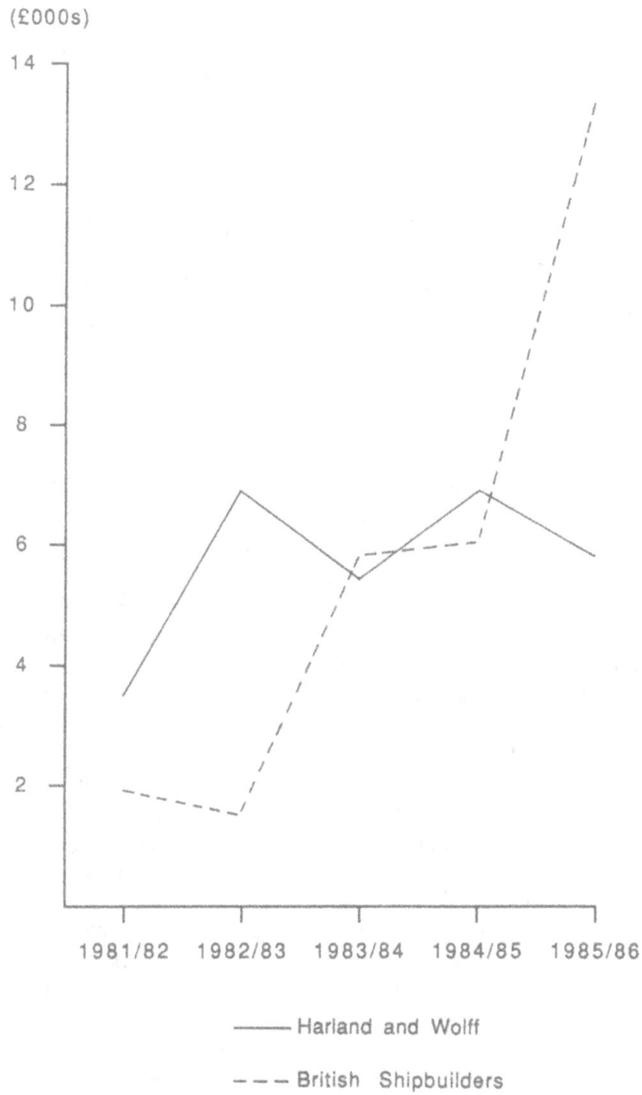

Source: Harland and Wolff Annual Reports, British Shipbuilders Report and Accounts 1985/86.

in 1985/86. Even if the provision of £43 m made by British Shipbuilders in the accounts for 1985/86 to cover the possibility that customer credit guarantees may be called upon is excluded (and this type of provision is in any case included in the comparative Harland and Wolff figures), total per employee trading losses in 1985/86 were £9,200, some 50 per cent higher than in Harland and Wolff in that year. If additional restructuring and redundancy costs incurred by British Shipbuilders in 1985/86 in connection with its merchant shipbuilding activities are included (as the equivalent figures are for Harland and Wolff) the loss per employee rises to £17,914 (see below). In discussing the scale and motivations for Government assistance to the shipbuilding industry in Northern Ireland in the remainder of this paper, therefore, it must be borne in mind that the scale of the problem and hence, by implication, the scale of the intervention necessary to maintain the industry in existence is not unique to Northern Ireland.

Government assistance

The pattern of Government assistance to Harland and Wolff broadly follows that of the company's financial performance since 1966 (Figure 6.5). The initial shift from profit to loss which occurred in the early 1960s, and the mounting trading losses which followed, were initially covered by transfers from the company's accumulated reserves. This, however, was only a short-term remedy and by end-1966 the company was close to insolvency: 'the company, trapped by contracts which were proving unprofitable, and with serious cash-flow problems, was fighting for its existence, certainly as an independent concern and possibly as a shipbuilder' (Moss and Hume 1986, 415). The Geddes Report (Shipbuilding Enquiry Committee 1966) had recommended a major reorganization of the British shipbuilding industry in 1966, by merging yards into larger groups with assistance from public funds, and the Shipbuilding Industry Board (SIB) was consequently established in June 1967 with the remit of stimulating reorganization and administering the funds to be provided for that purpose. However, despite early approaches from Cammell-Laird in Birkenhead Harland and Wolff was felt to be virtually large enough to be regarded as a group on its own and was therefore omitted from the groups which eventually came about (Todd 1984). At the same time the financial problems of the company were too immediate to await the formation and deliberations of the SIB. Accordingly, in 1966 the then Northern Ireland government made available a

Figure 6.5 Total financial assistance to Harland and Wolff 1966–1981/82 (constant 1981 prices).

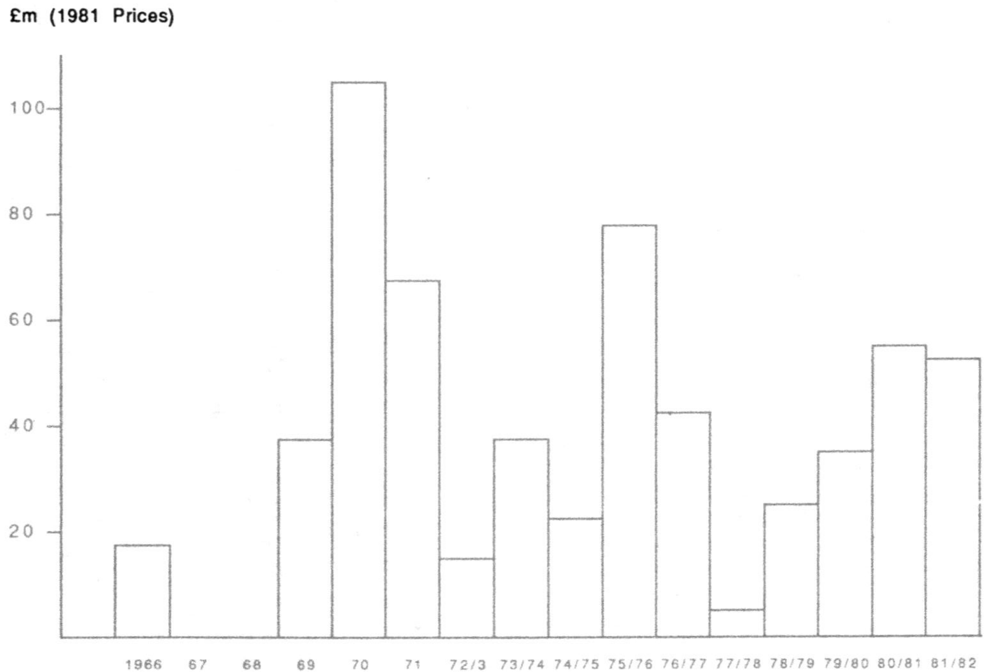

Source: Harrison 1988:216.

£3.5 m loan to prevent the physical closure of the shipyard. Following a restructuring of the board of the company, and a reappraisal of its operations and market, the building dock proposal was put to the SIB, who agreed to make a long-term loan of £8 m in 1969. Grants were also made by the Northern Ireland government in full relief of interest up to the end of 1970, and for the years 1971–74 inclusive interest was capitalized and included in the principal of the loans (Department of Commerce 1975).

As the financial position of the company continued to deteriorate, a thorough reappraisal of the position was undertaken by the government at the end of the 1960s. As an interim measure, the SIB made a special grant of £3.5 m to the company in 1970: this was considerably less than the £8.5 m the company thought it would need during 1970–1973 to cover actual and anticipated losses, but 'the problem was that the SIB only had about £3.5 million (in grants) left in the kitty, and it made that grant on the understanding that the government would take up the rest' (Sir Anthony Park, quoted in Hogwood 1979:122).

Public ownership and reconstruction

Overall, therefore, Harland and Wolff was a major beneficiary of SIB assistance, and accounted for 35 per cent of total SIB assistance in the period 1968–1971. As with much of the work of the SIB nationally, however, this assistance was made available reactively, after financial problems had become inescapably obvious and generally intractable, and concentrated on rescue operations (Hogwood 1979). Accordingly, in December 1970, faced with a further financial crisis in Harland and Wolff, the Northern Ireland government announced an interim rescue plan after it became clear that the losses anticipated in April 1970, when the SIB loan was made, would be greatly exceeded. The terms of this rescue plan can be summarized briefly.

The Northern Ireland government was to take control for a maximum period of three months, during which time it would guarantee overdraft facilities and appoint a director and financial controller to the Harland and Wolff Board. Proposals for the future of the shipyard were based on the retention of control by the existing company, and in March 1971 it was announced in the Northern Ireland House of Commons that the government had decided in principle to assist the company again, both by restructuring the membership of the Board and in the form of financial assistance. The aim of the rescue package was to ensure that the shipyard remained a viable and substantial provider of employment in Belfast. The statement of the Minister of Commerce in the Northern Ireland House of Commons on 3 March 1971, announcing this decision, concluded:

> In agreeing to provide financial support for the company the Government emphasised that public money cannot be poured indefinitely into any industry without regard to efficiency and viability. The Belfast Yard has the facilities to enable it to prosper and offer stable and secure employment once it has overcome its present difficulties. This is the justification for the public support now to be provided. Once it has been given, the responsibility for the company's continuing activities will rest wholly with the company and it will be up to management and the labour force to ensure that the community receives an adequate return. *There can be no question of further continuing support from public funds.*
> (Northern Ireland House of Commons Debate, 3 March 1971).

Final details of the financial assistance were announced on 6 July 1971: the Northern Ireland government was to subscribe £4 m for 47.6 per cent shareholding in Harland and Wolff, unpaid interest of £1.255 m on the £3.5 m loan made in 1966 was to be waived, and a grant was made under the Industries Development Acts (NI) 1966 and 1971 to write-off the actual and prospective losses on the company's order book as it stood at 3 March 1971. This figure was later ascertained to be £14.154 m, over and above the estimate of £10 m losses made in October 1970. Between 1969 and the end of 1971 Harland and Wolff had received approximately £210 m (1981 prices) in financial assistance from SIB and the Northern Ireland government. But the problems of the industry in Belfast were not unique. The Cammell-Laird group underwent significant restructuring under the aegis of the Industrial Reorganization Corporation in 1970 (Hogwood 1979) and Upper Clyde Shipbuilders went into liquidation in mid-1971 (McGill 1973; Foster and Woolfson 1986).

Although this assistance was considerable, a substantial proportion of it was provided in a form or through channels which were neither unique to the shipbuilding industry in Northern Ireland nor unavailable to other industrial undertakings in the region. Between 1966 and 1974, for example, 27 per cent of the total financial assistance made available to Harland and Wolff was in the form of standard assistance under statute, which was available to industrial undertakings generally in Northern Ireland, or to shipbuilders generally in Northern Ireland, or to shipbuilders nationally (including Regional Employment Premium and shipbuilders' relief). If the major grants paid in 1971 in support of the building dock related investment programme (Harrison 1988) under the terms of the Industries Development Acts are included this proportion rises to 33 per cent (Department of Commerce 1975).

In real terms, as Figure 6.5 makes clear, government assistance between 1969 and 1971 was higher than at any time before or since. Nevertheless it failed to prevent a further deterioration in the financial position of the company. In the wake of productivity and throughput problems in 1973, which had serious implications for slippage in the work programme and rapidly escalating costs, the government was approached for further financial assistance. Agreement was announced in principle in the House of Commons at Westminster on 19 November 1973, but detailed financial discussions were suspended with the General Election of February 1974. When negotiations with the incoming Labour government recommenced, it rapidly became clear that the company was continuing to fail to meet production targets and that previous proposals for providing financial assistance were inadequate (Moss and Hume 1986). In a statement to the Westminster House of Commons in July 1974 it was announced that the Government had decided to extend its control from 47.6 per cent to a substantial majority by extending the equity rather than by acquiring existing shares, although the possibility of full public ownership was not ruled out (House of Commons Debates 22 July 1974, cols 1060–71). The announcement was accompanied by the increasingly familiar declaration that 'this must not be regarded by those working for the company as an open-ended Government subventions' (ibid.).

Following the July 1974 statement, a review of the company's position revealed that the £38 m provision for estimated prospective losses on contracts entered into prior to 31 December 1973, shown in the company's published accounts, would have to be increased by £22 m to around £60 m in total (Department of Commerce, 1975). In a further statement it was announced that the only satisfactory way in which the company could be financially reconstructed was for the government to be the sole shareholder (House of Commons Debates, 26 March 1975, cols 496–507). The company was, therefore, taken into full public ownership under the Shipbuilding Industry (No. 2) (Northern Ireland) Order. The financial reconstruction of the company involved, in part, the writing off or capitalization of existing loans and the provision of up to £60 m of new public money. No financial assistance was to be given under the Order after 31 March 1979. To overcome this restriction in the light of the subsequent experience of the industry, the provisions of this Order were re-enacted in The Aircraft and Shipbuilding Industries (Northern Ireland) Order 1979. The provision of continued subventions is dependent on, first, the provision for further losses by outright grant under the terms of the 1975/1979 orders, and second, annual confirmation by the Department of Economic Development that 'the undertaking given by the Government in July 1974 to guarantee the liabilities of the company insofar as they could not be met by the company is still operative': as the company's Report and Accounts point out 'pending completion of the reconstruction, the company is being kept in funds by interim loans' (Harland and Wolff Annual Report 1984/85:7). The loans are free of interest, unsecured and without fixed repayment dates but subject to repayment at seven days' notice.

With the collapse of the world merchant shipbuilding industry in the mid-1970s, and the persistent inability of Harland and Wolff (in common with other western shipbuilders) to secure an adequate throughput of work at satisfactory prices, government support has continued at a generally high level. As Table 6.1 indicates, total assistance between 1966 and 1971 amounted to £229 m at constant 1981 prices; between 1972 and 1981/82 a further £366 m was made available – a total of almost £595 m (1981 prices) over a fifteen-year period. This has been expensive in terms of the employment preserved: over the period as a whole 146,258 man years of employment have been supported in the industry at a cost per job year of £4,068 (1981 prices). Between 1966 and 1971 over 58,600 man years of employment were

Table 6.1 Financial assistance to Harland and Wolff 1966–1981/82

	Total assistance £m (1981 prices)[a]	*Total man years of employment[b]*	*Cost per job year £ (1981 prices)*
1966–71	228.6	58,608	3,901
1972/73–1981/82	366.3	87,650	4,179
Total: 1966–1981/82	594.9	146,258	4,068

Sources: Department of Commerce 1975; House of Commons Official Report, 15 November 1982, col. 58; Harrison 1988.
Notes: (a) Financial assistance to the shipbuilding industry from all government sources, both standard assistance (including industrial development grants) and special assistance, inclusive of payments made under the Shipbuilding Redundancy Payments Scheme.
(b) Defined as the sum of employment in each year in the period.

supported at an average cost of £3,900 (1981 prices); between 1972/3 and 1981/82 the cost per job was £4,180 (1981 prices) for 87,650 man years of employment. This compares with the Northern Ireland Economic Council (1983b) estimate of approximately £4,000 per employment year created in the man-made fibres industry between 1959 and 1982 in Northern Ireland, assistance for which was provided under the industrial development legislation, and with an overall average of between £1,500 and £2,000 per man year of employment created in large firms under the industrial development programme (Department of Economic Development 1985). Although the marginal costs of continued financial assistance have risen in the 1980s (see p.140), these average costs per employment year created are not excessively out of line with those elsewhere in manufacturing industry in Northern Ireland. Given that the marginal costs of inward investment and large firm expansions in the 1980s are likely to have risen substantially (Industry and Trade Committee 1982), the maintenance of employment in Harland and Wolff, therefore, may not have been the least effective use of public expenditure in Northern Ireland during this period.

Public expenditure and shipbuilding assistance

The implications and significance of assistance to the shipbuilding industry in Northern Ireland for overall public expenditure in the late 1980s, in the light of the rapidly deteriorating financial position of the company (Figure 6.1), are illustrated in Table 6.2. These data have been taken from the Appropriation Accounts for Northern Ireland to set shipbuilding assistance within the context of the wider public expenditure budget in Northern Ireland. As the source of these data differs from that used to construct Figure 6.5 and Table 6.1, these figures are not directly comparable with those discussed above. In particular, shipbuilding related assistance as defined in Table 6.2 does not include financial assistance generally available to industry in Northern Ireland, which will be included under other expenditure sub-heads. 'Total assistance to industry' is here defined to include the package of selective assistance and standard capital grants which constitutes regional industrial development policy in Northern Ireland. It includes, therefore, all expenditure by the Industrial Development Board (IDB) and the Local Enterprise Development Unit (LEDU), including promotional and administrative expenditure, together with Department of Economic Development (DED) expenditure

Table 6.2 Expenditure on the shipbuilding industry and other industrial support in Northern Ireland, 1978/79–1987/88

	Assistance to the shipbuilding industry[a] *£m*	*SRPS*[b] *£m*	*Total shipbuilding related assistance* *£m*	*Cost per job year* *£*	*Total assistance to industry*[c] *£m*
1978/79	13.695	1.190	14.885	1,813	184.0
1979/80	23.056	2.340	26.296	3,487	194.6
1980/81	41.231	1.430	42.661	5,789	253.4
1981/82	40.124	1.280	41.404	5,887	184.9
1982/83	46.222	3.550	49.772	7,947	221.5
1983/84	40.047	4.212	44.259	8,118	193.6
1984/85	37.683	3.479	41.162	7,973	190.1
1985/86	36.610	2.539	38.969	7,893	226.5
1986/87[d]	68.157	2.000	70.157	16,704	241.3
1987/88[d]	40.661	2.000	42.661	11,376	193.8
Total 1978/79–1987/88	387.486	24.020	411,506	6,867	2,083.7

Sources: Harrison 1988:221; Department of Finance and Personnel 1987.

Notes: (a) Financial assistance to Harland and Wolff by way of grants and loans for working capital and capital expenditure, and the provision of subsidies to assist the company to secure shipbuilding orders.

(b) The Shipbuilding Redundancy Payments Scheme was established in 1978 and provides payments to eligible employees of Harland and Wolff who are made redundant or transferred to less well paid work in the company.

(c) Expenditure on industrial support and regeneration, general support to industry and miscellaneous services. Apart from assistance to the shipbuilding industry and SRPS the main items included under this heading are standard capital grants, selective financial assistance (industrial development programme), assistance to LEDU for small firm promotion, and assistance to the aerospace industry.

(d) Estimate.

on standard capital grants. Excluded from this comparison is other DED expenditure on the functioning of the labour market, including training programmes, tourism and energy policy. All figures in Table 6.2 are given in cash terms.

It is clear from Table 6.2 that total assistance to the shipbuilding industry, including expenditure incurred under the Shipbuilding Redundancy Payments Scheme, has risen sharply since the end of the 1970s: since 1980/81, total assistance has been over £40 m in almost every year, and provision has been made for assistance totalling £70 m in 1986/87, reflecting the continuing poor trading position of Harland and Wolff and the costs of restructuring and labour shedding which have been incurred. Over the ten-year period covered by the data in Table 6.2, and including the provision made for expenditure in 1986/87 and 1987/88, which may be subject to revision, total assistance to the shipbuilding industry will have amounted to over £410 m in cash terms. This represents a significant proportion of total assistance to industry in Northern Ireland (Figure 6.6). In 1978/79 total shipbuilding assistance (including SRPS) represented just over 8 per cent of total industry assistance as here defined. Relative to the company's share of manufacturing employment (6 per cent) this was not significantly in excess of what may have been anticipated. However, total shipbuilding assistance grew rapidly after 1978/79 in both absolute and relative terms, and by 1981/82 it accounted for over 22 per cent of total support for industry in Northern Ireland.

Despite a slight fall in the proportion, to around 17 per cent, in 1985/86 it is anticipated that the shipbuilding industry will account for a higher share of industry support in 1986/87 and 1987/88 than at any time in the past. As Figure 6.6 makes clear, this relative and absolute rise in total shipbuilding related assistance coincides with a relative and absolute fall in employment in the industry: by March 1988, for example, it is anticipated that total employment in the company will have fallen to around 3,750 as a consequence of the failure to win any new shipbuilding orders in 1987. In other words, between March 1982 and March 1988 shipbuilding employment in Northern Ireland will have fallen from 6 per cent to less than 4 per cent of total employment in the manufacturing sector.

The combination of falling employment and rising government assistance over the last decade has had considerable implications for the cost of maintaining employment in Harland and Wolff. In cash terms, the annual marginal cost per job maintained has risen from less than £2,000 in 1978/79 to around £8,000 since 1982/83. The scale of the company's losses anticipated in 1986/87, and the related provision for assistance to the industry, indicate that the

Figure 6.6 Financial assistance to the shipbuilding industry as a percentage of total assistance to industry in Northern Ireland 1978/79–1987/88.

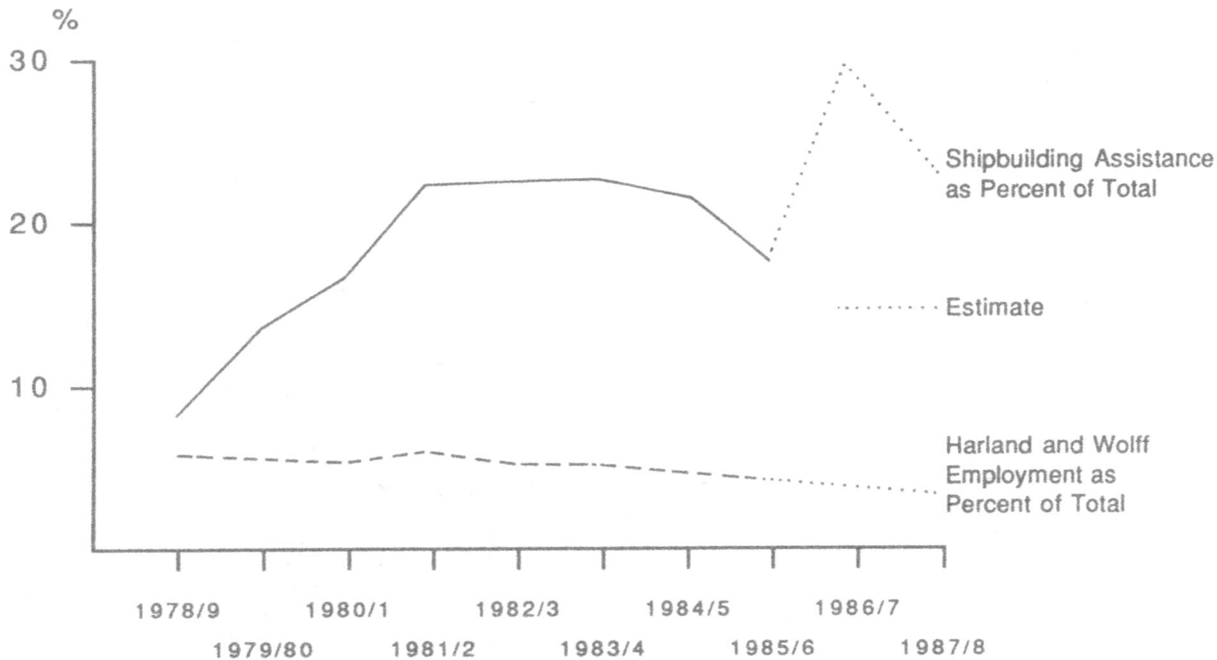

marginal costs per job maintained are anticipated to rise very substantially and to remain high in 1987/88 (Table 6.2). This is likely to have major implications for the continued provision of assistance on this scale to the industry (see p. 146).

However, the dramatic deterioration in the financial performance of the company cannot be considered in isolation from the problems facing the shipbuilding industry as a whole in the UK. It has already been indicated in Figure 6.4 that the trading loss per employee in British Shipbuilders' continuing activities exceeded £13,000 in 1985/86. The total trading loss for the year on British Shipbuilders' continuing business was £136.9 m. To this can be added £2.8 m additional provision in connection with the disposal of Scott Lithgow in 1984, and £53.6 m estimated restructuring costs arising from the closure of Smith's Dock Limited, the Troon yard of Ferguson Ailsa Limited, and the Wallsend facility of Clark Kincaid Limited, together with redundancies in other continuing companies, giving a total loss on ordinary activities before tax of £181.7 m, or £17,814 per employee in 1985/86 (British Shipbuilders Report and Accounts 1985/86). A further loss of £248.1 m was incurred on the sale of companies during the year, representing the 'bidders' views of the disposed companies' future prospects and of the market value of fixed assets as compared to their book value' (ibid. 38), giving a total deficit for the year of £429.8 m (£42,137 per employee in the continuing business).

In Table 6.1 it was calculated that between 1966 and 1981/82 total government assistance to shipbuilding in Northern Ireland from all sources came to £595 m at constant 1981 prices. If the data in Table 6.2 for the period 1982/3 to 1985/86 are adjusted to 1981 prices, the industry received approximately £165 m in this period (including SRPS) to maintain 21,815 man years of employment at a cost of £7,562 per job year. Overall, therefore, total government expenditure on the preservation of the shipbuilding industry in Northern Ireland between 1966 and 1985/86 has been approximately £760 m (constant 1981 prices), representing an overall average approximate cost per job year preserved of just over £4,500.

The political economy of industrial support

The level of this expenditure on support for the shipbuilding industry over such a long period of time raises two important questions. First, in terms of public expenditure in Northern

Ireland, has the level of support for the shipbuilding industry, which now accounts for over 20 per cent of total industry support in the region (Figure 6.6), 'crowded out' other potential applications of this expenditure which may have had a more beneficial impact on the regional economy? Second, and more importantly, given the oft-repeated declaration that each tranche of government assistance was positively the last on offer, why has the industry continued to receive financial assistance on this scale and for how long can this continue?

Displacement effects of shipbuilding assistance

The question of whether or not assistance to the shipbuilding industry has crowded out other, potentially more beneficial or cost-effective, uses of the sums involved can be approached at two levels. Most generally, it can be argued that the increased overall expenditure on trade, industry, and employment consequent upon the growing importance of shipbuilding assistance may have reduced expenditure on other programmes to a level lower than would otherwise have been obtained. However, in recent years public expenditure in Northern Ireland, as in the UK, has been tightly constrained. As the Northern Ireland Economic Council (1984) report on public expenditure priorities demonstrated, defining the counterfactual 'what would have happened if . . .' position is difficult if not impossible. Furthermore, since the late 1960s the very rapid growth of public expenditure in Northern Ireland reflects the increased expenditure on health and personal social services, social security and law, order and protective services: growth in these areas does not appear to have been retarded by the provision of assistance specifically to the shipbuilding industry (Simpson 1981).

In any case, as Table 6.2 makes clear, expenditure on total assistance to industry has fluctuated sharply, reaching a peak of £253 m in 1980/81 and was only 3 per cent higher in cash terms in 1984/85 than in 1978/79. If expenditure on the shipbuilding industry is excluded from these figures, the sharp projected rise in industry support in 1986/87 disappears: public expenditure on industry support excluding shipbuilding peaks in 1985/86 at £187 m (following the earlier peak of £210 m in 1980/81), and is projected to fall by almost 20 per cent in cash terms by 1987/88. Overall, public expenditure on industry, energy and employment (a much broader category than that discussed here) fell by 25 per cent in real terms between 1973/74 and 1984/85, compared with an overall real increase of 35 per cent in total public expenditure in Northern Ireland, leading one commentator to conclude that 'over the past decade top priority has been given to health, and this has been possible because industrial development, though even more important, has not been effectively prosecuted nor has its declining budget been fully expended' (Northern Ireland Economic Council 1984, 30).

The conclusion to be drawn from these considerations, taken collectively, is that the contention that shipbuilding-related increases in public expenditure have crowded out other uses of that funding cannot be substantiated. Indeed, if anything, persistent underspending of the budget allocation elsewhere in the industry support programme, largely due to persistent shortfalls in inward investment under the industrial development programme, has facilitated increases in public expenditure elsewhere in Northern Ireland which may otherwise have proved difficult to obtain. Furthermore, although the costs of employment maintenance in Harland and Wolff have been high in the 1980s (Table 6.2) relative to costs incurred elsewhere in the industry support programme, they do compare very favourably with the estimated cost per job year created through other public expenditure programmes: these range from between £4,000 and £6,000 for certain employment and training measures to between £10,000 and £26,000 per job year in health, education, and infrastructure provision (Northern Ireland Economic Council 1984). If allowance is made for deadweight and displacement effects in calculating the cost per job year created under the industrial development programme, 'conventional regional policy has cost more than £10,000 per job year (we divide the cost of each job created by the number of years it lasts for comparison with direct public sector employment) in Northern Ireland' (Canning *et al.* 1987:230). In the case of assistance to the shipbuilding industry in the region there is no deadweight, for without subsidy the company would close almost immediately, and there is no displacement within Northern Ireland as Harland and Wolff is the only company in the industry in the region. In terms purely of employment creation in Northern Ireland, therefore, redirection of public expenditure away from shipbuilding and into other programmes, including other forms of industrial development, would be less effective.

Given that there has, in fact, been no detrimental trade-off between support for shipbuilding within the overall trade and industry programme and public expenditure on other programmes in Northern Ireland, it may still be argued that the scale of the assistance made available to the shipbuilding industry has necessarily redirected expenditure away from other forms of support for industry within the trade, industry, and employment programme which may have provided more cost-effective employment generation than the preservation of shipbuilding.

Again, and in addition to the reservations of Canning *et al.* (1987) on the cost-effectiveness of regional policy in Northern Ireland, there seems to be little a priori justification for accepting this argument. Only 8 per cent of the total assistance to industry as defined in Table 6.2 is subject to cash limits and there is some provision for a roll-forward into the following financial year of a proportion of any shortfall in expenditure. Furthermore, the industrial development institutions (IDB and LEDU) have consistently argued in recent years that the availability of finance is not an immediate constraint on their job promotion performance: while LEDU has had considerable success in increasing both its target and attained levels of job promotion in the small firm sector in recent years (Northern Ireland Economic Council 1983b; 1987), the IDB, which is responsible for spending the largest part of the industrial development budget, has been consistently below target since its inception. Even if shipbuilding assistance were to be switched to other forms of industrial development (and the costs of the rundown and closure of the shipyard which this implies are ignored) the current market for industrial development in the form of either new inward investment or major indigenous expansion is severely constrained by the state of the regional, national, and international economies and by the intensification of competition among development agencies for the projects which are on offer. This implies that the historic average cost of job creation in Northern Ireland through selective assistance, estimated officially to lie in the range of £2,000–£4,000 (1984 prices) per additional job year created (Department of Economic Development 1985), may be considerably lower than the marginal costs of generating new employment in, potentially, higher risk projects in the future. The failure of the IDB to attain the modest job targets it has set itself, let alone increase these to compensate for the loss of employment in the shipyard if assistance were to be withdrawn, suggests that it is not realistic, therefore, to expect the release of finance from shipbuilding assistance to have more than a marginal impact on employment creation through the expansion of other sections of the industrial support budget. In view of these considerations the provision of continued assistance to the industry, in the particular circumstances of Northern Ireland, may well have been justified.

The rationale for shipbuilding assistance

There are signs, however, that the official climate is changing in Northern Ireland. In particular, as government in Northern Ireland seeks to stimulate a regional outpost of the new 'enterprise culture' being engendered in the UK as the cornerstone objective of industrial and employment policy, the attitude of officials and Ministers to the continued provision of subsidies to industry is undergoing a major change (Department of Economic Development 1987). Central to this new thinking is a belief that both the public and private sectors in Northern Ireland need to be aware of 'the dangers of substantial and prolonged dependence by industry on public subsidy' (Department of Economic Development 1987: 25). This DED report, however, also identifies a number of impediments to reducing the overall dependence of the regional industrial economy on subsidies. Two of these in particular are relevant here. First, they argue that there is a lack of awareness that dependence on grants is, in fact, a real problem, coupled with a corresponding general belief in the community that every firm in difficulty should be saved, irrespective of its long-term viability prospects. Second, there is a prima-facie justification for public subsidy to manufacturing and tradeable services arising from the requirement of firms in Northern Ireland to compete with firms in other grant-giving areas. In the context of the continuing need for subsidy in the shipbuilding industry in Northern Ireland, the relevant question is no longer one concerning the possible displacement effects of this expenditure on other programmes, but one of the rationale for continuing to provide assistance, for what period of time and at what cost.

There is no doubt, as this paper has shown, that shipbuilding assistance has been considerable in Northern Ireland in recent years. Between 1967 and 1971 capital reconstruction, SIB aid for investment in the building dock, and the 1970/71 package of assistance, together with other standard forms of industry or regional assistance, were equivalent to a subsidy rate (defined as total assistance used for operating purposes as a percentage of total revenue from sales) of 25.5 per cent in Harland and Wolff; only in Cammell Laird and UCS/Govan was the subsidy rate higher in this period, and these three companies were much more heavily subsidised than the rest of the UK shipbuilding industry (Denton 1976, Denton *et al.* 1975). In the late 1970s and early 1980s Harland and Wolff's total deficit, and therefore government assistance, has been equivalent to approximately 48 per cent of turnover, and this is expected to rise sharply in 1986/87.

This experience is not, however, unique (Carlsson 1983). For example, throughout the 1970s, and in particular after 1976, subsidies to traditional export industries, including shipbuilding, in Sweden rose rapidly (Hamilton 1981). Between 1976/77 and 1979/80 subsidies as a share of value-added in the Swedish shipbuilding industry were 69 per cent on average, and in 1978 and 1979 the industry received subsidies of such magnitude that they exceeded value-added in the industry, reaching a peak of 152.8 per cent of value-added in 1978/79. As Hamilton (1981:8) points out 'the implication of this is that inputs in the production process (steel, electric equipment, etc.) were worth more when they arrived at the shipyards than when they left in the form of newly built ships. Thus, in an economic sense inputs were destroyed in Swedish shipbuilding during 1978 and 1979'.

Public assistance to the shipbuilding industry has been necessitated by the existence of excess world capacity due to over-expansion during the pre-1973 boom conditions, the need for existing shipbuilders to modernize, and the entry and rapid expansion of new shipbuilding nations (Cragg 1981; Edwards 1982). The response of governments to this situation, which has affected industries other than shipbuilding (Pickering and Jones 1982; Strange and Tooze 1981; Pinder 1982) has been to introduce import restrictions, provide subsidies, introduce policies to modernize these industries, or, as in the case of the Swedish (Hamilton 1981), Japanese (Yonezewa 1980) and European shipbuilding industries, promote new activities into which their resources can be transferred (Pinder 1982; Gillis 1980). However, by 1978 the International Metalworkers Federation was arguing that the problems of the shipbuilding industry were more fundamental than these policies and actions implied, and could not

> be tackled by mere recommendations to reduce capacities or to restructure industry . . . In the pursuit of such action we must prevent by all means purely nationalistic approaches as well as short-sighted and precipitate measures . . . Adequate industrial adaptation measures are an indispensable remedy for reinvigorating shipbuilding and ship repairing . . . Permanent state aid, if only on account of its effects on international competition, cannot form the basis of any realistic shipbuilding policy. State intervention is at the most a contribution to put into effect comprehensive common planning
>
> (Quoted in Plant 1981:17)

The explicit assumption here that state aid for an industry, such as shipbuilding, which is facing conditions of considerable excess capacity, can be anything other than permanent is contradicted by the evidence from Northern Ireland, the UK, and Sweden, which is representative of the general state of the world shipbuilding industry (Todd 1986).

While industry-specific government assistance is generally provided on the implicit understanding that it is a temporary measure, 'over time, these subsidies often come to be regarded as a property right by their recipients . . . Consequently, many programs continue to expand, even though the circumstances that once justified their existence have long since passed' (Committee for Economic Development 1984:65). When these initial circumstances continue, as in the case of the major shift in the international competitive conditions in the shipbuilding industry, the pressures for the continuation of subsidies are even more intense. The potential dangers of a continuing level of public subsidy to a company, industry, or regional economy have recently been recognized by government in Northern Ireland. In particular the recent Pathfinder report argues, very much along the lines of the US Committee for Economic Development (1984), that

> grant seeking may become more important than profit seeking: subsidy may blur managers' focus on commercial objectives. Subsidy may be viewed as a safety net, resulting in complacency about business survival and development. . . . At worst, subsidy may breed yet more subsidy'
>
> (Department of Economic Development 1987:24)

While economic efficiency may well be a prime stimulus to protective subsidy introduction, a concern for the income of those directly threatened by unemployment is also a major motive (Flam *et al.* 1983), and is likely to become increasingly so the longer the subsidy is needed. Because of this the subsequent extent and duration of subsidization is not usually determined solely at the discretion of the government: it is, rather, the outcome of explicit or implicit bargaining with labour unions, political constituencies and capital owners, an outcome which is at least in part dependent on the authorities pursuing a maximization of political support strategy (Hillman 1982). That is, social justice considerations can account for the introduction of support for declining industries (Gray 1975; Cassing 1980), initially on a temporary basis, and subsequent lobbying by outside interests (unions, capital interests, political constituency interests) can successfully extend these subsidies into permanent or quasi-permanent support measures. It can be argued that in an economy in which:

> capital is sector specific, labour is imperfectly mobile, and wage rates are sticky, intervention to ease the adjustment of an industry which is inefficiently large as a result of foreign competition can yield a better outcome than that resulting from market forces alone
>
> (Forster and Rees 1983:240)

One kind of optimal policy which can be justified under such circumstances is a production subsidy which raises employment in the 'inefficient industry' above the level implied by market forces. However, if the subsidy becomes permanent, as has been the effective case in the shipbuilding industry, with the provision of both government assistance, in the form of unsecured loans to write off operating losses, and Intervention Fund subsidies on quoted contract tender prices, it may well inhibit adjustment to structural change and create a conflict between short-run gains in output (and employment above the market forces solution) and long-run efficiency losses because a permanent subsidy prevents efficient reallocation of resources in the longer run (Flam *et al.* 1983).

Conclusion

In the Northern Ireland context, of course, there is an additional dimension to the continued provision of assistance to Harland and Wolff, despite the repeated Ministerial declarations that each year's instalment of assistance is the last, which is consistent with both social justice and maximization of political support rationales for subsidization (Hillman 1982). Despite the considerable labour shedding of the post-war years Harland and Wolff is still one of the largest manufacturing employers in Northern Ireland and accounts for around 10 per cent of male employment in the Greater Belfast area. Accordingly, the government's attitude to providing continued assistance has, since the introduction of Direct Rule in the early 1970s, been complicated by the symbolic value which the yard took on in the context of local fears about government intentions to begin an economic withdrawal from Northern Ireland (O'Dowd *et al.* 1980).

Certainly for the unionist population in Northern Ireland the continuation of support from the national exchequer for one of the major employers of male Protestant workers in Belfast has become the key touchstone by which national government policy towards, and hence commitment to, the regional economy is judged. Accordingly, it still remains the case now as it was almost a decade ago, that 'Harland and Wolff's status as a state-owned entity in an area where special political considerations are involved will ensure that its survival will be a matter commanding the continuing attention of the British Cabinet' (Hogwood 1979:183). As a result, in this particular case, the economic justification for continued subsidization has been supplemented by, perhaps even supplanted by, politico-social pressures which are different in particular manifestation, but similar in general impact, to those governing the delivery of support for declining industries elsewhere.

The extent to which political changes, consequent upon the signing in 1985 of the Anglo-Irish agreement (O'Leary 1987; Bew and Patterson 1987), the new attitude in official circles in Northern Ireland to the continued provision of industrial subsidies in general, and the very much higher than usual losses to be announced by Harland and Wolff for 1986/87, will influence existing official attitudes to the continued subsidization of shipbuilding in Belfast will be one of the most important economic developments in the region during the next year or two. The scale of the problem is inescapably immense, but no worse, in relative terms, than that facing the rest of the non-privatized shipbuilding industry in the UK. The magnitude of the continuing subsidy required is substantial, but there is no evidence to suggest that it would be more efficiently deployed in other productive activities within Northern Ireland. It may well be, therefore, that Harland and Wolff, as a particular manifestation of a general sectoral problem, has enjoyed continued subsidization on the lesser of two evils argument, that not to subsidize would have been less desirable socially, politically and, perhaps, economically than subsidization itself.

References

Bew, P. and Patterson, H. (1987) 'The New Stalemate: Unionism and the Anglo-Irish Agreement', in P. Teague (Ed.) *Beyond the Rhetoric: Politics, the Economy and Social Policy in Northern Ireland*, London: Lawrence & Wishart.

Canning, D., Moore, B. and Rhodes, J. (1987) 'Economic Growth in Northern Ireland: Problems and Prospects', in P. Teague (Ed.)

Beyond the Rhetoric: Politics, the Economy and Social Policy in Northern Ireland, London: Lawrence & Wishart.

Carlsson, B. (1983) 'Industrial Subsidies in Sweden: Macro-economic Effects and an International Comparison', *Journal of Industrial Economics* 32, 1–23.

Cassing, J.H. (1980) 'Alternatives to Protectionism', in I. Levenson and J. Wheeler (Eds) *Western Economies in Transition: Structural Change and Adjustment Policies in Industrial Countries*, London: Croom Helm.

Committee for Economic Development (1984) *Strategy for US Industrial Competitiveness. A Statement by the Research and Policy Committee of the Committee for Economic Development*, New York and Washington, DC: Committee for Economic Development.

Cragg, C. (1981) 'Shipping and Shipbuilding', in S. Strange and R. Tooze (Eds) *The International Politics of Surplus Capacity*, London: Allen & Unwin.

Denton, G. (1976) 'Financial Assistance to British Industry', in W.M. Cordon and G. Fels (Eds) *Public Assistance to Industry: Protection and Subsidies in Britain and Germany*, London: Macmillan.

Denton, G., O'Claireacain, S. and Ash, S. (1975) *Trade Effects of Public Subsidies to Private Enterprise*, London: Macmillan.

Department of Commerce (1975) *Harland and Wolff Limited Belfast*, Belfast: HMSO.

Department of Economic Development (1985) *Review of Standard Capital Grants: Information Paper*, Belfast: Department of Economic Development.

(1987) *Building a Stronger Economy: The Pathfinder Process*, Belfast: Department of Economic Development.

Department of Finance and Personnel (1987) *Estimates for Services Under the Government of Northern Ireland for year ending 31 March 1988*, Belfast: HMSO.

Edwards, G. (1982) 'Four Sectors: Textiles, Man-Made Fibres, Shipbuilding, Aircraft', in J. Pinder (Ed) *National Industrial Strategies and the World Economy*, Totowa NJ: Allanheld, Osman.

Flam, H., Persson, T. and Svensson, L. (1983) 'Optimal Subsidies to Declining Industries: Efficiency and Equity Considerations', *Journal of Public Economics* 22:327–45.

Forster, B.A. and Rees, R. (1983) 'The Optimal Rate of Decline of an Inefficient Industry', *Journal of Public Economics* 22:227–42.

Foster, J. and Woolfson, C. (1986) *The Politics of the UCS Work In*, London: Lawrence and Wishart.

Gillis, M. (1980) 'International Experience in Assisting Distressed Industries', *Development Discussion Paper* No.108, Harvard Institute for International Development, Harvard University.

Gray, H.P. (1975) 'Senile Industry Protection: A Proposal', *Southern Economic Journal* 40:569–74.

Grunback, I. (1986) 'Harland and Wolff 125th Anniversary', *Lloyds List* Friday, 11 April:5–10.

Hamilton, C. (1981) 'Public Subsidies to Industry. The Case of Sweden and its Shipbuilding Industry', *Seminar Paper* No.174, University of Stockholm, Institute for International Economic Studies.

Harrison, R.T. (1983) 'Consequences of Technological Change: The Case of the Shipbuilding Industry', in D.L. Bosworth (Ed) *The Employment Consequences of Technological Change*, London: Macmillan.

(1985) 'The Regional Impact of Industrial Decline and Restructuring: The Example of the Northern Ireland Shipbuilding Industry', *Tijdschrift voor Economische en Sociale Geographie* 76:332–44.

(1986a) 'The Incidence and Nature of Redundancy in the Northern Ireland Shipbuilding Industry', *Environment and Planning A* 18:1125–36.

(1986b) 'Industrial Development Policy and the Restructuring of the Northern Ireland Economy', *Environment and Planning C: Government and Policy* 4:53–70.

(1988) *Organisation, Technology and Industrial Development: The Regional Impact of the UK Shipbuilding Industry*, Aldershot: Avebury Books.

Hillman, A.L. (1982) 'Declining Industries and Political-Support Protectionist Motives', *American Economic Review* 72:1180–7.

Hogwood, B.W. (1979) *Government and Shipbuilding: The Politics of Industrial Change*, Farnborough: Saxon House.

Industry and Trade Committee (1982) *Government Support for Trade and Industry in Northern Ireland*, House of Commons Papers—Session 1981–82 500, 398–i–ii. London: HMSO.

McGill, J. (1973) *Crisis on the Clyde: The Story of Upper Clyde Shipbuilders*, London: Dennis-Royster.

Ministry of Public Buildings and Works (1963) *Production of Building Components in Shipyards*, London: HMSO.

Moss, M. and Hume, J. (1986), *Shipbuilders to the World: 125 years of Harland and Wolff, Belfast 1861–1986*, Belfast: Blackstaff Press.

Northern Ireland Economic Council (1983a) *Economic Strategy: Historical Growth Performance* Report No.38, Belfast: Northern Ireland Economic Development Office.

(1983b) *The Duration of Industrial Development Assisted Employment* Report No.40, Belfast: Northern Ireland Economic Development Office.

(1984) *Public Expenditure Priorities: Overall Review* Report No.42, Belfast: Northern Ireland Economic Development Office.

(1987) *Economic Assessment: April 1987*, Report No.64 Belfast: Northern Ireland Economic Development Office.

O'Dowd, L., Rolston, B. and Tomlinson, M. (1980) *Northern Ireland: Between Civil Rights and Civil War*, London: CSE Books.

O'Leary, B. (1987) 'The Anglo-Irish Agreement: Meanings, Explanations, Results and a Defence', in P. Teague (Ed.) *Beyond the Rhetoric: Politics, the Economy and Social Policy in Northern Ireland*, London: Lawrence & Wishart.

Peck, F. and Townsend, A.R. (1984) 'Contrasting Experience of

Recession and Spatial Restructuring: British Shipbuilders, Plessey and Metal Box', *Regional Studies* 18:319–38.
Pickering, J.F. and Jones, T.T. (1981) 'The Problem of Excess Capacity in British Industry', *Occasional Paper* No.8104, Department of Management Sciences, University of Manchester Institute of Science and Technology.
Pinder, J. (Ed.) (1982) *National Industrial Strategies and the World Economy* Totowa, NJ: Allenheld, Osman.
Plant, R. (1981) *Industries in Trouble*, Geneva: International Labour Office.
Rowthorn, B. (1987) 'Northern Ireland: An Economy in Crisis', in P. Teague (Ed.) *Beyond the Rhetoric: Politics, the Economy and Social Policy in Northern Ireland*, London: Lawrence & Wishart.
Shipbuilding Inquiry Committee (1966) *Report of the Committee of Inquiry on Shipbuilding (The Geddes Report)*, Cmnd 2934 London: HMSO.
Simpson, J.V. (1981) 'A Functional and Economic Analysis of Public Expenditure in Northern Ireland', *Journal of the Statistical and Social Inquiry Society of Ireland*, 1981/82.
Steed, G.P.F. (1968) 'The Changing Milieu of a Firm: A Case Study of a Shipbuilding Concern', *Annals, Association of American Geographers* 58:506–25.
Strange, S. and Tooze, R. (1981) (Eds) *The International Politics of Surplus Capacity: Competition for Market Shares in the World Recession*, London: Allen & Unwin.
Teague, P. (1987) 'Multinational Companies in the Northern Ireland Economy: An Outmoded Model of Industrial Development?' in P. Teague (Ed.) *Beyond the Rhetoric: Politics, the Economy and Social Policy in Northern Ireland*, London: Lawrence & Wishart.
Thomas, D. (1983) 'Shipbuilding – Demand Linkage and Industrial Decline', in K. Williams, J. Williams and D. Thomas *Why are the British Bad at Manufacturing?*, London: Routledge & Kegan Paul.
Todd, D. (1983) 'Area Development or Sectoral Conflict? An Example of the Discriminatory Effects of Regional Policy in Britain', *Environment and Planning C: Government and Policy* 1:153–62.
(1984) 'Strategies of Growth, Diversification and Rationalisation in the Evolution of Concentration in British Shipbuilding', *Regional Studies* 18:55–67.
(1986) *The World Shipbuilding Industry*, London: Croom Helm.
Yonezawa, Y. (1980) 'Adjustment in Japanese Shipbuilding Industry and Government Shipbuilding Policy', *Discussion Paper 37*, The Japan Economic Research Centre.

7

Economic restructuring and services policy

J. Bachtler and P.L. Davies

Introduction

In recent years there has been a welcome upsurge in the research attention devoted to service sector issues. Although most researchers in the field justifiably complain about the 'Cinderella' status of the sector in industrial and economic research, recent work on macro-level employment and technological trends (Gershuny 1978; Gershuny and Miles 1983); on specific sectors such as financial services (Rajan 1984; 1986); business services (Marshall 1983); distribution (McKinnon 1983; 1985); and on the regional development implications of service development (Daniels 1983; Damesick 1986; Marshall 1985) has contributed to an improved understanding of what is happening within the service sector and its interrelationships with other sectors.

The policy implications of the development of services, however, have been afforded relatively little attention. The exception to this neglect is in the field of regional policy where the advocacy of less manufacturing/production-oriented policy measures was already evident in the 1960s and early 1970s in the debate on office location and relocation. More recently, the emphasis has shifted to arguing the case for including producer services within regional policy in response to the recognition of regional disparities in service provision and the role of producer services in regional growth (Daniels 1983; Marshall 1985).

This chapter is about the wider political aspects of government policy and services. It begins by examining some of the challenges currently faced by policymakers from the growth of services. It then provides a review of the extent to which there is a response to these challenges in the industrial strategies and policies pursued by the current UK Conservative government, i.e. the degree to which the service sector is a target of government policy at national, regional, and local level. In order to provide an indication of alternative political responses, the chapter also contains an examination of the policy prescriptions of other political parties in the UK. Finally, the chapter concludes with an outline of a 'policy agenda' and a summary of some of the key policy issues that confront policymakers involved in the development of services.

The challenges of the growth of services

The development of services and the emergence of what has been termed a 'service economy' – encompassing distribution, hotels and catering; repairs; transport and communications; banking, insurance and finance, business services, and leasing; public administration and other services – presents major challenges to policy and policymakers. The growing share of GDP, balance of payments and employment accounted for by service activities has been accompanied by fundamental changes in the relationship between different economic sectors, the structure and functioning of organizations and the nature of work.

Services account for over 56 per cent of UK gross domestic product (in current prices) – see Table 7.1 – contributing more than twice the value of manufacturing; in the Southeast region they account for around 70 per cent with financial and business services alone contributing more than 13 per cent.

In international trade terms, services – and, in particular, financial services – have made a significant contribution to the current account for the past twenty-five years. Although the contribution of some sectors has declined since the early 1980s, banking and financial services have continued to show a net increase in exports. In the latest 'Survey of prospects for invisible

Table 7.1 Gross domestic product by industry groups in the UK, 1984 (at factor cost; current prices)

	£m	*(%)*
Agriculture, forestry & fishing	5,966	2.1
Energy and water supply	31,541	11.3
Manufacturing	68,375	24.4
Construction	15,838	5.7
Services	158,189	56.5
Total	279,909	100.00

Source: HMSO (1986a) *Regional Trends*.

exports', estimated gross overseas earnings from private sector services totalled some £24.6bn in 1986, an increase of 4 per cent on 1985 (Montagnon 1986). The majority of service industries predicted increased earnings of between 5 and 15 per cent for 1987. Although some sectors, such as consulting engineers, were forecasting a significant fall in earnings, financial services, aviation and tourism were described as 'bullish' (British Business 1987).

For the longer term, however, the outlook may be less positive. While the absolute total of earnings from invisible earnings is rising, the British share of world trade in services is on the decline as a consequence of the growth of the overall market and the increased service activity among developing countries (Montagnon 1986). Moreover, a major threat is presented by competition from Japan where gross invisible earnings have been rising rapidly. In the financial sector, for example, the growing globalization of business and the concentration of ownership following deregulation is leading to an increasing dominance of financial markets by large Japanese and US institutions at the expense of (smaller) independent British firms (Hamilton 1986).

Within the UK, the growing significance of the services sector is most obvious in the changing employment structure, a dominance which has been developing for some two decades but which has become particularly evident as a result of the major job losses in manufacturing during the recent recession. In the industrial distribution of employees in employment, services represented a share of over 65 per cent in 1986, mostly in 'public administration and other services' and 'distribution, hotels and catering, and repairs'. While this share has increased by 6 per cent since 1979, the early 1980s represent the slowest period of service employment growth for over twenty years; in the 1959–66 period, for example, service sector employment was growing at the rate of 2.1 per cent each year.

The growth in service employment has been only partly caused by an increase in the number of jobs in service activities: a major component of change has been the rise in service occupations in other sectors of the economy, for example non-production employment in manufacturing firms. Taking into account these service occupations, it has been estimated that services are responsible for up to three-quarters of total employment in the UK (PSWP 1986).

As some of the main sources of job creation throughout the 1970s and during the early 1980s, services such as distribution, hotel and catering and business services are expected to continue growing until the end of the decade (Rajan 1986). This growth, though, is not likely to be universal and may not be long term. The 1986 survey by the Invisible Exports Council foresaw few sectors of the tradeable services sector with significant scope for much employment growth beyond 1990 (Montagnon 1986). Moreover, public sector services – the fastest and most consistent area of service employment growth throughout the 1960s and early 1970s – have been losing jobs since the mid-1970s (PSWP 1986). Given the current public expenditure constraints this trend is unlikely to be reversed in the foreseeable future.

The growing number of service jobs has involved a major change in the composition of the workforce and the nature of work. Much of the increase in service employment since the early 1970s is accounted for by female and (often also) part-time employment – while job losses in manufacturing have affected predominantly male, full-time employees (Fothergill and Gudgin 1983). Although the service jobs have created new employment opportunities for women, female workers (who comprise the majority of service employees) in services or non-production occupations in manufacturing are frequently subject to low pay, low status, poor conditions of employment, and high rates of turnover in response to market conditions or organizational change (Henwood and Wyatt 1986).

Many of these jobs are in the small firms sector, which contains a high proportion of service firms. Almost two-thirds of all firms are classified as service enterprises, over 80 per cent of which have a turnover of less than £250,000 (see Table 7.2). The service sector is also responsible for the majority of new business registrations. Over the period 1980–84, the industrial sectors experiencing the largest (net) increase in their stock of businesses were 'other services' (including advertising, management, computer, business,

Table 7.2 Distribution of firms by turnover, 1985

	Turnover size			*% total stock of businesses*
	<£250,000	*£250,000–£1m*	*>£1m*	
Agriculture, forestry and fishing	91.1	8.0	0.9	0.5
Mining and quarrying	55.5	23.3	21.1	0.1
Manufacturing	69.1	18.8	12.3	10.6
Construction	86.5	10.3	0.2	14.3
Services	83.4	11.4	5.1	65.4
All businesses	83.0	11.7	5.2	100.0

Source: Williams 1987.

and miscellaneous services) which increased by 30.6 per cent over the 1980–84 period; financial, property and professional services (23.4 per cent); and wholesaling (18.3 per cent) (Williams 1987).

However, in some service sectors the permanency of new start-ups is limited and many new registrations are regarded simply as replacements rather than genuine additions. In the retailing sector, for example, over 160,000 new retailing businesses were registered over the period 1980–84 but the net stock of businesses fell by almost 10,000 over the same period (Williams 1987).

Finally, there is the issue of the spatial distribution of services. Although there is a relatively even regional distribution of public service employment throughout the UK, private service jobs are strongly concentrated in the Southeast and especially – in the case of financial and business services – in Greater London. Further, recent employment changes in private service employment have favoured southern and eastern regions. Such differences in the location and growth of producer services, in particular, are said to be a major factor in explaining regional disparities. The availability of producer services is considered to influence the competitiveness, innovation and 'capacity for adjustment' of regional industry and, through the effect on occupational structure, may have consequences for the regional potential for entrepreneurship (Damesick 1986; Daniels 1986; Marshall 1985).

The processes of structural change which have led to the growing centrality of services – variously described as 'de-industrialisation' or 'industrial restructuring' – have considerable implications for policymakers. These range from the macro-economic questions of how to sustain output, employment, and trade in services at a time when the contribution of the manufacturing sector has been considerably diminished, to the detailed design of policy instruments for influencing the local development of specific firms. The objective of the following section is to examine how far government industrial policies are designed to influence the development of the service sector.

Government policy and services

National government policy

National government policy towards industry in the UK is currently governed by the objectives of a reduction in state intervention in the economy, the creation of a climate favourable to business, the improvement of international competitiveness, and the encouragement of innovation (DTI 1985). These objectives have been reflected in the privatization and rationalization of nationalized industries, the deregulation of markets and industries, and cutbacks in the growth of public expenditure. Spending on sectoral and regional support has been reduced in favour of increased expenditure on scientific and technological assistance, while the high profile of unemployment and the conditions of the inner cities has prompted a plethora of employment and training initiatives, as well as measures for urban infrastructure and environmental improvement.

The service sector, either in part or as a whole, has not been a specific target of these policy measures. Government strategy is opposed to discriminatory sectoral support and government policy statements have emphasized the role of market forces in determining the relative strength of each sector (Channon 1985). However, services have been affected by a range of government policy measures, notably through competition policy, the privatization programme and industrial support measures for improving efficiency, competitiveness, innovation, and productivity.

Reflecting current government priorities, perhaps the most significant impact on services has come through changes in competition policy. Internationally, the British government has been pressing for the liberalization of trade in services through the European Commission (via DGIV – the Trade and Competition Directorate) and through the forum of the General Agreement on Trade and Tariffs (GATT) which currently makes very little provision for services. Of particular potential benefit to the UK are said to be proposals for improving trade in insurance, re-insurance, and transportation (Aronson and Cowhey 1985; SDA 1986). To date, however, relatively little advance has been made in either forum.

More progress has been made at national level, where the government has initiated a range of deregulation and liberalization measures, most of which have affected services. Examples include: the deregulation of financial services, telecommunications and long-distance coach services; the removal of monopolies from house conveyancing, opticians and various mail services; the relaxation of advertising and competition controls on accountants, solicitors, surveyors, stockbrokers, and veterinary surgeons; and increased competition on air routes within the UK and between certain European countries (Conservative Party 1987).

This deregulatory philosophy has also been evident in the government's approach to the small firms sector – much of which is comprised of service enterprises. Small firms have been subject to two deregulatory White Papers 'Lifting the Burden' (HMSO, 1985) and 'Building Businesses . . . Not Barriers' (HMSO 1986b) which have involved the removal of legislation in areas such as planning, VAT collection and employment law, as well as simplifying business dealings with government. Small firms have also been the target of a range of measures to improve the availability of finance (through the Loan Guarantee Scheme, Business Expansion Scheme, and Venture Capital Scheme, for example) to provide exemption from taxation through capital gains, capital transfer, and income tax relief, and to improve advisory services.

At the other end of the corporate scale, services have featured prominently in the government's privatization programme. Between December 1979 and June 1987 over thirty companies or parts of organizations formerly in state hands were privatized, almost half of which could be classified as service activities. Most significant in employment terms were British Telecom, the National Bus Company, British Gas and British Airways; these firms together accounted for almost 500,000 employees (Steel and Heald 1985; Curwen 1986).

With respect to direct and specific industrial support, government incentive policy has affected services in two ways (Bienkowski and Bachtler 1987). First, incentive schemes which were formerly specific to the manufacturing sector alone have been modified to make them more applicable to services. Second, new schemes have been provided to promote usage of professional and business services. These encourage efficiency improvements in manufacturing firms as well as stimulating the demand for business services.

Most general investment support is now available regardless of sector, although retailing, wholesaling, and domestic services generally tend to be excluded. Much of the sector-specific support under Section 8 of the Industry Act 1972 has been abolished, the eligibility of other schemes has been widened to include services and, in some instances, changes have been introduced to make the form of support more appropriate to services. Most notable of these changes was the revision of regional policy support in 1984. Services, which were formerly restricted to applying for the Office and Service Industries Scheme (OSIS), were eligible for the standard regional assistance package. Since November 1984 a range of producer services – including advertising, market research, R. and D., consultancy and administrative headquarters – have been eligible for the Regional Development Grant (RDG) which offers an employment grant as well as a capital grant and waives the 40 per cent fixed asset ceiling applying to manufacturing projects. In addition, Regional Selective Assistance (RSA) has been modified to allow awards to be related to job creation or capital investment projects. Regional policy changes in 1988 meant that, while RDG ceased to be available, services are still eligible for RSA.

In the field of employment and training, the general support tends to be available to all firms regardless of sector. In certain areas, however, such as computer or engineering services, specific skill shortages have led to the introduction of special schemes organized by appropriate bodies such as training boards in the sectors involved. With respect to innovation policy, service firms involved in areas such as information technology, telecommunications, and scientific research can participate in numerous programmes sponsored by the Department of Trade and Industry and the European Commission, some of which sponsor collaborative work between industrial participants, consultants and research organizations.

The second area of financial support from which services have benefited is assistance in promoting the demand for services, through aid for business advisory services. The aim of this support is to promote a greater usage of business services, like design and marketing, to improve business performance. Service firms engaged in such consultancy and advice may qualify for subsidies to lower the cost of service supply. These advisory services include: the group of DTI Business and Technical Advisory Service (BTAS) schemes which fund consultancy projects in design, quality, and marketing; the regionally-restricted Business Improvement Services (part-funded by the European Regional Development Fund) which provide grants for using local general management, finance, and marketing service; and a range of specific consultancy schemes aimed at encouraging the diffusion of advanced technology throughout industry in areas such as microelectronics, advanced manufacturing technology, energy saving, and biotechnology.

Service firms are also increasingly eligible to use these subsidized services themselves. The BTAS services for example, which were previously restricted to the manufacturing sector, were extended to include services in 1985, and have recently replaced their former production orientation with a greater emphasis on marketing.

Lastly, although there is no major service-specific funding, two areas of the service sector which do have special schemes are the transport and tourism sectors. Mainly as a result of government deregulatory initiatives, assistance has been provided to encourage the development of private sector rail or water freight facilities and to subsidize private bus services. In the tourism sector, relatively small-scale support is available primarily for the development of tourist accommodation but also for the provision of health and recreation facilities.

Finally, public services have been directly affected by government employment policies, much of which consist of service employment. Between 1979 and 1984 public sector employment fell by over 7 per cent; for the Civil Service this represented a loss of 14 per cent (or 630,000 jobs). Although the National Health Service, the largest public sector employer with almost one million employees, experienced a minor increase in employment between 1979 and 1982, post-1983 expenditure cuts of £140 million were predicted as leading to the loss of 20,000 jobs; more radical proposals would increase this figure to 82,000. For local government employment the early 1980s saw a lesser percentage fall than at national level, but nonetheless involved a loss of 94,000 full-time and 27,000 part-time jobs (Beaumont 1985).

The service sector, therefore, has been affected by numerous aspects of government policy. This does not, however, betoken a comprehensive and concerted strategy for the service sector. Rather, it has its roots in a set of ideological beliefs which Conservative Governments have pursued with considerable determination for most of the period since 1979. The well-known tenets of this ideology are that inflation must be reduced in order to make Britain competitive, to be achieved by reducing the money supply and public spending, and also allowing the market to prevail wherever possible and encouraging the private rather than the public sector (Kavanagh 1986).

Regional and local government policy

The lack of any service strategy or extensive public debate on service policies at national level contrasts to a certain extent with the situation at regional and local level. Although the main concern of many regional and local agencies has been with the health of the manufacturing sector – unsurprising in view of the impact of the recession on many communities and regions – recent years have seen an increasing appreciation of the potential importance and contribution of services.

In Scotland, for example, the Industry Department for Scotland has been active in measuring output and employment in the Scottish service sector for some years (see Dewhurst, Lythe and Peterson 1984; 1985). From a policy perspective, the Scottish

Development Agency undertook an analysis of the state of the service sector in 1984 as a prelude to affirming the encouragement of services as a top corporate priority – along with technology, small firms, and local area initiatives and the creation of a Service Industries Division (SDA 1984). In response to the regional under-representation in private sector services such as business services, wholesale distribution, banking, insurance and R. and D., the SDA has been actively promoting various service initiatives in Scotland. A major area is the development of the Scottish tourist industry through projects such as the 1988 National Garden Festival in Glasgow and the 'Highland Gateway' Centre in Perth. Other strategies have involved the promotion of service exports (especially in the construction industry and the education sector), the development of business services (through the setting-up of a Distributive Trades Technology Advisory Centre in Stirling and support for the establishment of a Market Development Service for architects), and the identification of franchising as an area of considerable potential. Financial services are being given special attention with the establishment of a new SDA Financial Services Division during 1986/7 (SDA 1987).

A similar regional analysis of services was undertaken in Northern Ireland by the Northern Ireland Economic Council in 1982. The NIEC proposed that a range of producer services such as consultancy, financial, computer, and office services should be promoted more vigorously (NIEC 1982). Policymaker response has, however, not been forthcoming. The main industrial development support instruments continue to give only limited assistance to the service sector on the grounds that the sector is not 'tradeable' beyond Northern Ireland and that support would lead to job displacement.

At the local government level, local authorities are of major importance for the local service sector through their capacity as both service providers and service users, particularly of producer services. They have a range of responsibilities which involve services – the provision of public transport facilities and transport infrastructure; education and cultural facilities; housing services; leisure facilities; and social services. The functioning of local government, on the other hand, also involves the use of such services as computing, legal, and architectural services.

In response to nationwide industrial decline and diminishing regional assistance from central government, many local authorities (and indeed other local organizations) have become involved in the task of local economic development since the late 1970s and early 1980s. It is unclear to what extent this has involved a recognition of the service sector but the emphasis of activity appears to be mainly on the provision of manufacturing premises, factory conversion, industrial estates, enterprise workshops and nursery units (see Chapter 10). Examples of service-based measures however, do exist and include advance office building and service property development, leisure facility developments, financial support for business information and advice, training, education, and workforce support (LAA/NCVO 1984).

Local government involvement in service provision and usage, however, has been curtailed as a result of a continued reduction in central government contributions to local authorities through the Rate Support Grant in recent years. Many local authorities have experienced increasing difficulties in providing what they regard as a satisfactory range of local services and have found it necessary to reappraise the services that they provide in terms of their value to the local community and also their funding. In arguing the case for more funding with central government, local authorities have indicated the potential for developing services, both in tackling the problems of urban areas among the metropolitan authorities, and the tourism and leisure potential of the countryside by rural authorities (AMA 1986; ADC 1986).

Alternative political responses

Given the importance of political and ideological factors underpinning the current Conservative government's policy measures which significantly affect services – deregulation, privatization, public service cutbacks, etc. – it seems appropriate to refer to some of the alternative political positions (albeit only in the form of policy statements and manifesto commitments) which exist for an indication of other potential policy strategies. This section, therefore, examines the responses of the alternative political parties (the Labour Party, SDP/Liberal Alliance, and the Nationalist parties) to the growth of services in the British economy.

Through their policy documents, all the political parties have engaged in considerable discussion on the causes of, and remedies for, the problems of economic restructuring in the UK (Labour Party 1987; SDP/Liberal Alliance 1987; Scottish National Party 1987; Plaid Cymru 1987). Reference to services occurs in two areas.

First, there is the issue of training which is perceived by all the political parties to be of overriding importance in enabling the unemployed as well as those in work to acquire skills relevant to the job market of the 1980s. The training needs of the 'new' service industries and occupations, particularly those involving new technology, are identified as being a key area of emphasis. However, while each of the political parties have formulated detailed proposals for the types of training schemes envisaged, there are relatively few commitments to specific policy strategies or measures for the service sector. Actual proposals for training schemes are generally sector-neutral.

The second area where services are discussed by opposition parties is with regard to the provision of public services. Here, policy tends to be aimed at (a) creating new jobs, and (b) improving the quality of public services. These principles are applied selectively both to 'economically-deprived' areas like parts of Scotland and Wales, and to special interest groups like women and ethnic minorities.

Reflecting political philosophies, most policy proposals are committed to increasing expenditure on public services. In the field of health and social services, they identify additional resources for the National Health Service (more medical and research staff, more resources for preventative and non-hospital health care) and for social service activities (increased benefits). The main differences relate to how far the state should be involved. The Labour and Nationalist parties argue for almost total public sector provision and the Alliance allocate some of the burden to private medical expenditure.

Increased funding for education services is also a common theme. Proposals envisage a widening of access and greater investment in education facilities, notably for teacher training, nursery education, and higher education. They also indicate a desire for smaller education units (both schools and classes) and a greater range of options (particularly in the further and higher education field). While there is broad agreement on the principles, the degree to which the government should provide these services is again the main distinguishing feature. Thus, the Labour Party gives special emphasis to preventing the diversion of resources to private schools. By contrast, the Alliance wishes to preserve the right of those who wish to pay for independent education in the private sector.

Under the heading of transport, there is consensus also over the need for extra investment to renew road, rail, and port infrastructure to enhance the quality and quantity of transport services and to facilitate trade. Public provision of transport services is also highlighted by all the parties, with particular emphasis on local government responsibilities in this area.

The debate about the relative merits of public versus private ownership is most sharply focused on the attitude of the opposition parties to services provided by public enterprises. The Labour Party and Nationalist parties are, as a matter of principle, in favour of public control of basic utilities such as gas, electricity, and telecommunications. The Alliance is more equivocal, believing that the question of public ownership should be judged on the 'objective' criteria of competition and efficiency. On this basis, the Alliance is against the privatization of British Telecom, British Gas and the Central Electricity Generating Board, but supports the privatization of Rolls Royce and British Steel.

Finally, policy proposals focus on leisure, recreation and tourism as sources of income and employment generation. However, while the Labour Party and Plaid Cymru make only general commitments to expanding these industries under the all-embracing headings of 'environmental protection' and 'job creation', the Alliance and SNP have specific policies to promote leisure and recreation. Both propose the development of ministerial responsibilities for such activities to expand access and facilities, particularly from the viewpoint of export revenue.

Such proposals to expand public services are wide-ranging. Although in the absence of political power they can be little more than policy intentions, there has been some quantification of their expected impact. The Labour Party and the Alliance, for example, forecast that their proposals for public services will reduce unemployment by one million in two and three years respectively. Labour claims that its programme will increase public expenditure by £6bn net in each of the first two years of its period in office, and the Alliance predicts that public spending will go up by some £7bn a year net by the second year of its stewardship (*The Economist*, 23 May 1987).

These commitments to public service provision, of course, derive less from an appreciation of the role of services in the economy than from ideology. The Labour and Nationalist parties, for example, broadly favour the public provision of common goods and services rather than private control. Also, they affirm that the state is the most appropriate instrument through which economic growth can be achieved, and the effects of economic decline ameliorated. For the Alliance, the lesser commitment to public service provision is related to the combination of the Liberal Party's traditional views – which have generally been positive towards public investment – and the more market economy principles of the SDP (Owen and Steel 1986).

In addition, electoral expediency has contributed to the commitments to public services and training. Unemployment is universally recognized as the most serious social and economic problem in Britain (Moon and Richardson 1985). Opinion polls also show that most people would rather pay more taxes and receive better quality services, than the reverse (Gallup 1987). Opposition parties, therefore, have concluded that political and, more importantly, electoral popularity can best be achieved by advocating increased expenditure on public services, together with extensive training and retraining plans, and accompanied by assurances that such policies will create new jobs and also improve the quality of public services.

These ideological and electoral explanations for the 'alternative services policies' discussed above, however, do not constitute a structured response to the type of 'challenges' outlined earlier. There is, for example, almost no reference to private sector services such as finance and insurance. Indeed, the overall response of the opposition parties to services supplied by the private sector, with the exception of the Alliance, seems to be one of seeking to impose stringent state control over their activities. Hence, in the same way that the Conservative government has attempted to reduce the role of the state in all sectors of the economy (including those areas affected by industrial policy) mainly for ideological reasons, the Labour Party and the Nationalists' stance on expanding the influence of the state is similarly based on ideology and political considerations.

The obstacles to service policies

The conclusion to emerge from the preceding sections is that while there are major challenges to government from the growth of services, there is no 'service strategy' as such – certainly not at the national level, and in an early phase at the regional and local levels. A wide range of actual and projected policy measures affect services, yet there is little evidence of co-ordinated service-oriented thinking in these approaches. Policy measures have more of a political and ideological than economic development rationale. The same can be said of some of the alternative political responses, which propose a much stronger role for the public sector but again are derived basically from political standpoints. Such a conclusion, though, is hardly surprising given the political realities which shape the entirety of government involvement in society and the economy. On the other hand, the absence of co-ordinated strategies for services can perhaps also be attributed, at least partly, to other factors.

First, there is the question of lack of understanding and the conceptual problems of dealing with activities where output is non-physical and difficult to define. Much of the service economy is still a 'black box' with little knowledge in key areas such as the impact of trade on services. The lack of academic attention must be a contributing factor: it is perhaps no coincidence that the policy area where most overt consideration has been given to services is that which has been most intensively researched – that of regional policy.

Second, there is the issue of information. The lack of statistical data for services (compared to manufacturing), especially such basic information as input-output tables, makes it difficult to talk meaningfully about productivity in services or the interrelationships between manufacturing and services.

Third, the view that the economy is solely manufacturing-driven still has widespread currency. The contention is that services are wholly dependent on manufacturing and that services jobs are often not 'real' jobs. In this context there are sometimes references to a developing 'pizza economy' and 'lollipop jobs'. This derives partly from a concern with the serious implications of the decline of manufacturing, and the more limited tradeability of services. But perhaps it also reflects an excessive manufacturing and large-firm fixation on the part of both researchers and policymakers.

Fourth, there is the political standpoint which advocates that there is no need for a service policy. It is sometimes argued that many services are performing well unaided, that government has limited powers to intervene in the economy and that it should concentrate its involvement and resources on more urgent industrial and economic needs.

Fifth, there are the administrative problems associated with developing a service policy. Aside from the statistical and technical problems referred to earlier, the heterogeneous nature of the sector is such that an all-embracing policy may not be feasible, or even desirable. Moreover, the development of any policy would inevitably involve inter-departmental activity within government which would face major political and administrative obstacles (Self 1977).

Sixth, there is little political momentum for a policy for the service sector. The present government's philosophy on intervention is clearly a major hurdle. However, the sector's diversity means that there are no obvious representatives that encompass more than individual groups of activity, who could articulate the need for government intervention. There are few vocal pressure groups – with the major exception of the City – and both the CBI and the TUC are still largely dominated by manufacturing industry interests.

Finally, the lack of service policy is an illustration of the absence of an industrial policy, more generally, in the UK. In contrast to countries such as Germany and Japan, there is no tradition of a long-term, largely consensus-based and well-defined strategy for supporting industry in Britain. Among all the major targets for industrial policy – small firms, R. & D., sectoral support, structural change and adaptation, employment and training, export promotion, energy, environmental conservation and problem area development – there are few strategies which have been either co-ordinated or which have lasted unaltered beyond the lifetime of an individual government.

What kind of service policies?

The preceding sections have, in turn, reviewed the challenges to policymakers from the growth of the service sector, the existing policy measures from central, regional, and local government which influence service activities and some of the alternative political policy prescriptions. Reference has also been made to the obstacles to the development of service policies. This final section attempts to draw together some of the main points raised by this review and to suggest some of the key issues for a policy-making agenda.

The overriding priority for the development of a strategy for the service sector must be to encourage more debate and new thinking on the types of policy options available. Such a debate needs to be more sophisticated than the sterile discussion – reminiscent of the 1986 House of Lords deliberations – as to whether manufacturing is of more importance than services or vice versa. The debate is needed to help overcome the obstacles referred to above – the conceptual problems involved in thinking about and analysing a sector whose output is largely intangible, the lack of comprehensive statistics on service activities, and the bias towards manufacturing-oriented and large firm policies.

The starting point for this debate, therefore, should involve a recognition of the interrelationships between the different sectors of the economy and the need for an industrial policy which does not emphasize one sector at the expense of all others. Existing policy measures and policy delivery systems should, therefore, be reviewed from the viewpoint of sector-neutrality, to remove bias against services, and to give equal treatment with manufacturing, as has already occurred in regional policy and the Business and Technical Advisory Service schemes. There is general agreement on this issue across the political spectrum, including such representative groupings as the CBI and TUC which have both argued for policy to recognize the interdependence of manufacturing and services.

The future increase of employment in services is constrained by the restrictions on public services (the source of much past job creation) and the problem of modest or stagnant employment growth in private sector services. As opposition political parties have made clear, however, there is major potential in areas such as health and social services, education, transport, and leisure, recreation and tourism. Local authorities, which are major providers and users of services, have also indicated the opportunities for service development in dealing with both urban and rural problems. In part this potential has been recognized by the government, for example in the tourism sector, yet a major change in attitude towards public expenditure – particularly in health and education – is required if significant employment generation is to be achieved.

The majority of the self-employed are in service activities and a very high proportion of service enterprises are small businesses. Consequently, service firm development policies should be closely associated with policy measures for entrepreneurship and small businesses. Whereas new manufacturing firms may be more in need of financial aid, the emphasis of service support may need to be targeted more on advice and counselling (especially given the high rates of business failure in sectors such as retailing), marketing, sales and financial management. Policy instruments should also recognize the lower capital intensity of service firms and be tailored to meet specific needs such as the demand for working capital, employment-related aid, interest and rent relief.

For innovation in service activities and the generation of new service employment, the establishment of a national and international telecommunications and IT infrastructure has been identified as an important element. Hitherto, the government's policy has been to adopt an essentially 'hands off' approach. Although this liberalization of telecommunications may provide business with a competitive advantage and stimulate the development of new services, only the government can ensure that this is to the benefit of the whole country rather than just the core regions. The lack of a regional development dimension to telecommunications policy contrasts with the situation in other countries (such as France and Germany) where the development of telematics is seen as an important vehicle for regional development.

The increasing use of information technology in service firms and occupations highlights the need for appropriate education and training. Indeed, the training field is one of the common concerns of all political parties. However, discussion of national and vocational training in areas such as computing, electronics, and telecommunications tends to concentrate on the needs of the suppliers of IT rather than the users. Yet, with the increasing application of IT in such fields as office automation, a critical factor is the availability of information management skills – the ability to make use of, and exploit, the information proliferation. Among IT user firms there appears to be a significant shortage of such IT occupational skills (as well as multi-skilled technicians and maintenance staff), a deficiency which increases with ascent up the management hierarchy (LTPG 1985). More generally, the relevance of much management and business training may be questionable; there is evidence to suggest that there is frequently a considerable orientation towards the manufacturing sector, emphasizing traditional production concepts such as production control, product innovation, and stock control. In addition to IT usage skills, there appears to be a need for the development and use of service firm management and organization techniques and training.

A consequence of the changes in the nature of work has implications for a range of social issues, particularly the increase in female employment, frequently associated with part-time and casual work, and home/outworking. The employees involved often suffer problems of low pay, lack of employment rights, low levels of unionization, low status, few career prospects, and high turnover. Present government thinking, supported by business interests, advocates 'flexibility' and reliance on 'market forces' in the job market (for example, by reducing employment rights, union power, and minimum wage levels) (CBI 1986). However, alternative policy prescriptions emphasize the need for greater consideration of social issues with more protection for disadvantaged groups both in 'conventional' service industries such as hotels, catering and distribution, and in new information-based services such as computing (TUC 1986).

Finally, there is the question of regional disparities. The spatial distribution of service activities, particularly producer services, has received considerable attention in recent years. The potential (regional) policy responses have also been the subject of much research – which has been recognized in the strategies for relocating offices in the 1960s, the Office and Services Industries Scheme in the 1970s and, more recently, by the inclusion of selected producer services in the regional aid package since 1984. Future policy proposals advocate the continued spatial targeting of support for services in view of the place-specific and urban orientation of producer services (e.g. Daniels 1986) and the potential for provincial business service centres to counter the effect of the capital city (Damesick 1986). Taking such suggestions a stage further there may be a need for the consideration and development of 'regional service strategies' for utilizing and exploiting regional potentials and existing sectoral strengths in such areas as education, financial services, leisure, health care, commerce, R. & D. and corporate/administrative headquarters. The examples of Ireland (Fitzpatrick and McEniff 1984; Bannon and Ward 1985; RDO 1987); Denmark (Pederson 1986) and Sweden (SIND 1985; 1986; 1987) would be ones that the UK could surely profitably follow.

References

ADC (1986) *The Rural Economy at the Crossroads. A Review of Rural Needs and Problems in the 1980s*, London: Association of District Councils.

AMA (1986) *Programme for Partnership. An Urban Policy Statement*, London: Association of Metropolitan Authorities.

Aronson, J.D. and Cowhey, P.F. (1985) 'Services Trade: A Case for Open Markets', *Economic Impact* 2:11–17.

Bannon, M.J. and Ward, S. (1985) *Services and the New Economy – Implications for National and Regional Development*, RSA Irish Branch.

Barras, R. (1983) *Growth and Technical Change in the UK Service Sector*, London: Technical Change Centre.

Beaumont, P. (1985) 'Public Service Employment and Industrial Relations 1979–83', in P. Jackson (Ed.), *Implementing Government Policy Initiatives: The Thatcher Administration 1979–1983*, London, Royal Institute of Public Administration.

Bienkowski, M. and Bachtler, J. (1987) 'Grants Briefing: the Service Sector', *CBI News*, No.12, 12–25 June:8–10.

British Business (1987) 'Invisible earnings set to rise', *British Business*, 29 May 1987:12.

CBI Council (1986) *The CBI Response to the Report of House of Lords*

Select Committee on Overseas Trade (The Aldington Report), London: Confederation of British Industry.

Channon, P. (1985) *Speech to the CBI Council: Wednesday, 25 February 1986*, London: Department of Trade and Industry (Typescript).

Conservative Party (1987) *The Next Moves Forward. The Conservative Manifesto 1987*, London: Conservative Party.

CSO (1986) *Regional Trends* 21, 1986 Edition, London: Central Statistical Office, HMSO.

Curwen, P. (1986) *Public Enterprise – A Modern Approach*, Brighton, Wheatsheaf.

Damesick, P. (1986) 'Service industries, employment and regional development in Britain: a review of recent trends and issues', *Transactions of the Institute of British Geographers*, 11:212–26.

Daniels, P.W. (1983) 'Service industries: supporting role or centre stage?' *Area*, 15:301–10.

(1986) 'Producer Services and the Post-Industrial Space Economy', in R. Martin and B. Rowthorn (Eds) *The Geography of De-Industrialisation*, London: Macmillan.

DTI (1985) *Department of Trade and Industry AIMS*, Information Division, London: Department of Trade and Industry.

Dewhurst, J., Lythe, C., and Peterson, J. (1984) 'The Measurement of Output and Employment in the Scottish Service Sector (1962–1980)', *ESU Research Papers No.7*, Industry Department for Scotland.

(1985) 'An Analysis of Trends in Output and Employment in the Service Sector in Scotland', *ESU Research Papers No.10*, Industry Department for Scotland.

Fitzpatrick and McEniff (1984) *Technical Change and International Competitiveness in Service Industry, Implications for Ireland*, Education, Innovation and Entrepreneurship Research Programme, Dublin: EIE Publications.

Fothergill, S. and Gudgin, G. (1983) *Unequal Growth*, London: Heinemann.

Gallup (1987) *Gallup Political Index*, Report No. 326, October: London: Social Surveys (Gallup) Ltd, Table 11:17.

Gershuny, J. (1978) *After Industrial Society? The Emerging Self-Service Economy*, London: Macmillan.

Gershuny, J. and Miles, I. (1983) *The New Service Economy*, London, Frances Pinter.

Hamilton, A. (1986) *The Financial Revolution*, London: Viking.

Henwood, F. and Wyatt, S. (1986) 'Women's Work, Technological Change and Shifts in the Employment Structure', in Martin, R. and Rowthorn, B. (Eds) *The Geography of De-Industrialisation*, London: Macmillan.

HMSO (1985) *Lifting the Burden*, Cmnd 9571, London: HMSO.

(1986a) *Regional Trends*, London: HMSO.

(1986b) *Building Businesses . . . Not Barriers*, Cmnd 9794, London: HMSO.

Kavanagh, D. (1986) 'Margaret Thatcher: A Study in Prime Ministerial Style', *Studies in Public Policy* 151, Glasgow: CSPP, University of Strathclyde.

LAA/NCVO (1984) *Joint Action – The Way Forward*, London: National Council for Voluntary Organisations.

Labour Party (1987) *Britain Will Win*, Labour Manifesto, June 1987, London: Labour Party.

LTPG (1985) *IT Futures – what current forecasting literature says about the social impact of information technology*, Long-Term Perspectives Group, London: NEDO.

Marshall, J.N. (1982) 'Linkages between manufacturing industry and business services', *Environment and Planning A*, 14:1523–40.

(1983) 'Business service activities in British provincial conurbations', *Environment and Planning A*, 15:1343–59.

(1985) 'Business Services, the Regions and Regional Policy', *Regional Studies*, 19(4), August:353–64.

McKinnon, A.C. (1983) 'The development of warehousing in England', *Geoforum*, 14:389–99.

(1985) 'The distribution systems of supermarket chains', *Service Industries Journal* 5:226–38.

Montagnon, P. (1986) 'Job pessimism in trade in services', *Financial Times*, 13 November 1986.

Moon, J. and Richardson, J.J. (1985) *Unemployment in the UK*, Hants: Gower.

NIEC (1982) *Private Services in Economic Development*, Belfast: Northern Ireland Economic Council Report No.30.

Owen, D. and Steel, D. (1986) *The Time Has Come. Partnership for Progress*, London: Weidenfeld & Nicolson.

Pederson, P.O. (1986) *Business Service Strategies: The Case of the Provincial Centre of Esbjerg*, Commission of the European Communities, FAST Series No.19.

Plaid Cymru (1987) *General Election Programme. Winning for Wales*, Cardiff: Plaid Cymru.

PSWP (1986) *Uneven Development in the Service Economy: Understanding the Location and Role of Producer Services*, Report of the Producer Services Working Party.

Rajan, A. (1984) *New Technology and Employment in Insurance, Banking and Building Societies: Recent Experience and Future Impact*, London, Institute of Manpower Studies series: Gower.

(1986) *Services – the Second Industrial Revolution: Business and Jobs Outlook for UK Growth Industries*, London: Butterworth.

RDO (1987) *Strategy for Development of the Services Sector in the Mid-West Region of Ireland*, Mid-West Regional Development Organisation, Limerick.

SDA (1984) *Annual Report*, Glasgow: Scottish Development Agency.

(1986) 120, *Scottish Economic Development Review* 2.

(1987) *Annual Report*, Glasgow: Scottish Development Agency.

SDP/Liberal Alliance (1987) *Britain United. The Time Has Come*, London: SDP/Liberal Alliance.
Self, P. (1977) *Administrative Theories and Politics,* London: George Allen & Unwin.
SIND (1985) *Privat Tjanstesektor, Struktur och utvecklingsdrag*, SIND PM 1985:5, Stockholm: Statens Industriverk.
(1986) *Privata Tjanstesektoren, Regionala utvecklingsmojligheter*, SIND PM 1986:8, Stockholm: Statens Industriverk.
(1987) *Lanad Tillvaxti Tjanstesektorn?* Stockholm: Statens Industriverk.
SNP (1987) *Play the Scottish Card*, SNP General Election Manifesto 1987, Edinburgh: Scottish National Party.
Steel, D. and Heald, D. (1985) 'The Privatisation of Public Enterprises 1979–83', in P. Jackson, (Ed.), *Implementing Government Policy Initiatives: The Thatcher Administration 1979–1983*, London: Royal Institute of Public Administration.
TUC (1986) *Economic Review 1986*, London: Trades Union Congress.
Williams, D. (1987) 'Small Firms', *Midland Bank Review*, Spring: 16–23.

8

The relative competitiveness of small manufacturing companies in South Wales and Northern Ireland: analysis and policy

D.M.W.N. Hitchens and P.N. O'Farrell

Introduction

This chapter forms the second[1] (Hitchens and O'Farrell 1985) in a series of papers comparing small firm performance between four assisted and one non-assisted regions of the UK and Ireland. The regions include, in addition to those compared here, the Republic of Ireland, Scotland and a conglomerate of the non-assisted regions of East Anglia and Southeast England. The paper, by using a sample design based on matched pairs of firms (Daly, Hitchens, and Wagner 1984; O'Farrell and Hitchens 1986) in Northern Ireland and South Wales, and by comparing their markets, machinery, labour, premises, and certain dimensions of company performance, including growth rates, productivity, product quality, and price competitiveness, aims to identify regional factors inhibiting small firm growth and thereby recommend policy initiatives to be taken by Development Agencies. To do this an interview schedule has been developed to investigate six major growth related topics: (1) the characteristics of the firm; (2) markets served, including marketing methods used; (3) the competitive environment, including numbers of competitors and the basis on which competition takes place; (4) production detail, including how a product is made; (5) the age and type of machinery used; and (6) performance data including measures of growth, productivity, and selective price and non-price competitive characteristics of the main products manufactured.

Conceptual issues

Mason and Harrison (1985:4–5) have identified the 'need for some detailed studies of the . . . role and growth of new and small firms in contrasting regional environments' and have called for 'an examination of the locational and structural characteristics of successful small firms'. They have also argued that whereas there is now substantial research on new firm formation, equivalent research on performance of small firms in different regions is virtually non-existent (Mason and Harrison 1985). The local milieu may be an important influence upon the prospects for small firm growth and expansion: growth impediments are likely to vary in nature and scale between different regions. Venture capital availability is more limited in peripheral areas due to the centralization of the lending institutions and the distorted perception of risk by banks. Lower rates of economic growth and lower levels of income inhibit the opportunities for small firm expansion based upon local and regional markets; and small firms in the periphery may face less severe competition than those in core regions. Small firms in peripheral regions also suffer technical impediments to growth reflected in lower rates of innovation compared with similar sized firms in core regions (Oakey, Thwaites and Nash 1982). Labour supply bottlenecks – especially shortages of apprentice-trained craftsmen and managerial staff – vary between regional and sub-regional economies and may be a serious constraint upon growth. Furthermore, peripheral economies, such as South Wales, are typically dominated by large firms such as the British Steel Corporation, BP, and Ford which are not an ideal source of skilled labour for small firms. Del Monte and Giannola (1986) have also argued that one of the major impediments to the expansion of small firms in peripheral regions is the restricted supply of organizational and managerial skills. They also suggest that firms in less prosperous areas will be more vertically integrated than those in developed regions and that this lack of specialization reduces the competitiveness and growth of local firms.

Small independent firms are less well equipped than multi-plant organizations to anticipate and avoid impediments and also to resolve them; not only are their own problem-solving resources fewer, but also their limited management capacity may constrain their access to external public and private resources; while these latter resources may also be more scarce and of lower quality in peripheral areas.

At present an adequate explanatory framework within which to analyse the growth of the small owner-managed manufacturing enterprise has not been developed (O'Farrell and Hitchens 1986).

The research evidence presented in this chapter suggests that inadequate design, poor quality and lack of price competitiveness are major factors constraining the growth and threatening the survival of many small firms. However, theories of small firm growth implicitly assume that the production process is largely a 'black box' and that the firm can manufacture to the appropriate design, quality, and price for its specific market segment and can choose, therefore, whether or not to grow. In short, these models underestimate the difficulties that small firms have in meeting the competitive requirements of the market place. If a firm can solve its production problems successfully it will have overcome a major constraint upon its potential for expansion. Which firms achieve growth? Our thesis is that it will be those which can identify and act on the key criteria upon which to compete in certain segments, i.e. design, after-sales service, price, quality, delivery reliability, and so on, and can then build a competitive advantage based upon those criteria (O'Farrell and Hitchens 1986).

Research framework and small firms' policy

The research framework pays particular attention to those characteristics of the firm upon which public policy can or already does exercise an influence. First, only companies in tradeable or potentially competitive sectors are sampled because the volume of a firm's output is not subject to the constraint of local or regional demand. Such companies offer the prospect of additional employment in the region. The degree to which those companies sell beyond the regional market is compared and constraints on selling outside the region examined. Principal amongst these are transport costs on products and material inputs and 'logistic' difficulties arising from distance to main markets. The relationship between marketing and firm success is also examined.

The remainder of the analysis is concerned with supply-side characteristics. The price, quality, and design competitiveness of products produced by the firms are examined and factors affecting production. The latter include the adequacy and cost of premises, the quantity and quality of capital equipment used in manufacturing and the cost, quality and productiveness of the labour force. The analysis is set in the context of differences in regional aid made available to companies – more generous in Northern Ireland than South Wales – the implications of those differences are examined in the light of the comparative modernity of machinery, spaciousness of premises, etc. The overall thrust of the research is to understand the reasons for differences in performance to enable recommendations to be made on which agencies can act.

In order to achieve reasonable generality in the research a wide mix of products, manufacturing techniques and skills are sampled.

The sample and its characteristics

The analysis in this chapter is based on a sample of forty-seven Welsh firms and forty-four Northern Irish firms operating in four manufacturing sectors[2] – engineering, furniture, clothing, and miscellaneous trades (including electronics, printing, cosmetics, blinds, and toys). Northern Irish firms were sampled first[3] and matched at the second stage with firms randomly selected in South Wales (O'Farrell and Hitchens 1986). Matching was as close as possible with respect to product description, employment size category, and broad age group. An earlier pilot study had indicated the extent to which departures from a perfect match could be made without invalidating the comparison (Hitchens and O'Farrell 1985). Table 8.1 summarizes the industrial distribution of the sampled firms. The average size of firm visited was 23 employees in South Wales, and 20 in Northern Ireland, while the spread of employment ranged from just 2 to 100 in each region.

Table 8.1 Number of firms sampled by trade

Trade	*South Wales*		*Northern Ireland*	
Precision engineering	8		11	
Castings	3		3	
Other	10		5	
All engineering		21		19
Clothing	10		9	
Knitwear	2		3	
All clothing		12		12
Furniture	3		6	
Electronics	4		2	
Cosmetics	3		1	
Printing	1		2	
Toys	2		1	
Blinds	1		1	
All miscellaneous trades		14		13
Total		47		44

Source: Survey data.

Small firm growth

The central question addressed by the research is how does a firm's location influence its performance? Table 8.2 compares one aspect of performance between the two regional samples: the growth of firms over the period 1982–1986. It shows that, on average, employment at Welsh companies increased by 31 per cent compared with a *fall* of 15 per cent at matched Irish firms, reflecting a nominal sales growth of 84 per cent and 15 per cent respectively in the two regions. Numerically, only 53 per cent of Ulster firms increased output in real terms compared with 86 per cent of Welsh firms sampled. The results for specific sectors follow the same pattern.

Table 8.2 Small firm growth in sample companies, 1982–86

	Growth of nominal sales 1982–86		*Percentage of companies reporting growth in real terms*[a]		*Sample size*	
	SW %	*NI* %	*SW* %	*NI* %	*SW*	*NI*
Engineering	58	31	83	56	18	16
Clothing	65	31	83	75	12	9
Furniture	450	35	100	57	3	10
Miscellaneous trades	88	−21	88	15	9	6
All firms	84	15	86	53	42	38
Employment change						
All firms	31	−15			35	27

Source: Survey data.
Note: (a) Growth is defined here as a sales increase reported by proprietors to be over and above an increase in product prices over the period.
SW = South Wales
NI = Northern Ireland

In the engineering and clothing trades, growth of nominal sales by Welsh companies averaged twice that of Irish firms. A similar poor growth performance by Ulster firms was also found when a sample was matched with London companies (Hitchens and O'Farrell 1985).

The rest of the chapter examines contrasts in demand and supply factors facing firms in the two regions in an attempt to explain the observed differences in growth. In particular attention is focused upon the geographic structure of markets served by firms in the two regions, the cost of reaching those markets, the competitiveness of products manufactured and the cost and quality of buildings, plant and equipment, and labour used in making products.

Markets

The ability of firms to grow is partially dependent upon access to a suitable market, and the question therefore arises as to whether Northern Ireland's greater geographic separation from major population centres is significant in explaining the comparatively poor growth performance there. Three features of relative isolation were considered: the geographic distribution of customers served by Irish and Welsh firms, the cost of transporting products from the region in question: and comparative marketing, customer liaison and other logistic difficulties arising from the location.

Geographic structure of markets

Table 8.3 summarizes the geographic structure of the small firms' markets. It shows that almost three quarters of the output of all Northern Irish firms compared with only 45 per cent of sales of matched Welsh companies was sold to customers within the region. Similarly 'local' sales (within twenty miles of the factory)

Table 8.3 Geographic structure of small firm markets: percentages of the firms' output sold to local and regional markets

	Northern Ireland		*South Wales*	
	% local	*% regional*[(a)]	*% local*	*% regional*
Precision engineering	76	91	53	72
Miscellaneous engineering	68	77	46	55
Castings	62	93	10	22
All engineering	66	85	45	58
Clothing and knitwear	20	49	1	2
Furniture: kitchen & bedroom	45	100	83	100
Other (NI only)	20	48	–	–
Miscellaneous trades	53	68	24	51
All sectors	50	73	31	45

Source: Survey data.
Note: (a) Local market is defined as the area within a radius of 20 miles of the factory, while the regional market is defined as either that of Northern Ireland or South Wales, and in the case of the latter, additionally as an area within forty miles of the factory if that is larger.

accounted for one-half of the output of Irish firms but less than one-third that of Welsh firms.

The geographic pattern of custom varies considerably by sector. While a numerically higher proportion of Welsh firms sold outside the region (four-fifths as compared with two-thirds of Ulster firms, not shown in Table 8.3), the majority of companies in both regions had experience of selling to wider markets. When these alone are compared the penetration of extra-regional markets by Ulster firms is found to be lower and by as much as a factor of two in the engineering and clothing trades. A quarter of Welsh firms served export markets compared with only one-sixth of Northern Irish firms. All sectors except furniture were represented by firms with export sales: these were lowest in the engineering sector while a major dependence on overseas and especially American custom was found in the design and hand knitwear trade.

Two-fifths of Ulster companies sold to the Republic of Ireland. In engineering this involved tiny amounts, no more than 5 per cent of their trade, while in the other three sectors the proportion was larger ranging from 15 to 20 per cent of sales. A perceived fear of bad debts and the requirement, relatively commonplace in the Republic, personally to collect payment was said to act as a constraint on firms dealing more widely there. Knowledge of the reputation of potential clients was said to be especially crucial when dealing there in other than cash.[4]

Although Welsh firms sold more output outside the region in every sector, the disparity between Welsh and Irish firms was considerably greater in the castings and clothing and knitwear trades. Welsh foundries sold 78 per cent of their output outside South Wales compared with only 7 per cent of the sales of similar Northern Irish foundries to customers outside the Province. Similarly, 98 per cent of Welsh clothing and knitwear sales went outside the region compared with only 51 per cent of Ulster sales. In short, the Ulster firm was found to be more dependent than Welsh companies on the regional market; the earlier Anglo-Irish study reached a similar conclusion (Hitchens and O'Farrell 1985).

Transport costs

The more restricted geographical penetration of markets by Ulster firms raises the question as to whether this is a consequence of a lack of price competitiveness arising from the additional costs of distributing products to a mainland market. We measured transport costs (expressed as a percentage of the factory value of goods sold) to the main British market served outside the region.

Table 8.4 shows that despite difficulties in making comparisons transport costs are clearly small, of the order of 2 or 3 pence in the £ from both regions. In all trades Northern Irish costs are greater than Welsh transport costs but the differences are very small, ranging from 0.01 pence in the £ in precision engineering to 1.1 pence in other engineering.

Table 8.4 Transport costs to major British market locations outside the region[(a)] (expressed as a percentage of the value of goods sold)

	South Wales %	*Northern Ireland* %
Engineering: precision	1.2	1.2
All other engineering	1.4	2.5
Clothing	2.3	2.8
Furniture	–	6.8
Miscellaneous trades	1.4	2.9

Source: Survey data.
Note: (a) Table includes only those firms with extra-regional sales.

Logistic problems of supplying customers from a distance is potentially a greater problem for Ulster companies. In Wales access to the M4 motorway was said to be an advantage by firms not too far west or north of the system, although some reservations about the carrying capacity and continuation of the link with England via the Severn Bridge were expressed. The main advantage was one of ease of delivery of goods and of ease of access to customers. In engineering about one-third of all companies visited highlighted difficulties arising from the need for customer liaison, especially during the difficult early stages of interpretation of drawings and where periodic consultation was required on longer term jobs for other than standard products. The view was expressed on the basis of practical experience for many of the firms stated they sold to customers outside the region – including from Northern Ireland to Canada and the USA. It follows therefore that customer liaison problems are not insurmountable provided that the product is competitive on price and quality. With the exception of those engineering firms and companies manufacturing principally for the local market, only one firm, a producer of cosmetics in Ulster, claimed to experience serious difficulties[6] arising from location. It is therefore clear that in general it cannot be said that either transport costs to a major British market, or problems of customer liaison contribute in any significant way to explaining the faster growth, and larger markets, of Welsh relative to Northern Irish firms.

Cost of transporting materials

Measurement of transport costs on material inputs is being investigated with reference to a small sample of products selected as typical of material purchases of firms in the region. A direct comparison of material costs has not been possible because of variations between matched firms in the quantities and qualities of materials usually bought.

In a comparison of the delivered price of eleven inputs basic to the requirements of firms in the Northern Irish–Southeast England matched comparison, no variation in delivered prices by local stockists was found to exist between the two regions (Hitchens and O'Farrell 1985). Firms in the present sample reported that the cost of carriage was normally included in the price of their purchases and was only charged separately where small quantities were required. In both Northern Ireland and South Wales the main disadvantage arising from the location with regard to sourcing materials was said to be one of a lack of choice, and difficulties in obtaining 'odd ball' materials, such as particular shades of buttons and threads.

Marketing methods

The faster growth and greater geographical penetration of markets by Welsh companies compared with Northern Irish counterparts was not related to differences between firms in the two regions in methods of selling products. In 60 per cent of all cases, and typically in engineering, rudimentary sales methods were relied upon including advertisements in Yellow Pages, 'ringing round' and word of mouth. In the remaining cases more active strategies were adopted, including advertisements in trade journals, and the use of agents or a sales force. Those selling techniques were mainly found in the clothing, knitwear, furnishing, and miscellaneous trades.[7]

Extent of competition

Northern Irish firms claimed to be in competition with fewer than one-half the number of competitors recognized by their Welsh counterparts. This striking difference is explained by the local nature of the Northern Irish firms' market and its lack of exposure to national markets.

Businessmen were asked to rank the importance of price, quality, and delivery (and other factors such as design and flexibility) in competing for custom. In both Northern Ireland and South Wales firms considered the main requirement of the market place was for a quality product (reflecting in part the close matching of the firms compared). Ulster firms rated the reliable delivery of the product second in importance, and ranked price third. Welsh firms considered that price took precedence over delivery, and ranked that second. The ranking was broadly similar between trades, except where many Northern Irish clothing companies placed good delivery on an equal footing with quality as the most important criteria for gaining orders.[8]

Proprietors were then asked whether they considered their firm had any specific competitive edge in the market place. Only a quarter of Irish firms, compared with three-fifths of Welsh companies, claimed an advantage based on quality or workmanship – the factor identified by firms in both regions as the most important competitive requirement and therefore crucial for growth. In trades where design is important – furniture, toys, clothing, knitwear – few firms visited, in either region, claimed a leading edge, just under three in ten Welsh firms, compared with one in ten Irish companies.

Growth and the market place

Sixty per cent of Irish firms, compared with only ten per cent of Welsh companies, considered that a lack of demand for their product was an important constraint on growth.[9]

A second important factor affecting customer demand is the firm's willingness to respond to the changing market place. We found that twice as many firms in Wales (although they were as few as two in ten) achieved growth with new products, new designs or new markets. In Ireland the few firms that did respond in this way achieved above average growth in their sector.

A more typical Irish response to slow growth, and especially characteristic of small engineering firms, is to invest in new machinery to broaden the scope for custom. However, two in three of the Irish companies which undertook such investment no longer considered there was a growing market for their business, while four-fifths of all Welsh engineers were optimistic about the future (and they were less well equipped and expressed no need for new machinery).

Product price and quality comparisons

We compared the prices charged by firms in each region by asking businessmen to quote on the product produced by their matched counterpart (for a given specification and batch size). We also asked for a detailed comment on the quality and finish (and where appropriate design) of that product. In practice when the opportunity arose, several firms in the region evaluated and quoted a price on a product made in the other region. This enabled us to establish whether price quotations and quality evaluations differed between firms and were perhaps unreliable. In general, the quality assessments were highly consistent while price quotations were subject to somewhat greater variation, (although systematic differences were observed between regions). Analysis of the findings was helped and further reinforced by an independent price and quality judgement of mixed samples of Welsh and Irish products, (their origin undisclosed) made by the proprietors of matched firms in East Anglia and Scotland.

A total of 33 products manufactured by 26 Irish firms and 27 products made by 19 Welsh firms were evaluated. Product assessment is continuing, but to date all samples have been examined by a proprietor at a matched plant either in Northern Ireland, Wales, or East Anglia. Table 8.5 is restricted to price quotations and quality assessments made by Irish firms about Welsh products and by Welsh firms about Irish products. Products are classified as of satisfactory quality if the person evaluating them (usually the proprietor himself or production supervisor) stated that the item in question would pass inspection at his factory. Price quotations are shown as the percentage which are either equal to, or below, the actual price charged by the company making the product.

Northern Irish proprietors found fault with fewer than ten per cent of all Welsh products shown them, and in nearly three-quarters of cases they would charge higher prices[10] to manufacture the Welsh engineering products, and in 44 per cent of cases higher prices to make the Welsh clothing products. More Irish products were shown to Welsh firms so that Part B of Table 8.5 includes a miscellaneous product category (containing principally electronic components and cosmetics). Price quotations made by Welsh firms

Table 8.5 Comparison of price and quality of products made by firms in (a) Wales and (b) Northern Ireland
Part A Welsh Products

	% price quotations same or lower	*Judgement by Northern Irish firms*		
		number of products	*quality % satisfactory*	*number of assessments*
Engineering	27	12	93	17
Clothing	56	7	89	14
Total		19	90	31

Part B Irish Products

	% price quotations same or lower	*Judgement by Welsh firms*		
		number of products	*quality % satisfactory*	*number of assessments*
Engineering	67	15	18	21
Clothing	40	13	8	25
Miscellaneous	67	5	33	7
Total		33	15	53

Source: Survey data.

were lower or equal to those actually charged by Ulster firms in 67 per cent of cases in engineering and miscellaneous, while quotations made on clothing products were equal or less than those actually charged in 40 per cent of cases. Taking these quotations in conjunction with Ulster quotations shown in Part A of Table 8.5, we find that Welsh firms are on average cheaper at making engineering parts and miscellaneous products, while Irish clothing firms are slightly more price competitive than their Welsh counterparts.

What is most striking is that only 15 per cent of Ulster samples were considered to be of satisfactory quality as judged by the standards set by the Welsh firms for their customers, a proportion which does not vary greatly by sector (Table 8.5). When these findings, relating to quality, are viewed alongside the Welsh price quotations it can be clearly seen that the lower quality cannot be satisfactorily explained on the grounds of their cheapness in the market place. Northern Irish firms are not producing low quality goods at a low price. This is an important result because it helps explain the poorer performance of Northern Irish firms. The implication is that lower growth, less demand, and lower penetration of extra-regional markets by Northern Irish firms is due to a lack of price and quality competitiveness.

The criticisms made by the Welsh firms of the quality of Northern Irish products were confirmed by proprietors at the East Anglian companies. They were shown mixed samples of 26 Welsh and 11 Irish products. More Welsh products were shown to them because Irish products had attracted so much criticism in Wales and in London (Hitchens & O'Farrell 1985) that we wondered whether the Ulster businessman was a good judge of the Welsh quality. In the event Welsh products attracted criticism in only 12 per cent of cases while Irish products did so in 82 per cent of examinations in East Anglia.

What was the nature of the criticisms? In most cases the problem indicated was one of poor workmanship as a consequence of a lack of skill or supervision and of poor finish, especially with regard to attention to detail. In the main an examination for fundamental problems, for example by measurement of engineering pieces, could not be made without reference to the original detailed drawings, nor were clothing products measured for size or 'fit', or electronic components tested and so forth. Products were visually inspected.

We shall now summarize the most common criticisms made about Northern Irish products. First with reference to engineering products: 'finish unacceptable, . . . form doesn't look right, man who made it hasn't sharpened his tools properly'; 'unimportant feature is right and the important feature is wrong, suspect he doesn't care enough to do the job properly'; 'poor fettling finish, quality of casting looks suspect, there are holes in the surface'; 'cross jointed pattern or box fault metal has been stewed or not modified properly'; 'grinding operation is poor'; 'this has been milled with blunt cutters'; 'carelessness on the part of the skilled man'; 'cheap and nasty, poor quality toolmaking, problem of the man, bashed out'.

On clothing it was the stitching which attracted most attention. One garment maker quoted a price 50 per cent lower than his Irish counterpart and considered its quality 'diabolical'; another garment was said to be 'a bit rough, looks as though someone has made that in a garage, waist bands fraying out, not very good at all, got a rather nasty feel about it'; 'not bartacked off well, not trimmed, strictly not acceptable'; 'variation in size of stitch'; 'this has been done on a production line basis, but the operator doesn't know how to use the bartack machine, it ought to be a lot cheaper with the machinery he's got'.

Visual inspection showed up more fundamental faults in one instance – 'it's got two right sleeves'. In another case, a garment, though quite well made, suffered because 'the ribbing around the neck should be finished on the shoulder, the supervisor should have noticed and it would worry some of our customers'.

In knitwear, problems with 'linking' were noted: 'the shoulder join stitch is not whole all the way round, not quite our standard', and on machine setting 'the overlocker has jumped and missed a stitch because the tension on the machine is out slightly, an operator fault, and should not have been let through quality control, but it's better than a Taiwan product. The cuff sewing is not correct either.'

A cosmetic product was thought unlikely to sell because of its packaging and price: 'he's taken a lot of trouble to get his label straight, but he's greedy killing his market on price and he's better off without the box', another said 'the contents – the cream – isn't relevant, for a first sale labelling is everything and in this case its a bit ropey'.[11]

The work of two Irish engineering firms was particularly commended, about one it was said, 'this is a nice job, whoever has made it has made it well'; 'the quality is good he's taken time to grind it all round for presentation, quite neat'. In the clothing trade, too, a compliment was passed about one product which was 'quite well made for this kind of garment'. But the majority of Ulster products attracted criticism because sample products shown to Welsh proprietors were not of a standard acceptable to the customers of their firms. Problems with Welsh products were many many times fewer but where they occurred were usually to do with finish. In one engineering case the Welsh part was described by one of the commended Irish engineers as 'rubbish, upper range of rubbish, diabolical', and on another part 'rubbish work, no skill whatsoever, just a monkey on a machine'. In another case the finish on a product looked 'strange'. The stitching and machining of one Welsh blouse was also queried by an Ulster company: 'button holes untidy, threads, very reluctant to let it go out', but in the main Welsh products were not criticized by Irish companies on the grounds of their quality.

Design

We found that just under a third of Ulster companies attempted their own designs, compared with only one-sixth of firms in the Welsh sample. Design was found to be relatively more important in the clothing, furniture, and miscellaneous products (cosmetics and toys) sectors in both samples, although one in seven engineering companies (in both regions) manufactured their own specialist machinery too.[12] Innovative design was seen by many of these companies as a key to business growth and success.

Ulster clothing companies used both freelance designers in Belfast and design consultants in London to improve their range, but problems arose in a third of such cases because of a mismatch between the design adopted by the firm and the requirements of the market place. One company scrapped its new range because the London designs were too modern and 'would not sell' they were 'left with a lot of stock'. In another instance the Ulster company was too old fashioned, their sales were falling because 'our customers are dying'. Those businessmen feel out of touch because 'Northern Ireland is twelve months behind' and were puzzled and unable to sort out the different design requirements of customers located in other regions.

That problem was driven home when a range of blouses from six Welsh factories (made on a CMT basis) for the London market was shown to three Irish owners. In only one case was it recognized that 'this is what they want nowadays'. Further confirmation came from Welsh proprietors who thought the product made by those two Ulster companies were 'pretty but unadventurous' and indicated their 'conservative approach', while an Ulster skirt made by another firm for the 'older person' was thought too old fashioned – 'print is awful, colour is bad and pleated styles are out' – to sell in England.

One Irish furniture firm had similar difficulties adopting the right design for the different regional markets. They found 'Scotland more modern than Northern Ireland' and had 'problems designing for the English market'. In another case a Newry furniture company found difficulty selling Danish designs except in the Republic.

A better adaptation of fashion to the market place was found at three Ulster clothing companies which sold products nationally and internationally and designed in a variety of ways – either by the owners themselves 'by reading journals and travelling, or by engaging designers either local or from outside the Province'. One factor that linked those successful proprietors and marked them out from others in the Province was that all were immigrants (and of European stock).

Fewer Welsh firms were found with their own designs though many companies, especially in the clothing trade, complained of a local shortage of qualified designers. Those firms with their own styles attempted to take account of both the English and Welsh tastes. For example, a toy manufacturer made separately for the two markets while the cosmetics and knitwear firms made especially for the larger English market. This was not said to be problematic perhaps because of Wales' proximity to England. The marketing of those designs from Wales was said to pose much greater difficulties.

We have shown in this section that sample products from Ulster companies are not considered competitive by matched Welsh and East Anglian companies. That lack of competitiveness is primarily due to a poor quality of finish given the price charged by those Irish firms. In addition, Ulster firms had difficulty designing for markets outside Northern Ireland, though the number of firms attempting their own designs was found to be greater in the Province than in South Wales.

We now examine the production facilities, premises, wage rates, skills, and quality of the labour force in order to try and identify the major factors underlying differences in growth rates and price, quality and design of products in Northern Ireland and South Wales.

Buildings and machinery

We examined the comparative cost and quality of the firm's major assets – buildings and machinery – in relation both to the firm's competitive performance and also as a possible constraint on future expansion. The differences observed were much the same as those found when Ulster companies were compared with English firms (Hitchens and O'Farrell 1985).

Four features of the factory premises were compared: square footage of space available to each employee, numbers rented, rent and rates paid, and numbers of buildings judged to be unsatisfactory for whatever reason. These data are expressed in comparative Northern Ireland/South Wales ratio form and show that in all sectors the average square footage of factory space available to each employee was greater in Northern Ireland than South Wales, although the relative difference was smaller in the case of engineering.

Column two of Table 8.6 indicates that, with the exception of the engineering firms interviewed, more of the Irish businessmen owned their premises: 58 per cent of Welsh factories were rented against 44 per cent of Irish buildings. With the exception of the furniture trade, the rent and rates paid per square foot were

Table 8.6 Comparison of features of Northern Ireland/South Wales factory buildings by sector

	Square feet per person NI/SW	*Number rented NI/SW*	*Rent & rates £ per square foot NI/SW*	*Number of buildings unsatisfactory NI/SW*
Engineering	1.04	1.11	0.25	2.31
Clothing	1.52	0.43	0.69	0.54
Furniture	1.29	0.33	1.14	0.87
Other	1.97	0.83	0.29	1.11
Total observations: Northern Ireland/ South Wales	44/47	20/27	20/27	17/14

Source: Survey data.

considerably lower in Ireland: an Irish factory cost between 40p and 90p per square foot while Welsh factory costs ranged from £1 to £3.50 per square foot.

The Northern Irish owners were more likely to complain about the suitability or condition of their premises, and overall 39 per cent found them unsatisfactory compared with 30 per cent of Welsh businessmen. Most of the complaints expressed concerned rented accommodation, particularly amongst Northern Irish engineering firms.

About half the complaints from Ulster firms related to problems associated with the age of buildings, their state of repair and difficulties arising over proper maintenance. One-third of Welsh complaints also fell into this category. A fifth of problems with Irish factories compared with just under a third of Welsh complaints concerned room for expansion. But only one Welsh entrepreneur in the two samples considered that the general availability of factory space in the region was a major constraint on growth: it is therefore quite clear that lack of space for expansion is not an impediment to small firm growth in either region.

Machinery and equipment

We asked proprietors to itemize the most technologically up-to-date equipment they used and also to specify the age of the machinery in the factory. Table 8.7 shows that in the engineering, clothing, and miscellaneous trade sectors Ulster firms had, on average, substantially more modern equipment. In engineering and clothing the proportion of all machinery purchased by Irish companies within the last five years was 36 per cent and 61 per cent respectively, approximately treble the equivalent Welsh proportions of 13 per cent and 20 per cent. Only in furniture making did Welsh factories have newer machinery.

Table 8.7 Vintage of machinery

	Northern Ireland (per cent of machines)			*South Wales (per cent of machines)*		
	Under 5 Years	*Under 10 Years*	*No.*	*Under 5 Years*	*Under 10 Years*	*No.*
Engineering	36	48	17	13	37	21
Clothing	61	94	12	20	58	12
Furniture	29	59	7	39	77	3
Miscellaneous	70	77	7	37	63	5

Source: Survey data.

We saw more computer numerically controlled (CNC) machines at the Irish factories too: in engineering, for instance, we found on average one CNC machine per 4.5 persons engaged in the business, while in South Wales the equivalent ratio was one CNC machine availability to 29 persons.[13] Ulster firms in other sectors too were technologically more up to date. In clothing, for example, computerized embroidery machines had been installed, and CNC had also been applied to furniture making.

Grants were said to be 'a great help' in enabling the purchase of new and modern machinery in Ireland, while in Wales less emphasis was placed on their importance, 'we would have bought anyway' was a frequent remark: or where grants made a difference it was to purchasing at the margin, 'we would have bought some, but not all or settled for equipment of a lower specification or second hand'. For comparable Ulster firms, on the other hand, assistance had been on such a scale that without grants 'we'd have half fewer machines'. New machinery did not always have the desired effect: one engineering company had re-equipped 'for growth' although 'the bank manager thought the project foolish'[14] and since then not a single new job had been sourced. Another company in the clothing trade had replaced eight of their ten standard machines with computerized Japanese equipment; 'three machines fewer' would have been bought 'without LEDU grants', and while describing themselves as 'the best equipped in the British Isles' there was no further demand for their product. The investment was mistaken and for the last ten months the factory had placed its employees on short time.

Comparisons of Ulster small firms with London companies (Hitchens and O'Farrell 1985) also indicated much more modern machinery in the Province. In that comparison no clear association between investment and business success was discerned; indeed in a number of instances it was clear that advanced machinery was employed by Ulster companies to undertake work which English companies considered more appropriately suited to conventional machinery.

The more modern equipment found in Ireland seemed to have more to do with the generous financial assistance available there than with business success. While two-thirds of Welsh companies visited had received standard regional development grants, compared with only one third of Ulster companies, more than half the Irish companies had received the more generous selective financial assistance (from LEDU and IDB), compared with just 16 per cent of Welsh companies. Welsh factory owners did not express the view that their equipment was old or that they were undercapitalized, for although nearly a third (compared with half this number in Ireland) felt that their growth was restricted by a lack of finance, the investment required was for working capital needs, to employ salesmen, designers, to fund advertising and to move from CMT to own product lines, and not for a want of more modern machinery.

Labour

We compared the cost of labour and a number of qualitative characteristics of the labour force employed by sample firms in the two regions. The ratios in Table 8.8 refer to the relative wage cost of the highest grade of common labour employed on the shop floor

Table 8.8 Comparative wages paid by sector

	NI/SW
Engineering	0.97
Clothing	1.00
Furniture	0.88
Other trades	1.14
Average	1.00

Source: Survey data.

– a skilled man in engineering, a semi-skilled person in furniture making, a machinist in clothing, and so on.

On average there was no difference in wage rates, but there was some variation by industry. Clearly, Ulster firms were not at a disadvantage relative to South Wales because of higher labour costs.

We measured the proportions of persons designated skilled in the factories and found that this differed little between the two regions. For example, 90 per cent of the shop floor employees were craft trained in one branch of Ulster engineering compared with 95 per cent in comparable Welsh establishments. In another branch two-fifths of the workforce in each region was said to be trained. Employers pointed to the importance of differences in the degree of skill required by workers in different branches of engineering and clothing. Tool making required the finer craft skills, and in clothing the level of training needed to make duffle coats, workwear or ties was not as great at that required to stitch blouses. It was important, we were told, to make a correct judgement on how much skill was needed, and the consequent training requirements, to enable an employee to work to the quality standards required by the customer. 'If you don't have the skills you can't compete' was the way one Welsh factory owner put it to us; 'we associate quality with training' another said. One Irish engineering company commented, 'we have to train to get over our high reject rates'.

Problems arising from an unsatisfactory level of skill employed on the shop floor were identified by 23 per cent of Ulster proprietors. Three precision engineers drew attention to problems of a high scrap rate, in one instance said to be caused by carelessness; two foundries had problems with ability of employees to 'do the job', one particularly with their men 'letting anything through'; one knitwear firm claimed to have difficulty teaching linking skills (a quality characteristic criticized by the matched Welsh firms when shown the Ulster product); while a furniture firm had problems 'getting good clean joints'. Those Ulster problems were not mentioned by the Welsh entrepreneurs.

Labour force difficulties arising from a poor attitude to the job 'getting people to do a decent day's work' was mentioned by a quarter of Northern Irish firms, compared with under a tenth of Welsh companies. Difficulties of this kind were concentrated in the furniture and clothing trade, though semi-skilled persons working in certain 'other' engineering companies and miscellaneous trades are included. Difficulties with attitudes were linked to problems of trainability and of productivity for the company, but its symptoms included lack of interest in the work and absenteeism, in part a consequence of Ulster's troubles. Companies in or near West Belfast, Shankill, Short Strand, Lurgan, areas of Armagh and Newry seemed to have especially acute problems.

One cause of the difficulties was said to be the social security system, because the entitlement to state benefits could become a strong disincentive to work. An Ulster clothing firm lost its cutter when that employee's family had its fourth child. Problems of this kind were more particular to the (lower paid) semi-skilled employees in the sample where it was found 'hard to get people to work at the going wage'. In the clothing sector recruiting and retaining employees was difficult where it 'interfered with the husband's money'. One Welsh firm employed the recently redundant husband of a key worker as a sweeper so as to retain his wife's machining skills.

The rate of labour turnover at 14 per cent in Northern Ireland was 50 per cent higher than the average for South Wales. Twice as many (a quarter of) Northern Irish firms suffered an excessively high annual rate, above 20 per cent and those cases were concentrated in the clothing and furniture sectors. Where high levels of labour turnover were recorded at Welsh factories these were found in the clothing and miscellaneous trades. Absenteeism was a disruptive factor affecting a third of Welsh factories compared with just a tenth of Ulster companies. In such cases it was measured to exceed 10 per cent of available days lost. Two-thirds of both Welsh and Northern Ireland firms reporting a problem were engaged in the clothing trades.

We discovered differences in the emphasis placed upon the management of labour by proprietors in the two regions. Forty-four per cent of firms visited in Northern Ireland claimed a need to manage for productivity to 'coax work'.[15] In contrast, 39 per cent of factory proprietors visited in South Wales emphasized the need for supervision 'to watch the work to check quality'.

To manage effectively in Wales 'you have to be very very fair', we were told, 'because they are trade union minded'. Productivity problems were highlighted by two firms at the extreme north-west of the region. In those cases it was said 'the men aren't temperamentally suited' (because they were previously employed in nationalized industries). On our visits we noticed a further two cases where productivity seemed a problem, though not reported by management. These were cases where work practices appeared inefficient, and where equipment was double manned.

We measured productivity at sample establishments as sales adjusted for material inputs[16] per head of persons engaged in each

Table 8.9 Comparative productivity per person engaged: ratio of sales adjusted for material costs at sample establishments

	Range of estimates NI/SW
Engineering	0.90 – 1.04
Clothing	0.84 – 1.01
Furniture	0.87 – 0.97
Miscellaneous trades	0.86 – 0.96

Source: Survey data.

sector. The range[17] of comparative productivity levels found between the matched Ulster and Welsh firms shows that only in the clothing and engineering trades were any Northern Irish firms found with comparable levels of sales per head. In general, productivity was found to be lower when measured this way, despite the more up-to-date equipment found in the Ulster factories.

A shortage of quality skills was reported to be a major constraint on growth by nearly half the Welsh firms in the sample, compared with a fifth of Ulster firms. Most difficulty arose in the engineering and clothing sectors where a shortage of intermediate skills was emphasized. About a third of Irish engineering companies visited highlighted this as a problem compared with more than three-fifths of Welsh engineers. The source of the difficulties ranged from the poor standards of persons applying 'out of training centres' where the 'lecturer didn't know', to the narrow training provided by larger companies sufficient for their own needs, but inadequate given the wider range of work carried out by the small firm. A Port Talbot engineer 'short of skilled labour for two years' was especially 'bitter' because his market 'comprised ex-steel men and they've forgotten how to work': 'it takes two years to train them to the required standards'. Shortages were further exacerbated where men 'were being lost to higher pay' offered by larger local companies. In one South Wales valley an employer paid significantly higher wages than were available for the same job in an adjacent eastern valley because his costs had been bid up by the presence of Hitachi and NCB;[18] a similar case was quoted by an Antrim engineer.

In clothing, the problem of obtaining required skills was claimed an impediment to growth, affecting more than half the Welsh clothing companies visited, compared with just 10 per cent of comparable Northern Irish firms.

Although skill shortages were felt more acutely by Welsh firms, reflecting their faster growth rates, they also trained fewer persons than their Irish counterparts. Overall we found twice as many trainees at Ulster firms than at Welsh companies: in engineering, for instance, there were three times the number found in Wales, and in furniture and miscellaneous trades more labour was currently being trained to semi-skilled standards. That greater training effort was enabled by grants and was carried out despite the fact that 30 per cent of firms there, against half that number in Wales, reported problems regarding the suitability of recruits for training.

The cost of training worried Welsh businessmen which perhaps explains why less is undertaken there. Two Welsh companies disagreed with the off-the-job training modules required by the EITB, and leading to an unnecessary 'absence from work' to follow 'irrelevant college courses' and thereby implying a cost to the employer. In one case the Welsh engineer gave his 'own kind of apprentice training' to avoid 'time lost through day release'. In another case a Welsh company would not train because it 'couldn't fit with MSC standards', again regarding the off-the-job component of training requirements.

Difficulties in obtaining foreman and technician grades were mentioned by two firms in each of the Irish and Welsh samples; a further two firms in Ulster and three in Wales had difficulty recruiting middle managers, including marketing men, to assist growth by building a management team. Another firm in Wales emphasized problems attracting designers.

In comparison with South Wales companies, Ulster firms were not found to be at a disadvantage due to higher labour costs, nor to the number of persons designated skilled at the factories, but we doubt the quality of those skills in Ireland and suspect that their deficiency bears a causal relationship with the poor quality of products produced there (Hitchens and Jones 1986).

While labour turnover was found to be higher in Ireland, absenteeism was found to be greater in South Wales. Northern Irish firms managed for productivity while Welsh management concentrated on supervising the quality of output. Productivity was measured to be lower at the Northern Ireland companies. Shortage of skills was the major problem affecting the growth of companies in South Wales. That problem was felt less acutely in Northern Ireland where firms grew at a slower rate and more training was undertaken by the firms themselves.

Summary, conclusions and recommendations

This paper has reported on a matched comparison of 44 small firms in Northern Ireland (35 per cent Catholic, 59 per cent Protestant, 6 per cent Jewish owned) and 47 small firms in South Wales. A comparison of growth rates showed that on average employment at Welsh factories rose by 31 per cent between 1982 and 1986, compared with a fall of 15 per cent at the matched Irish companies. The sales growth of Welsh firms averaged five times that of Ulster companies, and nine-tenths of Welsh companies recorded growth compared with only one-half of their Ulster counterparts.

A comparison of the geographic structure of markets showed that only a quarter of the output of Northern Ireland firms was sold outside the region, compared with more than half of that of Welsh firms. Higher transport costs from Northern Ireland to a mainland market were not found to be the explanation for the narrower market served by the Ulster firms. Furthermore, firms in both regions competed for orders principally on the basis of quality and not price.

The logistic difficulty of supplying to mainland customers from Ulster is a potentially greater problem, but the majority of firms in both samples were doing it anyway; it was the penetration of those wider markets that was lower from Ulster firms. The real explanation for the Irish firms' narrow markets was that their products were not competitive. Nor were they likely to become competitive, since 60 per cent of Ulster firms, compared with just 10 per cent of Welsh companies, considered a lack of demand for their product to be the main constraint on their growth.

The explanation for the poor performance of Ulster firms became clear when an exchange of products was made between the matched Welsh and Irish companies. Northern Irish businessmen found fault with fewer than 10 per cent of Welsh products shown them, while Welsh proprietors criticized the quality of 90 per cent of the Ulster products. (Mixed samples of both Welsh and Irish products were shown to owners of matched factories in East Anglia without disclosing their origin, and evaluations by those managers confirmed these findings). Price comparisons indicated that the poorer quality of Ulster products could not be explained on the grounds of a lower price: more than half the products would have been made as cheaply or cheaper by the Welsh factories. In most cases criticisms related to a poor finish arising from a lack of skill or supervision in production.

Innovative design was seen by many companies as the key to growth and business success. Few Welsh companies undertook their own designs but those which did tried to suit the English market. Ulster companies were more likely to attempt designs but had difficulty sorting out the fashion or design requirements of different regional markets.

Lack of performance by Ulster companies could not be traced to disadvantages arising from the cost or quality of the firms' major assets – its buildings and machinery. Buildings were cheaper and more spacious in Ireland though they attracted more complaints about their condition. In neither region was the availability of factory space reported to be a constraint on growth.

Ulster firms had substantially more modern equipment than their Welsh counterparts. Not only was it newer but also technologically more up-to-date, with more found to be computerized. Both Welsh and Irish companies received standard regional development grants, but half the Ulster companies (compared with one-sixth of Welsh firms) had received generous selective financial assistance (from LEDU and IDB), and two-thirds of Irish companies claimed that their purchase of machinery was strongly influenced by those lavish grants. Welsh factory owners did not express the view that they were under-equipped; indeed 75 per cent of owners claimed they were unaffected by grants. They would have bought the machinery they had anyway. The growth of Welsh firms was not impeded by a want of more modern equipment, and it cannot therefore be imagined that the performance of Ulster firms was constrained by a lack of modern machinery either.

The key to understanding differences in performance between firms in Northern Ireland and South Wales lies in the characteristics of their respective labour forces. The cost of labour (wages) was similar in the two regions; the proportions of persons designated skilled was similar too. The level of skill and the standard of (on-the-job) training, both of which were argued by businessmen to be critical for product quality and, therefore, business success (Hitchens and Jones 1986), was lower at the Ulster companies. Not only was that the implication of our findings on the comparatively poor product quality of those Irish firms but, in addition, a quarter of Ulster proprietors recognized the fact for themselves. They reported an unsatisfactory level of skill employed on their shop floor. No Welsh firm said this.

More than twice as many Irish owners complained of labour force difficulties arising from an unacceptable attitude to work which they linked to problems of trainability and productivity. Production at Welsh firms on the other hand was more likely to be disrupted by absenteeism. Nearly half the Irish companies visited claimed the need to manage for productivity to 'coax work' while in contrast 40 per cent of Welsh companies emphasized the need for supervision to maintain quality standards. Labour productivity was measured and found to be lower in all sectors in Ireland (despite the more modern equipment).

A shortage of high quality skills was the main constraint affecting the growth of nearly half the Welsh companies in the sample. Fewer, only a fifth, of Irish companies made similar complaints, reflecting partly slower growth, but also more training: they had twice as many trainees at their factories, a consequence partly of a higher level of labour turnover found there and more generous training grants. Welsh firms were reluctant to train because of a dislike of the off-the-job component of training schemes and the high cost of the training provision.

The deficiencies of the Ulster firms are widespread: narrow markets, lack of competition, lack of price, quality, and design competitiveness, labour problems, but good machinery and equipment. Hence, a lack of competition, poor and weak management, poor training, and generous financial assistance must each bear some responsibility for the lack of performance by Ulster firms. Irish companies had fewer than half the number of direct competitors reported by Welsh firms and were, therefore, selling to a softer regional market. Both real and perceptual barriers make that market relatively sheltered. Difficulties in selling beyond Ulster were identified as arising from a problem with the quality of the products produced, and the responsibility for poor quality must ultimately be with the owner-manager. It was emphasized by the proprietors of factories in both London and South Wales that the manager sets the standards and it is then the duty of the supervisor or foreman to carry them out and maintain them on the shop floor. Many Ulster managers are clearly unaware of those external standards. Having identified the need to raise standards their achievement requires an improvement in skills (through better on-the-job training) of factory employees, including foremen. In short, the poor quality identified here results from an interaction of poor standards and poor quality skills of managers, supervisors and shop floor workers.

Raising standards is a priority for government agencies in Northern Ireland; indeed many firms complained that they received no advice – 'we were thrown in at the deep end' – although they had 'done well out of LEDU' but judged by the performance of comparable firms in South Wales and London, the generous provision of financial assistance (through LEDU and IDB) cannot be said to have improved the economic performance of those Ulster companies. On the contrary, the tangible evidence of that expenditure in plant and machinery indicates a degree of waste.

Recommendations

The major recommendation is for small firm agencies to provide advice, especially with regard to: (1) Efficiency, with emphasis on the appropriate mix of machinery and skills; (2) Training – to raise the overall quality of skills at all levels; to raise firm owners' awareness of the importance of design and quality and the lack of price and quality competitiveness of Northern Ireland's (small firm) products; (3) Development of quality control systems with special emphasis on the cost of building in quality and avoiding rejects; (4) To provide feedback, preferably through a form of inter-firm comparison so that firms are aware of their performance relative to other similar firms in the UK; (5) Consideration might be given to setting up a Northern Ireland Quality Standards Institute which would advise firms and admit to membership companies producing products of a minimum and consistent standard.

Such a strategy should emphasize the importance of advisory systems as against the traditional grant incentives used in Northern Ireland and Wales.

Appendix I

The sample

The Northern Ireland Trade Directory (published by the IDB) was used as a sampling frame in conjunction with the Yellow Pages and local information obtained from businessmen. Firms visited were located in counties Down, Antrim, Armagh, Londonderry, and Tyrone. All but four companies agreed to co-operate. The sample of firms in South Wales was drawn from an area bounded in the east by Cwmbran and Abergavenny; in the west by Ammanford in Dyfed; and in the north by Ystradgynlais, Hirwaun, and Tredegar. Industrial directories for each county (except South Glamorgan), the WDA list of firms, and Yellow Pages were used as sampling frames from which randomly to select matched firms. The response rate, with only one firm refusing to co-operate, was extremely high.

Interviews with managing directors were of a similar duration in each region, lasting from an hour and a half to half a day. Dr Hitchens undertook all the Northern Ireland visits, while Dr O'Farrell participated in many of the Welsh interviews. The general level of co-operation in both regions was uniformly high.

Notes

1. Further papers will deal with pairs of regions in turn.
2. A fifth sector – food processing – is currently being added to the list of comparisons.
3. Twelve of the Ulster companies in this comparison were included in the comparison with Southeast England (Hitchens and O'Farrell 1985).
4. Local demand is especially important for factories making custom-built wooden kitchen and bedroom furniture, and no less so in Northern Ireland than in South Wales, because there is a need not only to supply the high build-to-value units but also to fit them. This product is partially non-trade at the lower end of the market, permitting relatively inefficient local firms to survive. There is important competition especially from France and West Germany in the quality market segment. Window blinds are similarly made for the local market.
5. The difficulty in measuring such costs arises because destinations differ and costs differ according to whether own transport is used, whether a full load and a return load is likely, and so forth.
6. The difficulty that company was experiencing will be shown to have more to do with the product they produce than the company's location.
7. Rather more Welsh engineers adopted active marketing methods – such as the use of a salesman – than their Irish counterparts, whilst the reverse was the case in clothing where more Welsh factories sampled were producing on a cut-make and trim (CMT) basis.
8. Ulster clothing firms matched with London companies also gave less priority to quality; Northern Irish firms ranked price as of greatest importance in gaining orders.
9. It was only in the clothing sector that the market outlook of Irish firms was at all comparable with that of Welsh firms, despite their lack of penetration of markets outside the Province. One firm in that group emphasized the avoidance of competition as a means of overcoming their own competitive disadvantages arising from poor finish: 'We feel we are more competitive selling to people living in the countryside'.
10. On average Irish engineering companies charged at an hourly rate 7 per cent greater than that of their Welsh counterparts.
11. The proprietor of that firm considered his lack of success to be one of marketing failure and a need for capital to launch the product. In his eyes: 'it's unique; each time you take a step (to open the box) you'll like what you see. Unfortunately the shops mightn't accept it.'
12. Design entered into the way engineering jobs were approached. In one of the two Ulster cases where the workmanship was commended, it was the design of the job which was thought lacking by comparable precision engineering firms in Great Britain. That Ulster entrepreneur had never undertaken an apprenticeship himself, but had moved from the retail trade into engineering as a result of experience gained from a hobby. Similarly, in one foundry instance the 'crossjointed pattern or box fault' was said to be a design fault.
13. Even with fewer advanced machines we came across one Welsh

company which had such difficulty programming the lathe that it was decided to use the machine in a conventional way for one-offs.

14. This firm's Welsh counterpart used standard machines and considered these up-to-date. Their growth outstripped that of the Irish company and was achieved by undertaking further manufacturing stages of the product so the firm had become more vertically integrated.

15. This was clearly not always the case. One manager, while recognizing the benefits of timed work, allowed machine operators to 'stop the clock themselves'. In another Ulster case, the careful introduction of work study had improved output by 50 per cent. Occasionally Northern Irish management connected the syndrome leading to poor productivity with poor quality too; 'lack of interest in the job goes hand in hand with poor output'.

16. While we did not find any difference in the cost of raw materials used by firms in the two regions, an adjustment must be made to turnover in order to take account of those cases where companies working on a sub-contract basis receive 'free issue' materials, thereby affecting the comparability of their turnover figures with those companies which have purchased those inputs.

17. The range rather than the average productivity difference is shown in order to capture the detail of the matched trades. An average for each sector would require a weighting of those matched trades to reflect their importance in order to obtain an average productivity difference for the sector.

18. Interestingly, an employer of semi-skilled workers in the miscellaneous trades sector benefited from training provided by Hitachi, 'they get shot of them and it's no trouble recruiting them'.

References

Daly, A., Hitchens, D.M.W.N., and Wagner, K. (1984), *Productivity, Machinery and Skills in a Sample of British and German Matched Manufacturing Plants*, London: National Institute for Economic and Social Research.

Del Monte,A. and Giannola, A. (1986), 'Relevance and nature of small and medium sized firms in Southern Italy', in D. Keeble and E. Wever (Eds) *New Firms and Regional Development in Europe*, London: Croom Helm.

Hitchens, D.M.W.N. and O'Farrell, P.N. (1985) 'Inter Regional Comparisons of Small Firm Performance', *Working Paper* 24, Queen's University, Belfast.

Hitchens, D.M.W.N. and Jones, I. (1986) 'Adult Training in a Sample of British Industrial Establishments', Report to Manpower Services Commission, October 1986.

Mason, C.M. and Harrison, R.T. (1985) 'The Geography of Small Firms in the UK: Towards a Research Agenda', *Progress in Human Geography* 9:1–37.

Oakey, R.P., Thwaites, A.T., and Nash, P.A. (1982) 'Technological Change and Regional Development: Some Evidence on Regional Variations in Product and Process Innovation', *Environment and Planning A* 14:1073–86.

O'Farrell, P.N. and Hitchens, D.M.W.N. (1986) 'Inter Firm Comparison in Industrial Research: The Utility of a Matched-Pair Design', *Papers in Planning Research*, No.9, Heriot Watt University.

Local policy initiatives

9

International comparative aspects of government intervention in local economic policy

W.F. Lever

Introduction

The growing recognition that, in European countries, there exists an urban problem in addition to a regional problem, has led to the emergence of urban policies, many of which focus on the economic regeneration of the larger cities. Local government is most frequently, although not always, the administrator of such policies. This is a relatively new role for local government which hitherto has been more concerned with policies pertaining to housing, planning and the environment. There has therefore been considerable interest in sharing and comparing results between local authorities in a number of countries, either on their own initiative, or by commissioning research studies through universities or through an international agency such as OECD (Davies 1986).

One such transnational study originated in the United Nations-sponsored Habitat Conference held in Vancouver in 1976, and the Seventh Conference of the Mayors of Major World Cities in Turin in 1978. On the initiative of the Mayor of Turin, the European Co-ordination Centre for Research and Documentation in Social Sciences, based in Vienna, was requested to co-ordinate a programme of research concerning the nature of urban social and economic change and policy responses. The use of the Vienna Centre was significant because the intention was to develop a programme of studies covering cities in both Western and Eastern Europe. The project was launched in 1980 with the cities of Turin, Cologne, Glasgow, Krakow, Lille, and Dresden participating. Since 1980 the city of Lille has withdrawn and the city of Tallinn in Estonia has joined, representing the USSR. The deliberate choice of cities from Eastern Europe extended the range of the project but at the same time increased the difficulties of comparative work. It became clear that there was a considerable community of interest in matters pertaining to the environment and to housing and transportation, for example, but much less coincidence in confronting economic problems. Whereas the western cities had all experienced sharp rises in unemployment, the eastern cities were still more concerned over labour shortages. This lack of a common problem base is likely to remain a continuing difficulty in east-west studies (Cherry 1986). Experience suggests, however, that such east-west comparative exercises can be valuable, and at times there is more scope for comparison between east and west than might be anticipated. The recent study by Dangschat and Blasius (1987), for example, shows the similarities in housing allocation policies between Warsaw and some western European cities.

Given that the focus of study is the impact of government intervention on local economies, this analysis restricts itself to the three western European cities in the project namely Glasgow, Turin and Cologne. In each of these cases it is possible to trace government intervention at three levels – local, regional and national – into local urban economies. In each case the intervention works in two ways: (i) to induce the private sector to make decisions, which it presumably would not otherwise make, to adjust local investment output and employment, and (ii) to use its own powers within the public sector to boost local economies.

The European urban system

The measurement of the scale of the urban problem within western Europe has been facilitated by the production of statistics on a common basis. A number of studies (e.g. van der Berg 1982; Hall and Hay 1980) have used these data on population change to identify trends in European urbanization and counterurbanization by relating the experience of individual cities to a general urban life-cycle model. This usually shows a period of rural to urban shift, with population growth in the metropolitan core, followed by net suburbanization, followed by a period of total population loss (Cheshire and Hay 1986). More recently attention has turned towards economic problems, rather than mere demographic change, and the study by Cheshire, Carbonaro, and Hay (1986) seeks to use both indices to measure the relative health of a large number of west European cities. This study uses population change as one measure, and develops a 'problem index' as the other. The problem index is a dependent variable regressed from

Figure 9.1 Problem score 1 against population decline index

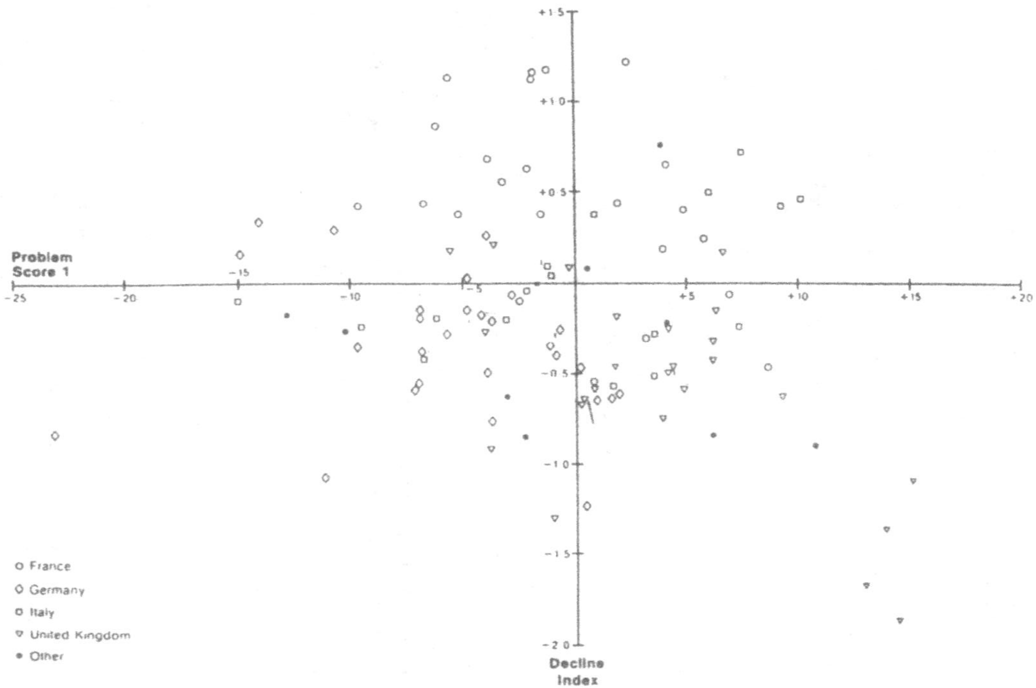

three measures: the unemployment rate, 1977–81, the net population change due to migration, 1971–81, and a 'travel demand' index which is based upon new hotel construction. Graphing 103 cities against these two indices produces the scatter shown in Figure 9.1. From this it is clear that there is no linear relationship between the two, and the four quadrants have distinctive populations. The lower right quadrant is predominantly British (population decline, high problem scores), the upper right is predominantly Mediterranean (population growth, high problem scores), the lower left quadrant is predominantly German (population loss, low problem scores) and the upper left quadrant is Franco-German (population gain, low problem scores). In terms of Figure 9.1 the three cities provide a broad spread of experience from Glasgow through Turin to Cologne. In terms of the problem score Cologne is ranked 25th out of 103, Turin is ranked 67th, and Glasgow is ranked 101st. Although the intention of the Turin Project was to study similar cities, and the Cheshire, Carbonaro, and Hay study appears to show how divergent they are, the rationale for their selection within the project lies in their relative positions within the national city groupings. Thus, as Figure 9.2 shows, Glasgow within the UK emerges as the third worst city, with only Sunderland and Belfast having more acute problems. In the case of Turin, only Genoa is in a worse overall position, although a number of south Italian cities, such as Naples and Cagliari, have worse problem scores. Cologne is more centrally placed within the ranking of West German cities where the worst overall scores are to be found in the cities of the Ruhr (Wuppertal, Essen, Duisburg) and in Saarbrucken. Nevertheless, Cologne is a city with problems when measured in terms of unemployment, relative to the national average.

The urban economic problem

In all three cities the main changes in the urban labour market are net employment loss, the shift from manufacturing to services, and the suburbanization of workplace location. As Table 9.1 shows, all three cities have suffered declines in total employment in the period 1970–85; however, the decline in Clydeside (−19.0 per cent) was much sharper than that in Cologne (−9.5 per cent) and Turin (−6.1 per cent). The second difference is that in Clydeside the decline of 1970–85 merely accelerated a decline which had been under way since the 1950s, whereas in Cologne and Turin the decline only started in the 1970s. The shift into services is a fairly

Figure 9.2 The study cities in their national context

Table 9.1 Employment totals in Cologne, Turin, and Clydeside, 1950–1984/85

	Cologne	*Turin*	*Clydeside*
1950	277,474	–	844,000
1960	460,627	700,000	840,882
1970	483,230	727,400	789,514
1980	456,400	718,950	685,538
1984/5	437,500	683,000	640,000

Source: Survey data.

uniform phenomenon as Table 9.2 shows. Cologne and Clydeside both had roughly two-thirds of their workforces employed in services by the mid-1980s, although Clydeside had effected a more rapid switch in the period since 1960, reflecting the more rapid rundown in industrial employment. Turin lags behind in the percentage of employment in services because of its higher

Table 9.2 Percentage in service sector employment in Cologne, Turin, and Clydeside, 1960–85

	Cologne	*Turin*	*Clydeside*
1960	53.3%	37.1%	47.9%
1970	58.4%	42.7%	58.6%
1980	65.6%	51.2%	62.7%
1985	68.0%	53.8%	66.0%

Source: Survey data.

proportion engaged in agriculture. Thus by 1985, the percentage engaged in service occupations in Turin was equal only to that of Cologne in 1960 and of Clydeside around 1965. On this basis one would expect Turin's service sector component to continue growing at a faster rate than those of Cologne and Glasgow. In each case, the growth of the high service sector employment has been constrained by the growth of a nearby city with a more bouyant service/adminstrative role: Düsseldorf in the case of Cologne, Milan in the case of Turin, and Edinburgh in the case of Clydeside (in which case, given the greater centralization of government and the economy in the national capital, London might also be considered a more active rival for service employment than either Bonn/Berlin or Rome).

The decline in employment, coupled with population growth in the case of Cologne and Turin, until recently, has inevitably led to higher rates of unemployment, as Table 9.3 shows. In each city the overall rate of unemployment has climbed sharply so that in Cologne and Turin it is now between 12 and 13 per cent and in

Table 9.3 Unemployment: cities and national ratios

	Cologne	*FRG*	*Ratio*	*Turin*	*Italy*	*Ratio*	*Clyde-side*	*GB*	*Ratio*
1970	0.3%	0.4%	0.75	–	–	–	5.0%	3.0%	1.67
1975	2.7%	2.7%	1.00	5.4%	3.2%	1.68	6.2%	3.7%	1.67
1980	6.4%	3.5%	1.82	8.2%	5.3%	1.55	11.5%	6.6%	1.74
1984	13.0%	9.6%	1.35	12.3%	9.9%	1.24	17.6%	12.6%	1.40

Source: Survey data.

Clydeside it is 17.6 per cent. Whereas the rate for Clydeside has consistently been above the average for Great Britain as a whole, the rates for Cologne and Turin have moved from below their respective national averages in the early 1970s to above those averages by 1980. The last feature to note in Table 9.3 is the tendency for the unemployment rates in the cities to converge towards their national averages in the period 1980–84. Whereas the city rates were between 55 and 80 per cent above the national rates in 1980, the relative disadvantage had shrunk to 24–40 per cent in 1984.

Within the overall unemployment totals there are certain similarities between the three cities. First, in each case the inner, core city has a higher rate of unemployment than the surrounding ring. Thus in Clydeside, for example, Glasgow's unemployment rate in 1985 was 21.3 per cent compared with 15.7 per cent in the outer metropolitan area; for Turin the equivalent figures were 15.5 per cent and 10.9 per cent. Second, the number of long-term unemployed has risen. Thus in Cologne the proportion of those out of work for more than one year rose from 19.6 per cent in 1980 to 37.0 per cent in 1983, whereas the figures for Clydeside were 27 per cent in 1979, 35 per cent in 1982, and 46 per cent in 1985. Third, there is in each case a growing proportion of young workers amongst the unemployed. Thus in Clydeside in 1971 those aged between sixteen and nineteen made up 8.2 per cent of all the registered male unemployed and 12.7 per cent of the female unemployed. By 1981 the figures were 9.8 per cent and 12.7 per cent, but by 1986 the figures were 29.1 per cent and 29.1 per cent respectively. Lastly, the employment compositions of the unemployed workers reflect the fact that Clydeside's depression started before that of Cologne and Turin. Thus, whilst it is clear that many of the unemployed in the latter two cities are prime workers released by the manufacturing sector, in Glasgow's case there is a much wider spread of 'last occupation' amongst the unemployed. Within Clydeside, of 140,000 unemployed in 1983, the largest group (32,000) were unclassified, reflecting the fact that they had had no employment since terminating education, followed by construction (20,000), distribution (15,000), miscellaneous services (13,000) and public administration (9,000). The 'old' industries of steel, shipbuilding and mechanical engineering jointly accounted only for 10,000.

The three cities, whilst sharing the economic depression which followed the oil price rise of 1974–75, and which was intensified in 1979, ascribe their major economic problems to different causes. In Turin, a single sector, motor vehicle manufacture, and indeed a single company, Fiat, is seen as the major component of industrial decline. The dependence of the Turin area economy on the car and the car-related component industries can be measured from the fact that out of 400,000 workers in manufacturing industries in 1971, over half were directly or indirectly involved in the production of motor vehicles. There has been major restructuring in the car industry, especially within the Fiat group of companies, as new technologies have been introduced to meet intense competition from foreign manufacturers. Product innovations have included changes to engine design and changes in bodywork and transmission to save weight by using new lighter materials. The increased mechanical efficiency of the newer vehicles has placed strains on component suppliers. Restructuring has taken the form of reducing production costs by saving on labour cost, first by using more capital intensive techniques and, second, by saving on material input costs by improved product design and better inventory control. The new materials have called for changes in labour skills: for example, plastic parts cannot be welded but must be joined chemically.

A programme of capital reinvestment by Fiat has led to locational shifts (Amin 1985). The restructuring of the labour force has led Fiat to close several plants in Turin, including the major Lingotto plant, and to shift production into southern Italy thereby avoiding the labour problems which had developed in Turin and attracting government incentives to industry in the Mezzogiorno. This process has also allowed Fiat to establish a number of less vulnerable establishments after the workers' struggles of 1968–72. For example, the plant at Cassino was equipped with four independent production lines each manufacturing a different model, thus overcoming the problems of single-line, single-product systems typical of the older Turin plants. In addition to the job losses from the Fiat plants in Turin, there are the considerable direct multiplier effects in the components industry. Fiat sources about 60 per cent of its components in the Turin area, although the component firms are not solely dependent upon sales to Fiat. Fiat has sought to reduce the number of component suppliers in the Turin area from 1,200 in 1980 to 850 in 1985, concentrating on the higher quality, more technological and less labour intensive suppliers. At the same time Fiat has reduced its in-house production of components. The net result on the Turin economy has been the loss of about 30,000 jobs by Fiat itself, between 1980 and 1984, and a loss of about 20,000 jobs, out of a total of 55,000 in the component industry over the same period (Enrietti, Follis, and Fornego 1985).

In the case of Cologne, the job loss is largely attributed to the city's industrial structure. The decline in manufacturing employment of 62,000 jobs between 1970 and 1982 is very largely concentrated in the mechanical engineering, vehicles, electrical engineering, and chemicals sectors, which together make up 70 per cent of the city's manufacturing employment. This employment is concentrated into a relatively small number of major industrial plants which have restructured in order to face increased foreign competition. The failure to compete effectively is attributed to financial difficulties which occurred after the 1973 and 1979 oil price rises, but more particularly to difficulties in competing in world markets given the growing strength of the Deutschmark. For example, the mechanical engineering sector in Cologne is dependent upon export sales for 55 per cent of all turnover, and the vehicles sector is 60 per cent dependent upon exports, whereas the corresponding figures for the Federal Republic as a whole are only 45 per cent and 47 per cent (Stadtentwicklung 1984). At the same time, enterprises in Cologne have been affected by the general movement of manufacturing industry to the southern Länder such as Bavaria and Baden-Württemberg.

Finally, in Clydeside's case the industrial structural explanation of employment loss has not been found adequate. As Table 9.4 shows, for the period 1971–81 only about one quarter of the net loss of 100,000 jobs could be explained in terms of the national economic performance and the conurbation's industrial structure. Indeed the city of Glasgow at the conurbation's core had a positive structural component. The structure alone would have accounted

Table 9.4 Shift-share analysis of Clydeside, 1971–81

	Initial employment (000s)	*Change (000s)*	*National (000s)*	*Structural (000s)*	*Residual (000s)*
Glasgow city	463	−63.8	−10.7	+8.2	−61.3
Outer conurbation	327	−40.1	−7.6	−17.7	−14.7
All	790	−103.9	−18.3	−9.5	−76.0

Source: Census of Population, 1971, 1981.

for less than 10 per cent of the job loss. The residual, measuring the conurbation's competitive weakness, accounts for 76,000 of the job losses with much of this concentrated into the inner city. In fact the competitive performance of the outer ring of the conurbation was actually positive in the period 1971–78 but in the period 1978–81 there was some convergence in the performances of the inner and outer cities as the former improved relatively and the latter worsened (Lever and Mather 1986). The failure of the Clydeside economy to sustain employment, or even to restrict decline to national average levels, is attributed to operating cost differentials in which the conurbation is found to have low levels of productivity per worker, particularly in the inner city, so that firms are disproportionately disadvantaged by wage rises above the rate of price inflation and have low levels of net capital investment per employee. In addition, the rate of new establishment formation is found to be low relative to the rest of Scotland and the rest of the UK. This low birth rate has been variously attributed to low levels of entrepreneurial ambition in a regional economy historically dominated by large employers in steel, shipbuilding, and heavy mechanical engineering, a lack of premises due to urban renewal, low levels of capital availability due to the conservatism of the regional banking system, and uncertainties in the urban environment due to road-building and residential clearance programmes on a massive scale.

A similar shift-share exercise for the city of Turin for the period 1971–81 also produces a wide range of negative differentials which show that of the 15.6 per cent job loss between these years, only 0.4 per cent was attributable to structural composition and 15.2 per cent was the competitive differential. Of this latter figure, 32 per cent was attributable to the motor vehicle industry and a further 14 per cent was attributable to the linked machine tool industry. Significantly, in Turin as in Clydeside, the service sectors also showed negative differentials in some cases.

Government intervention in local economic policy

The extent and nature of government intervention into local, urban, or metropolitan economies can be seen as a function of the degree of centralization or decentralization in the national administrative system. The Committee on Urban Affairs (OECD 1983) has recently drawn attention to the increasing decentralization of most systems in the developed nations, and this in its turn has led city governments to play an increasing role in economic development. Between the national and metropolitan levels of government in each of our three cases is a regional level of government, namely the province of Piedmont in the case of Turin, the Land of Nordrheinwestfalia in the case of Cologne, and the Scottish Office/Scottish Development Agency tier in the case of Clydeside. This study deals successively with the national, regional and local levels of intervention in the three metropolitan economies.

i) National

Under the heading of national urban policy there are two main components – actual urban policy and incidental regional policy which may have urban effects. Under the heading of formal regional policy only Clydeside qualifies to receive selective assistance. In the Federal Republic, regional economic policy has had a number of objectives, including support for areas whose natural market areas have been truncated by international frontiers with eastern Europe under the Zonenrandgebeit programme and the Regional Action Programme, focusing assistance on industrial development centres (gewerbliche Schwerpunkte). These, too, tend to lie on the margins of the Federal Republic along the Baltic coast, in the Alps, and along the frontier with the east. Within Nordrheinwestfalia, regional assistance has not been available to the heavily urbanized core including Cologne but has been restricted to the peripheral areas such as the Saarland and the Sauerland (Krumme 1974).

Similarly, in the case of Turin, regional policy has tended to favour the peripheral regions and to exclude the largest cities. Thus within Piedmont, the areas in receipt of assistance are the mountainous areas linking to the Val d'Aosta and Liguria and small areas classified as Depressed Areas which attract soft loans. The Turin Metropolitan Area qualifies for no assistance under the regional policy system (Allen *et al.* 1975). In a sense the current development of Italian and German policy is similar to that of Britain prior to 1960 when larger cities tended to be excluded from coverage as higher unemployment rates were to be found in rural and small town areas.

In the case of Clydeside, the full range of regional policy assistance is available but recent study has shown (Lever 1986) that it tends to be anti-urban in effect, and certainly in the case of Clydeside, to work against the inner city. For example, in the period 1979–83 some £100m of Regional Development Grant (RDG) and some £36m of Regional Selective Assistance (RSA) were received by the Clydeside conurbation. Of these totals, however, Glasgow with 55 per cent of the employment, received only 31 per cent of the RDG monies and only 22 per cent of the RSA. This imbalance is not explained by the differing industrial sectoral composition of the two areas, as in the twenty major industrial sectors only four had higher per capita levels of assistance in the inner city than in the outer area. However, it would be wrong to minimize the impact of regional assistance within the Clydeside conurbation, for it can be estimated that some 19,000 jobs have either been created or maintained by regional policy in the period 1979–83, in the context of a total registered unemployment figure of approximately 140,000. Within regional policy, only the Office and Service Industries Scheme (OSIS) appears to favour the inner city, and here the job creation level in 1979–83 was much lower, with only 900 jobs assisted. A further contribution to economic policy within the Clydeside conurbation from its assisted area status is the area's eligibility for aid from the EEC. The conurbation in the period 1975–86 received some £125m of grant aid from the European Regional Development Fund for infrastructural investment, making it the second highest user (on a per capita basis) of ERDF monies after the Mezzogiorno (Calderwood 1987). In addition, the conurbation received some £154m in loans from the European Investment Bank, although the net saving to the area amounted to no more than perhaps £3–5m overall in terms of marginally lower interest rates, and some £25m from the European Social Fund to help fund a labour subsidy scheme to take on unemployed workers, some 13,000 of whom have benefited within the conurbation between 1975 and 1986.

Under the heading of formal Urban Aid, much has been channelled through Manpower Service Commission projects and through the Scottish Development Agency. However, some direct Urban Aid funding has come to the conurbation by way of funding to support Community Business, with a 75 per cent grant once approved by local authorities. It is impossible to obtain total Scottish Urban Aid expenditure on community businesses, but McArthur (1984) estimates that in 1984–85 twelve organizations in the conurbation received £440,000, £262,000 in recurring revenue over a 3–5 year period, £139,000 in capital grant and the remainder in nonrecurring revenue (Keating and Boyle 1986:122).

ii) Regional

Under the regional level of intervention, there is a great diversity amongst the agencies intervening in the economies of the three cities. In the case of Turin, the role of the province of Piedmont is a relatively restricted one. Since 1976, when Decree 902 was passed, Piedmont has had the role of monitoring and granting soft loans to small and medium-sized enterprises, although the funds are provided by the national government and by the private banks. In the period 1976–80, some 700 requests for loans were received by Piedmont, although not all of these came from the city of Turin, and preference was granted to requests coming from the 'inadequately developed' parts of the province. The majority of loans were requested for modernization projects: far fewer companies were planning extensions or new plants. Most of the requests (hence most of the investments) were made by medium-sized companies (51–300 workers). Most of the extensions and new plants were planned by the smaller companies. The effect of Decree 902 has been to increase the average plant size of manufacturing industry in Piedmont, and thus by creating scale economies hopefully to create a more competitive sector. In net terms, however, Luzzati and Bottiglieri (1985) found that many of the investment plans had already been carried out and applications for soft loan finance were being made retrospectively.

Also at the regional level, the Piedmontese Regional Financial Institute (Finpiemonte) was established in 1976 with the purpose of contributing to infrastructural development and the organization of services. These regional finance companies have two main purposes – the provision of risk capital and the creation of regional infrastructure (Cottino 1982). Finpiemonte's capital now stands at £10m, but the statutory maximum grant of £500,000 per project means that private sector financing has to be involved in most cases. Projects include the assembly and servicing of land for industry, the construction of advance factories, the industrial promotion of Piedmont, housing improvement, and the creation of an industrial leasing company.

In the case of Cologne, the role played by the Land of Nordrheinwestfalia is somewhat different to that in Piedmont. Development plans for Cologne identified as key sectors information processing and the development of high technology industry. It was recognized that the city alone should not attempt a programme based on these areas but that the Land should draw up a scheme of integrated projects. In consequence, the Land (in conjunction with the Federal Government) has funded a science park linked to the University of Cologne with special emphases on biotechnology and microelectronics. Cologne University is the leading university in the FRG for biotechnology, with links to the Max Planck Institute and to major chemical and pharmaceutical companies. In order to expand the information processing industry, the Land has helped to found an Information Technology Centre (with similar ones in Aachen and Seigen) to offer computing software developments to subscribing member firms, and training programmes. The Land has also become the major funder of enhanced communications technology through a project to lay cables and provide satellite communications services to the major information processing companies such as banks, insurance companies, Lufthansa, and publishing companies.

The regional scale of intervention in the Clydeside economy is largely the province of the Scottish Development Agency. The SDA, founded in 1975, currently has an annual operating budget of about £130m, assets valued at £173m in terms of land and buildings, and £42m in terms of investments in companies. The SDA has no particular remit within the Clydeside conurbation but the clearest evidence of its intervention lies in the four area-based programmes in Glasgow, Clydebank, Motherwell, and Coatbridge. As Table 9.5 shows, the gross investment value of the four areas is about £853m of which the SDA will provide £120m, private sector industrial and commercial development will total £203m, private sector housing development will total £193m and the balance, £337m, will come from the remainder of the public sector. Thus, although the SDA is the smallest of the four partners in the area-based projects, its catalytic role has been widely recognized (Moore and Booth 1986a).

Without the designation of area-based programmes, based in the SDA's view on 'areas of potential', the massive private sector development would not have been attracted. The SDA now claims that the SDA:private sector gearing ratio has risen from 1:2.2 in 1983–84 to 1:5.1 in 1984–85 and to 1:7.0 in 1985–86. The total number of jobs created in the area programmes, as Table 9.5 indicates, is almost 10,000, but this total does not include a

Table 9.5 Area-based projects in the Scottish Development Agency

	GEAR	*Clydebank*	*Motherwell*	*Coatbridge*
Period	1976–87	1980–[a]	1982–87	1983–88
Total investment	£500m	£79m	£223m	£51m
SDA investment	£63m	£25m	£21m	£11m
Private industry	£97m	£23m	£71m	£12m
Private housing	£87m	£29m	£65m	£13m
Jobs	4,000	3,000	1,400	800

Source: SDA Annual Reports.
Note: (a) No completion date.

considerable number of construction jobs, nor does it take into account the direct and indirect multiplier effects. The investment function of the SDA is not focused particularly upon west central Scotland. Of investments made by Scottish Development Finance and financial help offered through the Small Business Division, a total of 1,064 by 1987, Glasgow establishments had received only 147, and the outer conurbation only 142. This total of 289 is considerably less than the 'fair shares' ratio which Clydeside might expect if financial assistance to companies was distributed randomly throughout the area for which the SDA is responsible.

The SDA, through its agency Locate In Scotland (LIS), has centralized all the attraction of inward investment, depriving local authorities (except the New Towns) of the power to engage in promotional activities on the grounds that the multiplicity of local authorities seeking to attract investment was confusing. LIS's main promotional role is exercised overseas with a budget of £2m per year and offices in New York, San Francisco, Chicago, and Houston and an agency in Tokyo. Some 9,000 new jobs and 10,600 additional jobs in existing companies were attributed to the work of LIS in 1981–84 throughout Scotland (Lever 1986). However, LIS has no specific brief for Clydeside, and indeed argues that its best chance is to offer the most attractive sites to possible investors rather than hamstring itself by rigidly offering the most depressed and needy locations. The consequence has been a bias away from the inner city areas like Glasgow. Henderson calculated (1980:187) that Glasgow's share of immigrant industry employment was some 34,000 jobs short, cumulatively over the period 1945–70, and LIS has undoubtedly reinforced this trend. The only exceptions within Clydeside are the two New Towns, Cumbernauld and East Kilbride, which have proved able to attract inward investment (Henderson 1984).

Regional development agencies such as the SDA would appear

to have greater expertise and flexibility in creating or responding to special projects than is the case with local authorities. The SDA has become involved in a number of unique area-based developments, in addition to those listed in Table 9.5, each of which has had special needs and requirements to which the SDA has been able to respond. Sector-based, but areal, developments have occurred at Motherwell and west Glasgow. In the former case a Food Park has been established with some twenty companies on a site whose excellent motorway access has made it a natural choice for food distribution depots. However, there are some externalities, such as food analytic testing facilities, which are unique to the site. On the west side of Glasgow the SDA was instrumental in setting up the West of Scotland Science Park in 1983, which now has twenty companies at a final cost of £6m. The local authorities and the city's two universities are joint partners in the venture. The SDA also played a role, with the local authorities and development companies, in setting up the Scottish Exhibition and Conference Centre (SECC) on reclaimed dockland close to the city centre, and a similar site on the other side of the Clyde housed the International Garden Festival in 1988. Lastly, recognizing the employment potential of the city's Central Business District and the investment and income multiplier effects, the SDA has been involved in a study of the CBD both to attract corporate office headquarters to the area, and in a parallel development to encourage new and refurbished housing for white-collar workers in the CBD.

iii) Local authority

First, on the basis of the Clydeside and Cologne cases, it is almost possible to propound a law of inverse power: the stronger the regional development agency the weaker the city government's role in economic development. However, the city of Turin conflicts with such a rule – or introduces a third element, that of central government. Certainly in the Clydeside case, there is evidence that legal powers have been removed from the local authority and conferred on the non-elective regional agency, as in the case of attracting inward investment. Second, where resources for industrial development are limited, increased spending by one agency must necessarily be accompanied by lower spending elsewhere in the system. Last, there is an attitudinal point: where a strong regional development agency is operating and operating successfully, then there is often a tendency for local government to relax on the basis that there is little more that it can usefully do. Thus in the Clydeside conurbation, the presence of the Scottish Development Agency has enabled some local authorities at the district level to allow the SDA to do the economic development work and merely act as a support agency. For example, Clydebank District Council has had much of its developmental role taken over, firstly by the SDA's Taskforce, set up to deal with the problems caused by the Singer Sewing Machine Co. closure, and subsequently by the Enterprise Zone.

In the eleven district councils which make up the Clydeside conurbation, there are several different strategies. Three of the district councils are predominantly white-collar suburbs whose male unemployment rate in 1981 was about 7 per cent: they have little or no economic development policy, nor do they see the need for one. The two districts which contain New Towns had a male unemployment rate of 12.5 per cent: through their development corporations these two areas have retained powers of attraction of inward investment and have aggressive strategies of seeking foreign and British companies. This is in marked contrast with many older local authorities who have tended to concentrate upon smaller indigenous firms in their areas. At the other end of the spectrum, Glasgow, with a male unemployment rate of 23.5 per cent in 1981, has been forced to develop an integrated economic assistance plan over and above whatever the SDA may do in its area. Outside Glasgow, the worst male unemployment rates are found in Clydebank (20.8 per cent), Motherwell (19.6 per cent) and Coatbridge (Monklands DC) (22 per cent). Each of these three has been chosen as the site of one of the SDA's area-based programmes and to an extent each has been willing to let the SDA make the running in local economic development. Rather in limbo are the two other district councils, Hamilton and Renfrew, where the male unemployment rates were 17.8 per cent and 14.3 per cent respectively. These two areas have failed to attract SDA support in the form of an area-based programme but the district councils have not established cohesive economic development plans of their own.

In some cases the failure of local authorities to create their own programmes of assistance reflects either a lack of expertise in business, or a reluctance of Labour-controlled councils to be seen to be working with the private sector. The 'solution' to these problems has in a number of instances been to help in the creation of an Enterprise Trust where public sector money and private sector expertise are brought together. Examples from within the conurbation include the Lanarkshire Industrial Field Executive

(LIFE), Monklands Enterprise Trust (MET), Glasgow Opportunity (GO), and the Trust for Action, Cumbernauld and Kilsyth (TACK) (Moore and Booth 1986b). Glasgow District Council is perhaps the only lower tier authority of a sufficient size and with sufficient expertise to create an integrated Economic Development Plan. This Plan looks forward three to five years and is rolled annually. Significantly, however, it has a spend less than that permitted by legislation, and 80 per cent of its total expenditure of £6m goes on land, site preparation, and buildings. The remainder goes on rent relief, financial assistance to co-operatives and worker-managed enterprises (WMEs) and on contributions to Enterprise Trusts. Direct financial assistance to firms in the form of grants, loans, or loan guarantees, do not form part of the Economic Development Plan.

Whilst to an extent this study has created the impression that the presence of a powerful and successful regional development agency like the SDA is seen as beneficial by local authorities, it is not an entirely unmixed blessing. In some cases local authorities will argue that (i) with the SDA's scale of resources, the local authority could do as well, (ii) the SDA's objectives may conflict with the local authority's – e.g. in terms of land use planning, and (iii) the SDA has no specific remit for particular areas outside the area-based projects, thus a town like Hamilton or Renfrew may receive very little benefit from the SDA. A more difficult issue for local authorities to confront as a consequence of the SDA's intervention is the treatment of what the local authority regards as a priority area, but which is not taken into an SDA area-based programme. Thus in the case of Glasgow, the SDA has focused its efforts on the inner city's eastern sector (Glasgow East Area Renewal) and, in a rather different way, on the city centre and related developments such as the SECC and the Garden Festival site. Away from GEAR, the city of Glasgow identified two other inner city areas, one north-west of the city centre (Maryhill) and one south of the city centre (Govan-Kinning Park). These two areas are the subject of joint programmes between Glasgow District Council and Strathclyde Regional Council but receive no special treatment from the SDA. Glasgow District Council and Strathclyde have attempted to bend mainline programmes into these areas and, based on public sector expenditure per head indices, they appear to have been successful. However, such success almost inevitably generates claims from other areas for similar treatment. More recently, Glasgow District Council, recognizing the shifting locus of deprivation from the inner cities to the peripheral public sector housing estates, has designated

Easterhouse and Drumchapel as areas to receive priority treatment. Nevertheless, there is no evidence to date that mainline programmes have been disproportionately 'bent' into these areas (Jolliffe 1985). Just as in the SDA's case where area-based programmes have been designated in areas of 'potential' rather than economic disaster areas, Glasgow District Council tends to use the same terminology. Again there is similarity in the dilemmas in which the SDA and Glasgow District Council find themselves in terms of knowing how and when to withdraw special status for designated areas.

In Cologne, it has been argued, the absence of a regional development agency should generate a much higher level of city government intervention. First, the city government uses Federal funding for job creation and for training to, and sometimes beyond, the limit of permitted expenditure. Second, the city uses its own budget to create and maintain employment. In Cologne, out of approximately 500,000 jobs, 10 per cent are directly or indirectly city financed. This figure includes the administrative staff of the city, city-run enterprises (hospitals, ports) and local businesses in which the city is an important shareholder (the local savings bank, public utilities and public transport). This total of employment has recently been expanded by about 1,000 by the creation of a city-wide programme of landscaping, environmental improvement, and graffiti-cleaning (Wohnumfeldverbesserung). Land assembly and infrastructural provision has always played an important part in German economic development policy, and the city's DM30 million annual programme is about three times that of the city of Glasgow on a per capita basis (although this makes no allowance for the SDA's contribution in Glasgow). This heading covers derelict land reclamation schemes, some of which are financed by the Land, refurbishing vacant industrial premises and the establishment of small industrial parks (Gewerbehöfe). The city has developed a programme of business advice both to assist the rate of new firm formation and to help maintain the existing business stock (Bestandspflege). For new businesses, potential entrepreneurs such as retailers and craftsmen are offered a range of advice extending from suitable locations to financing and marketing, and in some cases supplementary courses are run to enable businessmen to enhance their qualifications. For continuing businesses the city has identified a large number which are being run by the third generation in the family and where there is no direct successor: in these cases the city seeks to find new owners and managers. Other firms come to the attention of the city through its environmental improvement programme which involves identifying firms which may have adverse effects on residential areas through smoke, noise, pollution, etc. (Gemengelagen) and who will require advice and possibly financial assistance to overcome the problem through relocation or filtering.

A city such as Cologne has inevitably developed its own policies towards high technology, although some of these are funded by the Federal Government. A Centre for New Firms and Innovations (Gründungs-und-Innovationszentrum-GIZ) has been set up, providing accommodation for innovative, newly established firms and for the promotion of broad technology transfer. This is now privately managed but works in conjunction with the city's Chamber of Commerce and banks. Rents charged are market rents but management and other professional services are subsidized for three to five years, a period felt adequate to develop new products and to test their market competitiveness. Paralleling this, the city has established an Information Technology Centre to help small- and medium-sized businesses to install computing equipment and to retrain staff. The city has commissioned a number of sectoral studies designed to lead to commercial developments in areas in which the city is known to have a competitive edge – banking and finance, solar energy, and biotechnology. The last two reflect specialisms within Cologne University. It is significant that whereas in Cologne the city commissioned the studies, similar studies for Clydeside were undertaken by the SDA. Lastly, Cologne pursues a vigorous programme of promotion to attract inward investment, again a role currently played by the SDA in Glasgow's case.

In Turin, the city's involvement in local economic development policy is significantly less than in the Glasgow and Cologne cases. Italian cities have few legal powers to intervene in local economies, this role largely being played by the national government and the regions. Prior to 1971 there was little interaction between the private sector of industry and municipal government, but Law 865 passed in that year authorized the municipal authorities to produce their own plan for new industrial plant (known as PIPS) and to expropriate the necessary land. However, analysis of subsequent events in Turin, and elsewhere, suggests that the Law has been less effective than was originally anticipated. By the time the first PIPS came into operation, the Turin economy had swung from growth to recession, and few companies were making long-term plans requiring major new sites. Currently some fourteen PIPS are operating in Turin, and analysis shows that the process is unduly cumbersome and has the effect of raising land prices. Only about 60 per cent of industrial development within the city conforms to

PIPS proposals and monitoring reports use phrases such as 'the behaviour of the property developer appears to be less predictable than first imagined'. PIPS do have some advantages, however: they do permit some scale economies in the provision of municipal services to be realized, and they are now increasingly being linked to developments in particular manufacturing sectors, thereby offering the possibility of external economies. In theory, the long-term objective of the PIPS programme is that it becomes self-financing on a rolling basis.

Away from the PIPS, the city of Turin has normal land use zoning powers. Land zoned for industry under the city's three-year development plans is still under pressure of demand but significantly the pressure is coming from property developers rather than from industrialists *per se*, and this creates some problems over long-term control and the ultimate type of land use (e.g. office development on sites zoned for warehousing). Thus, whilst the municipal government of Turin may hold views on social welfare, job creation, and a desirable employment structure for the city, it has few powers outwith land use planning with which to confront these issues.

Conclusion

A transnational comparison of three cities has been attempted and the degree of government intervention in their local economies evaluated. Intervention in each case occurs at three levels – national, regional, and local. The ratio between these three levels and the effectiveness of the intervention varies widely. In Clydeside the regional dimension, through the SDA, has come to dominate; in Cologne, city government appears the strongest force; in Turin, national policies and processes have had the most impact.

References

Allen, K.J. *et al.*, (1979) *Regional incentives in the European Community – a comparative study*, EEC: Brussels.

Amin, A. (1985) 'Restructuring in Fiat and the decentralization of production into southern Italy', in R. Hudson and J. Lewis (Eds) *Uneven Development in Southern Europe*, London: Methuen.

Calderwood, R. (1987) 'Economic development and the EEC', *Strathclyde Economic Trends*, 14:1–5.

Cherry, G. (1986) 'Problems in cross-national research: an East European

perspective', in I. Masser and R. Williams (Eds) *Learning From Other Countries*, Norwich: Geo Books.
Cheshire, P., Carbonaro, G. and Hay, D. (1986) 'Problems of urban decline and growth in EEC countries', *Urban Studies* 23:131–50.
Cheshire, P. and Hay, D. (1986) 'The development of the European urban system 1971–81', in H.J. Ewers, J.B. Goddard, and H. Matzerath (Eds) *The Future of the Metropolis*, Berlin: de Gruyter.
Cottino, G. (1982) 'Financing investment in the city from public and private resources', in B. Allan (Ed.) *Making the City Work*, Glasgow DC.
Dangschat, J. and Blasius, J. (1987) 'Social and spatial disparities in Warsaw in 1978', *Urban Studies* 24:173–91.
Davies, H.W.E. (1986) 'Working with international agencies', in I. Masser and R. Williams (Eds) *Learning From Other Countries*, Norwich: Geo Books.
Enrietti, A., Follis, M. and Fornego, G. (1985) 'The restructuring of the car components industry in the Turin area', in C. Villain-Gandossi (Ed.) *Turin Project International Report*, European Co-ordination Centre for Research and Documentation in Social Sciences.
Hall, P. and Hay, D. (1980) *Growth centres in the European urban system*, London: Heinemann Educational.
Henderson, R.A. (1980) 'The location of immigrant industry within a UK Assisted Area', *Progress in Planning*, 14(2):109–226.
(1984) 'The employment performance of established manufacturing industry in the Scottish New Towns', *Urban Studies* 21(3):295–315.
Jolliffe, C. (1985) 'Bending main-line programmes: the utilisation of main programmes for urban regeneration', *Inner City in Context Working Paper* No.8, University of Glasgow.
Keating, M. and Boyle, R. (1986) *Remaking Urban Scotland*, Edinburgh University Press.
Krummer, G. (1974) 'Regional policies in West Germany', in N. Hansen (Ed.) *Public Policy and Regional Economic Development*, Cambridge, Mass: Ballinger.
Lever, W.F. (1986) 'Old policies in a new role', in W.F. Lever and C. Moore (Eds) *The City In Transition*, Oxford University Press.
Lever, W.F. and Mather, F. (1986) 'The changing structure of business and employment in the conurbation', in W.F. Lever and C. Moore (Eds) *The City in Transition*, Oxford University Press.
Luzzati, E. and Bottiglieri, B. (1985) 'Local government and economic policy interventions', in G. Cardetti (Ed.) *Project Turin International*, European Co-ordination Centre for Research and Documentation in Social Sciences.
McArthur, A. (1984) 'The Community Business movement in Scotland', *Centre for Urban and Regional Research Discussion* Paper 17, University of Glasgow.
Moore, C. and Booth, S. (1986a) 'Unlocking enterprise: the search for synergy', in W.F. Lever and C. Moore (Eds) *The City in Transition*, Oxford University Press.

(1986b) 'The search for effective area strategies', in W.F. Lever and C. Moore (Eds) *The City in Transition*, Oxford University Press.
OECD (1983) *Managing Urban Change: Vol.II, The Role of Government*, Paris: OECD.
Stadtentwicklung (1984) *Der Kölner 'Ruck nach vorn': neuere Ansätze zur Stadtentwicklung und Wirtschaftsförderung in Köln*, Köln: Amt für Stadtentwicklungsplanung.
van der Berg, L. *et al.* (1982)*Urban Europe: A Study of Growth and Decline*, Oxford: Pergamon.

10

Assisting local economies: an assessment of emerging patterns of local authority economic development activities

J. Sellgren

Introduction

Local authorities have historically taken an interest in the affairs of their local economy and indeed economic intervention by municipal authorities can be traced back into the nineteenth century. These early attempts at intervention were primarily concerned with securing public health and in making provision for a range of municipal utilities. Early attempts on the part of local governments to alleviate economic problems were developed during the depression of the inter-war years. However, it has been argued that the role of central government in maintaining full employment after 1945 retarded the growth of local economic development measures (Local Government Training Board 1986a). Chandler and Lawless (1985) argue that despite this by 1970 local authority economic development had developed a static characteristic form, with authorities offering land and premises for incoming or expanding industries, and on occasion providing rent concessions or key-worker housing, and often advertising the values of their area in order to attract relocating or expanding firms. However, in recent years and particularly since about 1973, economic development has expanded rapidly within authorities; largely in response to the impact of economic decline upon local areas and the impact of rising local unemployment, together with a perceived lack of concern for manufacturing by central government (Coulson 1986).

Local authority economic development work may be defined as any action taken deliberately by a local authority to alleviate what it perceives to be a local economic problem. However, their ability to act to undertake such activities is constrained both by the legal powers which define local authority actions and the resource base available to fund their work. It is suggested by Young (1985) that the growing interest amongst local authorities in economic development has been taking place through the operation of three distinct processes. The first, termed *rippling out*, refers to the shift in activity levels from the older conurbations and the assisted areas to the non-urban areas and to the more prosperous regions. The second, *filtering down*, is the growing concern for economic development shown by the minor authorities. The third process, termed *diversification*, is concerned with the widening range of activities practised by local authorities and particularly the growth of more interventionist development strategies. This chapter divides into three sections which seek to explore the action of these processes in order to examine recent trends in local authority economic development activities. The first reviews briefly the range of powers and resources available to local authorities in the UK to undertake economic development activities. The second assesses the range of activities which have been undertaken by district-level authorities and explores the regional variations which exist in the operation of these activities. The final part makes a summary analysis of local economic initiatives by illustrating the contemporary patterns of such activities from an original survey of over 200 local initiatives.

Local government powers

The activities of local government are circumscribed by the *ultra vires* doctrine which has been developed to ensure that public authorities act only in an authorised manner. In addition, local authorities are bound by the rule of law. Even where statutory authorization is available, it is still possible for a decision to be declared *ultra vires* where the authority has contravened some principle of common law. Thus authorities may exceed their powers in a manner which the courts maintain Parliament did not intend. Economic development is an activity for which local authorities have no specific powers. However, they may undertake such activity under a variety of statutory powers. A study by JURUE (1980) classified four types of power that may be used for economic development activity:

(i) Statutory duties for employment services.
(ii) Statutory duties for other services which are not primarily concerned with employment objectives but may have an incidental effect upon them.
(iii) Permissive powers given to local authorities which may be used in certain circumstances to undertake employment initiatives.

(iv) Local powers arising either from Local Acts or from Special Acts which apply only to some local authorities or within specified areas.

In addition to the statutory provisions, local authorities are also able to draw upon their common-law powers to do anything which is reasonably incidental to their statutory functions.

The statutory duties for services and major permissive powers which may be used by local authorities to assist local economic development are shown in Appendix 1 at the end of the chapter. It is argued that the statutory services provided by local authorities allow intervention into the supply side of a variety of elements of the local economy. For example, the aggregate supply of labour may be influenced through policies affecting key workers, housing, transport, schemes to increase labour availability, and day nurseries to increase female participation rates. The quality of the labour force may also be affected by the education curriculum and provision of training by the authority. While the provision of transport infrastructure is vested in central government, local authorities may be able to influence access in more local terms through zoning and traffic control decisions as well as through the management of transport systems required by local industry and commerce. In the execution of these statutory duties, the local authority is drawing upon fairly large resources in both financial and manpower terms. Local government is frequently a significant local employer and also a consumer of goods and services; a factor which may also be used for the benefit of the local economy.

In recent years, however, a number of authorities, notably those which have been identified as the New Left have rejected the liberal democratic principles upon which the provision of public goods and services has been based. Their approach has been characterized by a rejection of five popular tenets of traditional economic development policies; first, competitive promotion whereby local authorities vie with each other to attract mobile industry. Second, they have rejected a generalised approach to wealth creation through the provision of land and buildings. Third, the arms length relationship with the private sector has been rejected in favour of a more direct interventionist strategy whereby the authorities seek to influence directly the decision making of private firms. Fourth, they have rejected attempts to regenerate the local economy through small firms alone, and last, the division between economic and social policy has been rejected, thus production has been assisted where it is both consistent with wider social objectives and can provide long-term profits (Gilhespy *et al.* 1986).

Local authorities also have permissive powers which allow those wishing to do so to undertake a variety of additional activities. The most important of which are as follows: Sections 2, 3 and 4 of the Local Authorities (Land) Act 1963 which enable authorities to undertake or support the provision of land, buildings, and infrastructure and to provide advance factories, warehouses, or small units. Under the Local Authority Superannuation Regulations 1974 and 1984, authorities are empowered to invest up to 10 per cent of their superannuation funds in unquoted securities and this may include local firms. The Local Government Act 1972 and Local Government (Scotland) Act 1973, provide a variety of powers which local authorities may be able to utilize for economic development work and these include: appointing staff (Section 112/64) and thus they are able to appoint persons to industrial development posts; publishing information, arranging lectures, holding discussions, or mounting displays on matters relating to local government (Section 142/88). Further, the authority can engage in a variety of activities to collect and circulate information relating to the area and thus to promote it. Sections 111/69 of these Acts make a general provision which empowers local authorities to do anything conducive or incidental to the discharge of any of their functions and this may include setting up economic/industrial development units. Local authorities are also empowered to engage in some limited municipal enterprises, these include powers to establish and maintain municipal restaurants, markets, and slaughterhouses, and also to provide a varied range of goods and services which may be used by other local authorities or public bodies.

The most widely publicized permissive power which may be used to undertake economic development is Section 137 of the Local Government Act 1972 (in England and Wales, and its equivalent Section 83 of the Local Government (Scotland) Act 1973); under these provisions local authorities are able to incur expenditure in the interest of their area or its inhabitants up to a maximum of a 2p product of the rates. However, this power has been reviewed on a number of occasions, most recently by the Widdicombe Committee (Widdicombe 1986). Research by Ramsdale and Capon (1986) undertaken for the Widdicombe Committee noted that, on average, local authorities in the UK are using 66.8 per cent of the total resources which they derive from Section 137/83 for economic development. It is estimated by Ramsdale and Capon that the increase in expenditure on economic development from 1981/82 to 1984/85 under Section 137/83 was some 405 per cent at constant prices. In actual terms, this represented an increase from about £17m in 1981/82 to about £90m in 1984/85 (at 1984/85 prices). However, the pattern of spending indicates that it is the lower tier, district and borough authorities which have made increasingly widespread use of the resources available to them under Section 137/83 for economic development over the last decade. The future of Section 137/83 was considered by the Widdicombe Committee and while they received evidence to suggest that there were problems with the power as it stood, they felt that it was a valid measure, providing a means of making discriminatory spending in 'the interest of the area'. It was recommended that the existing position relating to Section 137/83 could be clarified by maintaining the notion of ensuring that benefits accrue to the local area, but 'defining more precisely the degree of benefits which must be achieved' (Widdicombe 1986:8.85). They also felt that the yield from any discretionary power needed to be regulated. Clearly these recommendations would not preclude the continued use of a discretionary power for economic development, although the way in which the yield would be calculated and limited would place a financial constraint upon the use of such a power.

Financial and staff resources

Economic development is not a constituent of block grants, and so council expenditure for this has come from the rate fund or capital allocations, both of which are heavily constrained by central government policy. Figures showing the level of expenditure on economic development have been published for local authorities in England and Wales since 1978–79 by the Chartered Institute of Public Finance and Accountancy (CIPFA)[1] (unfortunately, comparable figures are not available for Scotland). An analysis of the data for local authorities in England and Wales reveals that there has been a steady increase in the level of expenditure made on economic development over the last decade. Table 10.1 shows the amount spent by county and district authorities per caput over this period. It should be noted that these figures are for expenditure made on capital account and therefore may (for individual authorities), fluctuate from year-to-year. It is clear, however, that there has been a considerable growth in the resource commitment to economic development by authorities at both county and district level. In general terms, the proportion contributed by county and district authorities has maintained itself at the level where the districts have provided about 80 per cent of the total expenditure.

Table 10.1 Capital expenditure (per caput) on economic development: England and Wales

	1977–78	1978–79	1979–80	1980–81	1981–82	1982–83	1983–84	1984–85	1985–86
	£	£	£	£	£	£	£	£	£
County	0.38	0.53	0.68	0.98	0.77	1.06	1.14	1.16	0.84
District	1.75	2.09	3.31	4.03	2.95	4.34	4.00	4.50	4.25
Total	2.13	2.62	3.99	5.01	3.72	5.40	5.14	5.66	5.09

Source: CIPFA.

These figures may be further disaggregated by authority type, distinguishing the Greater London Council (GLC), Metropolitan Counties, Shire Counties, London Boroughs, Metropolitan Districts and Shire Districts. The figures for the three types of county-level authority show a considerable degree of similarity in terms of the average capital expenditure per caput on economic development. However, at borough/district level the picture is more complex. While the London Boroughs appear to have traditionally a very high level of capital expenditure on economic development the other metropolitan districts appear to have increased their level of spending more rapidly only since 1979–80. While the non-metropolitan districts have only had a fairly low level of expenditure throughout the period, their budgets have grown less rapidly than the metropolitan districts, although in the years prior to 1979–80 they had a higher average per caput expenditure level.

An analysis of expenditures made on revenue account (see Table 10.2) confirms the importance of the district level authorities. However, there are clear indications that the overall levels of current expenditure over the last five years have not been falling, which would suggest that government measures to curb public expenditure have not impacted upon the economic development activities of district authorities.

Although complementary figures to those collected by CIPFA for England and Wales are not available for Scotland, the Local Financial Returns made by local authorities to the Scottish Office do identify an additional category for Industrial Promotion within

Table 10.2 Mean net current expenditure per 1,000 head of population on economic development: England and Wales

	1980–81	1981–82	1982–83	1983–84	1984–85	1985–86
	£	£	£	£	£	£
County	374.12	442.86	575.82	628.00	726.65	698.16
District	1,518.74	1,579.68	1,378.90	1,396.36	1,419.15	1,535.53
Total	1,892.86	2,022.54	1,954.72	2,024.36	2,145.80	2,233.69

Source: CIPFA.

the figures for planning services.[2] The accounting conventions applied to this expenditure vary from those used by CIPFA since only the revenue account element of industrial promotion is classified and this is broken down into two components, net expenditure and loan charges. For the purpose of assessing the level of expenditure in Scotland, the net expenditure for industrial promotion has been divided by the total population for regional and district authorities to produce a total net expenditure per caput. The results of this are shown in Table 10.3.

Table 10.3 Mean net expenditure per caput on industrial promotion: Scotland

Region			
1982–83	1983–84	1984–85	1985–86
£	£	£	£
2.02	1.53	1.02	1.53
District			
1982–83	1983–84	1984–85	1985–86
£	£	£	£
0.66	0.86	1.33	1.32
Total			
1982–83	1983–84	1984–85	1985–86
£	£	£	£
2.68	2.39	2.35	2.85

Source: Scottish Office.

In the case of the Scottish district authorities it was notable that the total number of authorities making an expenditure on industrial promotion increased from eleven in 1983–84 to twenty-eight in 1984–85 (and thirty in 1985–86). The very widespread participation by district authorities in Scotland does mask the exception of eight districts in which the responsibility for all industrial promotion work is vested in the regional authority and in two cases where the function was jointly managed (Municipal Yearbook 1987). However, one distinct feature which the Scottish data illustrates is that whereas in England and Wales the districts contribute about 80 per cent of the capital expenditure and about 70 per cent of the current expenditure on economic development, in Scotland the resources are drawn more equally from the two tiers of local government. From the limited nature of the time series it is not possible to make any firm assessment of the trends in the level of expenditure by local authorities, although it is very clear that there has been a very rapid increase in the number of authorities making expenditure on industrial promotion, particularly at the district level.

The data published by CIPFA also provides details of the numbers of staff engaged in economic development (these are based on budget estimates). From this it is possible to calculate the average number of staff involved in economic development (full-time equivalents) for counties and districts of England and Wales. Although this shows a much higher application of staff in county authorities, the figures are more revealing if the two classes are further disaggregated by authority type; this is shown in Table 10.4. While these data indicate the growing staff resource commitment in all types of authority they do identify differences between different types of authority. The very high numbers of staff employed in economic development in the former GLC is apparent; but it is also clear that until their abolition, there was a rapid increase in the number of persons employed in economic development by the other metropolitan counties. These latter saw almost a threefold increase in the size of their economic development staff over an eight year period. Although the number of persons working in economic development in the shire counties has always been less than in their metropolitan counterparts, these have nonetheless seen a doubling of staff over the period. The district level authorities have seen a far less dramatic growth in economic development staff. Amongst these authorities differences between types of authority are also apparent, with much larger numbers of persons being employed in the metropolitan districts (and particularly in the London Boroughs) and a much smaller number in the shire districts. However, the rate of growth in economic development staff in the shire districts has been more dramatic than in the metropolitan districts.

Since economic development is not a statutory function of local government, it has tended to evolve from existing functional departments. An analysis of the department in which the economic development officer is located provides some insight into this. Table 10.5 shows the results of an analysis based upon data from the Municipal Yearbook for all local authorities in Britain. It is clear that the largest proportion of EDOs are situated within planning departments. This frequent association of economic development with planning is perhaps not surprising, but it may betray a particular attitude to the means by which economic regeneration is to be achieved, that is through favourable policies relating to physical infrastructure, land and buildings, roads and housing. The same is also true of authorities where the responsi-

Table 10.4 Mean net staff numbers employed in economic development: England and Wales by authority type

	1978–79	1979–80	1980–81	1981–82	1982–83	1983–84	1984–85	1985–86	1986–87
Greater London Council	241.10	237.60	229.60	246.30	256.30	237.00	299.50	–	–
Metropolitan Counties (Excl. GLC)	10.10	15.84	17.98	21.57	21.15	25.98	26.70	27.33	–
Non-metropolitan Counties	4.93	5.54	5.73	6.92	6.35	8.90	10.42	9.83	10.75
London Boroughs	8.94	8.19	8.44	8.53	8.92	10.56	10.34	8.93	10.35
Metropolitan Districts (Excl. London Boroughs)	9.31	7.79	9.29	9.75	10.69	13.53	12.00	14.26	18.65
Non-metropolitan Districts	1.65	1.66	1.83	1.95	1.76	2.40	2.47	2.48	2.72

Source: CIPFA.

bility for economic development has been vested in the estates and surveyor's department. However, in a significant proportion of authorities economic development has been placed within the chief executive's department. This department is normally responsible directly to the council, acting as a support service for all other departments, frequently regulating and co-ordinating their activities. In a large number of authorities they also provide central services such as research and information, legal and clerical support, as well as dealing with administrative matters relating to the authority as a whole. Locating the economic development function within this department may well be a recognition of the cross-cutting nature of the activities involved with economic development in relation to the major functional departments of the authority, and the need to draw upon resources from a variety of departments such as planning, surveyor's, education, social services, treasurer's, and technical services in undertaking economic development work.

It is also clear that a great many authorities have appointed a person to a specific economic development post and that there has been an increasing tendency for authorities to do so. In a survey by Mills and Young (1986) of the 233 authorities replying to their questionnaire, only nine authorities had created a separate economic development department. Their study also showed that 27 per cent of EDOs were planning officers and that 41 per cent were economic development officers located within planning departments. Combining this with the information provided in Table 10.5 for the developments over time, it may be suggested that what has occurred is that responsibility for economic develop-

Table 10.5 Department responsible for economic development: England, Scotland, and Wales

	1980 %	*1981* %	*1982* %	*1983* %	*1984* %	*1985* %	*1986* %	*1987* %	*1988* %
Economic development	24.7	24.2	24.8	27.9	28.6	31.1	33.4	33.5	38.4
Planning	38.5	38.8	38.5	36.5	36.5	32.3	32.0	33.5	31.9
Estates & surveyors	9.7	10.5	10.1	10.6	9.7	9.7	9.9	8.5	7.4
Research & information	1.0	0.7	0.5	0.5	0.2	0.2	0.2	0.0	0.2
Chief executive	15.0	15.6	16.1	15.6	15.0	14.3	14.9	14.7	13.9
Technical services	3.9	3.6	3.6	3.4	3.5	2.8	3.0	3.2	2.8
No specific officer	7.3	6.7	6.5	5.5	6.5	9.5	6.4	6.7	5.4
Treasurers	0.0	0.0	0.0	0.0	0.0	0.0	0.2	0.0	0.0

Source: Municipal Yearbook.

ment has been developed as an extension of the statutory planning role of local authorities. Officers who have taken a key role in economic development as part of their existing responsibilities have increasingly devoted greater amounts of their time to this role and in many instances this has been recognized by designating this person as an economic development officer. In a recent paper, the Local Government Training Board (1986a) stressed the need for one officer to take overall responsibility for economic development. It is suggested that this officer should become the focal point of regular meetings and exchanges of information with counterparts in neighbouring authorities, in the other tiers of local government, and with trades unions and the voluntary sector. It has already been argued that the economic development role of local authorities has been developed from the characteristic planning orientated activities of the early 1970s to make far more widespread use of the range of statutory and permissive powers available to local authorities. It can thus be suggested that this broadening of activities has necessitated the appointment of an officer (or officers) to be responsible for economic development and to formulate and co-ordinate policy actions.

Local authority economic development activities

A survey of county and district level local authorities in England and Wales was undertaken by Mills and Young (1986) in the spring of 1984. This survey asked a series of questions relating to the period since January 1980 concerning a range of activities with which authorities have become engaged to promote local economic development. Their findings are shown in Table 10.6

Mills and Young found that the provision of sites and premises was a widespread activity amongst local authorities, but with the exception of a few very active authorities, these were generally

Table 10.6 Economic development activities: percentage of responding authorities engaging in these activities since January 1980

Activity	%
Sites and premises	82%
Financial assistance	48%
Promotion/marketing	73%
Research for economic development	55%
Business development	88%
Other economic development initiatives	86%

Source: Mills and Young, 1986.

small-scale activities concentrated at the lower end of the industrial property market (for a more detailed empirical assessment of local authority provision of factory premises, see Perry 1986 Chapter 4). In looking at authorities' use of financial assistance to industry, the survey was able to identify the purpose for which grant and loan monies were given. In general the pattern tended to show a bias towards assistance with land and premises, particularly for conversion or improvement of land and buildings or for rent relief on industrial properties. It was noted that well over half of the authorities which provided detailed information had budgets of £100,000 or less for financial assistance. Local authority promotional and marketing schemes were largely devoted to advertising and involvement with trade fairs and exhibitions. The most frequently cited economic development activity was business development (88 per cent of authorities). Clearly, however, this is a very broad category covering a wide array of activities and services, and as defined in the survey it encompassed activities ranging from the provision of information on site availability to financial advice and assistance to ethnic minority enterprises. When broken down by category, the area of business advice showed the very strong emphasis placed upon the traditional roles of providing information upon industrial sites and financial advice to industry. The final category considered by the survey included a wide variety of additional activities including tourism development, temporary employment schemes, training, and voluntary sector initiatives.

It is clear from the analysis of financial and staff resources that in England and Wales much of the implementation of local economic development work lies in the hands of the district councils. In Scotland it would appear that the financial responsibility for economic development is shared more equally between the two tiers of local government. While the county councils may be important in setting guidelines and co-ordinating local projects it is the district level authorities which have been responsible for the delivery of local economic development strategies; although it is impossible to make absolute rules about the role played by particular tiers of local government. In seeking to explore the relationship between different levels of local government in England and Wales, the Local Government Training Board (1986b) noted that in general higher spending in one tier produced associated spending in the other, which is what would reasonably be expected in areas with acute economic problems. However, there were exceptions where high-spending districts were coupled with low-spending counties, while several of the higher-spending counties included districts that spent almost nothing on economic development. The conclusion drawn was that the pattern which has emerged is extremely complex and that in many places both counties and districts are active in economic development, often undertaking similar work, although usually having different emphases. In other areas, counties have taken the lead and the districts play a supportive role. A more common situation, however, is for some of the districts in a county to be extremely active and the county involved with some joint activity with those districts, but the county concentrating its activity on areas covered by the less active districts. It is suggested by the Local Government Training Board (1986b) that there is a theoretical argument for economic development activity to be undertaken by the lowest possible tier of government since this will bring responsibility for the service as close as possible to local communities. This should also allow for consideration of local variations and encourage quick responses to the local situation. However, where economies of scale may exist then there is a case to be made on grounds of increased efficiency for the activity to be undertaken at a higher tier. Clearly, however, the issue of scale will affect different types of activity in different ways and it is thus likely that a division will occur between different levels of government in the types of activity performed.

Table 10.7 shows the percentage of district councils in Great Britain (excluding the three Scottish Island authorities), engaging in certain types of economic development activities over the last four years, taken from the Industrial Development Guide (Cambridge Information and Research Services Ltd). It shows very similar patterns of activity to those identified by Mills and Young (1986). It demonstrates very sharply that the trend in all areas of economic development work has been upward. However, certain types of activity have grown faster than others in recent years. In addition, local authorities' own provisions have been augmented through their support for local enterprise agencies. Most notable in this respect is business advice, which in 1983 was offered by less than 40 per cent of authorities, currently being available in over 75 per cent of districts. It is also clear that since 1983 more local authorities have become involved with offering both sites and premises; much of this has been under the provisions of the Local Authorities (Land) Act 1963. It is argued that these are intended to make provision in cases of market failure, where property developers see such development as either uneconomic or unprofitable. Fothergill, Monk and Perry (1987) argue that local authority funding for factory building has increasingly been available only on a selective and limited basis through specific government initiatives, and most notably the Urban Programme. Clearly, however, there is a greater tendency for smaller units and sites to be made available, which may suggest that this is an area for which the demand has been greater and for which local authorities are better able to operate (at a smaller scale).

Table 10.7 Activities engaged in by local authority districts in Britain

	1983 %	*1984* %	*1985* %	*1986* %
Serviced land	64.6	65.9	66.6	63.5
Factory development	32.1	40.2	38.9	37.6
Nursery units/workshops	63.5	70.8	74.3	75.8
Loans/grants	51.0	57.4	58.7	58.9
Rent concessions	42.4	46.2	47.3	46.2
Key-worker housing	71.2	76.5	75.6	73.4
Business advice	38.5	55.6	63.1	75.8
Sites up to 2 acres	85.9	89.0	93.0	93.6
Sites 2–10 acres	86.6	90.6	92.1	92.5
Sites over 10 acres	64.0	72.5	72.1	75.4
Premises up to 2,500ft^2	90.8	95.2	97.1	98.7
Premises 2,500–10,000ft^2	93.0	96.3	95.6	95.8
Premises over 10,000ft^2	74.1	81.1	82.6	83.3

Source: Cambridge Information and Research Services Ltd, 1983, 1984, 1985, 1986.

Another important growth area has been in the provision of nursery units and workshops, these being mainly small serviced premises for new business start-ups and often being associated with additional assistance in the form of rent and rate concessions. In recent years there has been a shift away from the provision of solely the factory space itself and increasingly towards the development of managed workshops. These attempt to provide a comprehensive business environment for new and small firms; and are often undertaken in association with other agencies. Managed workspaces are being created by local authorities, large corporations, and private speculators (these frequently involve the conversion of old industrial premises into small units). A recent estimate by the National Managed Workspace Group put the numbers of businesses associated with managed workspaces at around 18,000 (personal communication). Providing serviced land is an area in which local authorities have traditionally played an important role through their statutory responsibilities for planning. They have thus been able to co-ordinate the development of infrastructure and new industrial sites and ensure that adequate land is brought forward for development. Some two-thirds of authorities offer this as part of their economic development package. It is interesting to note that factory development is in general a less favoured option for local authorities and is an area, along with the provision of serviced sites, which has seen a decline in activity. Mills and Young (1986) suggest that the provision of sites and premises, although a widespread activity, in general tends to be only a very basic service to the industrial development process.

Loans, grants, and other financial incentives, such as rent and rate concessions, have also been used by an increasing number of authorities over the past four years, but these activities still seem to have a relatively low priority. Much has been made of the role of the local authority in providing subsidy to business, particularly through rent concessions and by providing premises at reduced rents; however, it seems that this is not necessarily a part of all local authorities' economic development packages. This form of activity has often been associated with attempts to attract footloose business activity, but has frequently been subject to criticism on the grounds that it distorts competition. Also, by offering subsidies to attract firms to their areas, local authorities may be engaging in a 'zero-sum' game, since it is argued that these activities do not stimulate additional growth but merely serve to redistribute business activity towards areas offering favourable subsidies (Harford 1979). However, this is an area of activity which has come under pressure as a consequence of increased expenditure constraints, as well as being undermined on theoretical and ideological grounds.

While local authority economic activities have seen change over time, there are also quite considerable regional variations in the provisions made by local authorities for economic development, these variations are shown in Table 10.8. In general, the level of local authority economic development activity is higher in the areas with the worst economic problems. In particular, in the South-east, East Anglia, and to some extent also the South-west, local authorities are less heavily involved with local economic development – this is particularly the case in the provision of financial support for business (through loans and grants, and rent concessions). Despite the presence of the Scottish Development Agency (SDA)[3], local authorities in Scotland are very active in economic development. The vast majority of district authorities in Scotland offer sites and premises and can provide serviced land and factory space despite the very extensive programmes operated in these areas by the SDA. One area in which Scottish authorities have lagged behind their English and Welsh counterparts, however, is in providing business advice services. This may be due in part to the existence of the SDA's Small Business Division and the support provided by the Highlands and Islands Development Board (which undertakes most of the economic development work in the Highlands and Islands area).

In Wales, local authorities are very active in all aspects of local economic development work. Although the Welsh Development Agency is engaged in developing industrial sites and premises and also with providing loan and equity finance, this does not seem to have discouraged local authorities from offering their own support programmes. In Mid-Wales further support for business is available from the Development Board for Rural Wales[4] which provides not only financial assistance but also has a major commitment to factory construction and also offers a business advisory service. In general, in both Scotland and Wales, the development agencies and local authorities perform complementary roles, frequently engaging in collaborative projects.

In England, the South-east has seen little overall activity in local direct support for economic development in recent years. Outside the new and expanding towns there is little public sector investment, other than in small units and workshops. However, fewer than 20 per cent of authorities in the South-east are prepared to build large premises and the level of financial support has contracted, possibly due in part to budgetary constraints. The exception to the general pattern in this region has been the work of the former GLC, already seen in resource terms to have been very heavily committed to local economic development. The GLC perhaps epitomized the New Left approach discussed above and its London Industrial Strategy (Greater London Council 1985) demonstrated the most coherently developed statement of these principles. This strategy made it clear that while seeking to tackle unemployment within London and to strengthen and improve public services, it sought to 'show how this (can) be done in the interests of the people who live and work in London and in ways which involve working people in the process of planning and restructuring' (Greater London Council 1985:vii). In this view planning involved the identification of new products to meet social needs based upon existing local skills to create new markets and in which the authority's role may be to provide some initial pump-priming or other assistance. In other regions, more than three-quarters of the local authorities are active in the provision of nursery units/workshops. Financial support schemes are normally available in over one half of localities in the form of loans, grants,

Table 10.8 Activities engaged in by local authority districts in Britain: by region in 1986

	SW %	*SE* %	*EA* %	*Y&H* %	*EM* %	*WM* %	*N* %	*NW* %	*Wales* %	*Scotland* %
Serviced land	56.5	30.5	80.0	73.1	80.0	66.7	89.7	86.5	67.6	92.5
Factory development	23.9	13.7	35.0	38.5	27.5	36.1	72.4	62.2	51.4	71.1
Nursery units/workshops	60.9	60.3	85.0	73.1	85.0	86.1	93.1	81.1	86.5	90.6
Loans/grants	39.1	25.2	50.0	80.8	90.0	52.8	96.6	75.7	75.7	88.7
Rent concessions	23.9	16.8	50.0	57.7	52.5	44.4	89.7	64.9	62.2	79.2
Key-worker housing	84.8	40.5	95.0	84.6	80.0	91.7	86.2	78.4	97.3	86.8
Business advice	87.0	69.5	80.0	80.8	90.0	83.3	79.3	81.1	70.3	60.4
Sites up to 2 acres	100.0	81.7	100.0	100.0	100.0	100.0	96.6	97.3	94.6	98.1
Sites 2–10 acres	95.7	82.4	100.0	96.2	97.5	94.4	96.6	100.0	94.6	96.2
Sites over 10 acres	67.4	57.3	75.0	84.6	92.5	86.1	89.7	83.8	78.4	86.8
Premises up to 2,500ft^2	100.0	96.2	100.0	100.0	100.0	97.2	100.0	100.0	100.0	100.0
Premises 2,500–10,000ft^2	100.0	96.9	90.0	92.3	97.5	94.4	100.0	97.3	94.6	90.6
Premises over 10,000ft^2	80.4	87.8	75.0	80.8	85.0	86.1	82.8	97.3	81.1	67.9

Source: Cambridge Information and Research Services Ltd, 1986.
(SW=South West, SE=South East, EA=East Anglia, Y&H=Yorkshire & Humberside, EM=East Midlands, WM=West Midlands, N=North, NW=North West.)

or rent concessions. Assistance for new and existing small businesses is available in most districts. Activities are normally greatest on smaller sites of less than two acres.

It is clear that local district councils have become increasingly involved in economic development; however, it would appear that their activities have to some extent been constrained by restraints upon public expenditure. Many local authorities have therefore become involved in working with other agencies such as the MSC, voluntary bodies, and educational institutions to establish local initiatives which are run independently from, but nevertheless receive considerable support from, the local authority. Local economic development involves drawing together and co-ordinating a variety of resources in the best interests of the local community. The nature of the problem of achieving this aim is summarized in a discussion document circulated by the Local Government Training Board:

> Clearly the financial and professional resources available currently to local authorities for economic development are minute in comparison with the scale of investment required nationally. This is not to say that they are ineffective, but rather to recognise that local authorities could achieve more if greater resources were available. However, resources are constrained, which makes it imperative that the local authority is ensuring it is securing all potential sources, and deploying its own resources to best effect.
>
> Local Government Training Board 1986a:14

Local economic initiatives

Local economic initiatives are the specific projects through which local economic development may be undertaken and these encompass a wide range of activities from assisting existing firms and encouraging new firm formation to labour training and direct employment. An analysis was made of local economic initiatives detailed by the Local Economic Development Information Services (LEDIS).[5] LEDIS provides information on a number of issues; finance, involving sources and total expenditure budgets; timing, plotting the formulation of objectives and the stages of their implementation; organization, describing the legal structure and staffing of the initiatives; details of the project's role in wider policies or programmes; and an assessment of its performance, suggesting possible lessons to be learned. The kinds of initiatives that LEDIS has examined include enterprise agencies, private sector initiatives, co-operatives, examples of youth enterprise, and projects targeted towards disadvantaged groups. It has also charted the work of a number of local authorities and multinational companies and a range of training and advice-giving initiatives.

Table 10.9 shows the types of activity being undertaken through the initiatives in the survey and the percentage of cases in which they are being practised. The results indicate the importance of information and advisory services as part of local economic development work. Nearly 80 per cent of the initiatives in the sample had associated with them some form of advisory facility. A large number of initiatives are aimed to assist business through local advice centres, such as the enterprise agencies. Others may offer advice and information as part of a package, for example, many of the managed workshops in the survey had some form of advisory facility associated with them. Labour training initiatives and those which assist in sales and marketing may also have an advisory function. Since information plays such a crucial role in local economic development, it is hardly surprising that nearly 35 per cent of initiatives use some form of advertising to communicate with clients. While some of these represent campaigns by local authorities to attract industry to their areas, the large majority are schemes which promote the work of the initiative itself. Therefore, it is difficult to make general conclusions about advertising.

The survey showed a large number of initiatives to be engaged directly in assisting with sales and marketing by providing sales outlets for products, undertaking market research on behalf of

Table 10.9 Local economic initiatives: types of activity

Type of activity	*% of cases*
Information and advice	79.9
Labour training	44.3
Provision of land/premises	39.7
Advertising	34.7
Provision of finance	25.6
Sales and marketing	21.0
Direct employment	18.3
Company formation	12.8
Equity investment	7.3
Provision of land	5.0
Loan guarantee	1.4

Source: LEDIS survey.

small businesses, or by offering advice on matters relating to marketing; usually, however, by some combination of these activities. This points again to the emphasis placed upon information as a basis for local economic development. Sophisticated marketing methods and research techniques may well be beyond the means of many small and medium sized firms but accurate market information is essential in a competitive environment. Further, many of these firms may be considering expanding their markets, often overseas, and require advice on how to develop a marketing strategy and in dealing with the extra administrative work which such an expansion would entail. It may well be that this is an area where support has previously been lacking and therefore in which there is considerable potential for local economic development work to be undertaken. Fourteen initiatives were actually offering retail outlets for local producers, particularly in the area of cottage industry activities.

Training forms all or a part of the work of about 45 per cent of the surveyed initiatives. It has been argued by Chandler and Lawless (1985) that the development of local training programmes has been a consequence of a perceived lack of central government policy or its inherent weakness in terms of local labour training requirements. Despite this view, however, the major role played by the MSC in labour training, acting through a variety of schemes, most notably the YTS and Community Programme was reflected by this survey. However, there were also a large number of initiatives which were not associated with the various MSC programmes but which involved some form of training either in production or management functions. The survey identified eighteen such initiatives as being set up by voluntary organisations. These, together with the work of the MSC, comprise a very significant number of the training placements listed in LEDIS and this would seem to confirm that there is a very considerable amount of training now being undertaken outside the company (possibly as a consequence of the reduction of apprenticeship places and the restructuring of vocational training). The survey showed that it was common for other agencies to become active in this area (often supported by MSC funds) and thus be able to influence directly the nature of training provided with MSC support. In addition to training courses, a large number of training workshops have been set up to provide training as well as employment (these are often similar in content to the schemes run by the MSC) attempting to provide the skills required by local business and to provide some assurance of long-term employment placement.

The provision of factory space has been a favoured approach for regional policy and for local authorities, the latter having statutory powers to engage in this. The survey revealed a great deal of factory development being undertaken not only by public agencies but also by private developers. However, the most notable feature of these developments were that the facilities offered frequently extended beyond merely the provision of factory space itself. Far more frequent was the development of managed workshops. These were often run as companies offering a variety of centralized services to tenants. In these units overheads such as telephone, secretarial support, cleaning, and maintenance may be managed centrally and their cost forming part of the floorspace rental. These central services may also fulfil a business advisory role in addition to physical support services. Many of the workshops were housed in converted industrial premises which had been redeveloped at low cost and were frequently eligible for grants and other assistance towards the cost of the conversion work. Conversion of property, particularly for use by small businesses, may offer a very cost-effective means of providing accommodation. An estimate by Green and Foley (1983) has suggested that the average cost of converted units is about £2.17 per square foot, as against £15 per square foot for newly-built premises.

Provision of finance comprised an element of the work of about one quarter of the local economic initiatives sampled. Providing finance to local business, or indeed other initiatives, may form an element of this type of policy action. Many initiatives may thus be serving to pump-prime business enterprises as a means of stimulating indigenous growth potential. Fifty per cent of the initiatives which were identified as having been involved with assistance by providing finance, were doing so by means of grants. The rest were using loans or other arrangements whereby conditions for returns were set prior to funds being released. The high level of commitment to these forms of assistance would suggest that there is a strong belief amongst those responsible for managing and running initiatives that financial resource constraints operate to retard economic development. Confirmation of the somewhat indirect and non-interventionist strategy which is distinctive of some approaches to local economic development activity is reflected in the very small number of initiatives (28) which have been involved with providing finance. Only a few (16) of these have made finance available by taking equity stakes in companies, and this may reflect either an unwillingness by potential financiers to invest such venture capital or an unwillingness or inappropriateness on the part of potential recipients to accept such forms of investment.

Only forty initiatives (18.3 per cent of the sample) were identified as being involved with direct employment, that is schemes set up to employ people rather than encourage or stimulate others to do it. This reinforces the notion that there is a preponderance of initiatives engaged in the stimulation rather than the actual creation of jobs as their primary objective. A number of these were training workshops which attempted to combine labour training with work experience. Clearly, however, these lie on the margin between initiatives and new enterprises but may be included in LEDIS since they illustrate rather novel forms of enterprise.

The contribution of local authorities to initiatives

The survey was able to identify the contribution made by local authorities to local economic initiatives in a number of ways. Of the 220 initiatives in the sample, almost a third (68) were set up by local authorities; however, only half of these were being managed and run by the authority and its officers. The other half being spun-off as independent activities with their own staff and legal identity. Thus while the local authority may be an important primum-mobile it is not necessarily managing a large proportion of the initiatives which it sets up.

The survey showed that in terms of financial support to initiatives local authorities were the most significant contributors. They offered support to 61.2 per cent of the sample or 135 out of a total of 219 initiatives. This may well suggest that local authorities are attempting to diversify the range of activities to which they provide support and may thus be able to have some influence over a large proportion of the economic development activities within their local area. The survey also indicated that leverage was occurring between different financiers, particularly between local, national and also the European Community. Such a finding is not particularly surprising given the nature of the rules by which such schemes are operated. However, it is illustrative of the extent to which schemes which are eligible for government agency funding may be able to secure funds from more than one programme. Particularly in their early stages of development, projects may be unattractive to the commercial lender as there is inadequate collateral, or an inability to demonstrate creditworthiness. In the analysis which follows, those initiatives which were set up by local authorities (68) are compared with the rest of the sample (151). Table 10.10 indicates the types of activities which local authorities and other agencies have become involved in setting up.

In rank terms both the local authority and the non-local authority initiatives showed broadly similar patterns of activity; however, a more detailed analysis revealed distinct variations in the proportion of activities initiated by the two groups. These indicate the way in which schemes initiated by local authorities may be characterized by a certain mix of activities and favoured approaches to local economic development. Thus while the activities of labour training, advice and information giving, and land and premises provision predominate in both groups, it is clear that the area of land and premises provision is one which is particularly favoured by local authorities. While providing land and premises is an activity in which local authorities have had considerable interest and for which they have statutory powers, there has been an increasing tendency for small factory developments to be undertaken in partnership with private developers. Advertising and giving advice and information show a very marked similarity between the two groups. As has already been stated, both of these activities are an integral part of most economic development initiatives. Advice and information being a part of the services offered by the vast majority of initiatives and advertising also being widely used to disseminate information about the area or the scheme.

It appears that initiatives set up by local authorities are more

Table 10.10 Type of activity for initiatives set up by local authority and non-local authority agencies

Type of activity	*% of cases local authority*	*% of cases non-local authority*
Information and advice	79.4	80.1
Labour training	42.6	45.0
Provision of land/premises	51.5	34.4
Advertising	36.8	33.8
Provision of finance	30.9	23.2
Sales and marketing	26.5	18.5
Direct employment	14.7	19.9
Company formation	4.4	16.6
Equity investment	11.8	5.3
Provision of land	8.8	3.3
Loan guarantee	4.4	0.0
	Total cases 68	Total cases 151

Source: LEDIS survey.

likely to offer some form of financial assistance either by direct provision of money through grants or loans, or alternatively, by taking equity stakes in firms or by providing a loan guarantee. The role of local authorities as being significant sources of funding for local economic development in general terms has been noted. This analysis would seem to suggest that where local authorities have set up initiatives, they have given some emphasis to the role of financier and thus to assistance through monetary contributions rather than more direct forms of intervention. The LEDIS analysis found companies to be assisting a large number of initiatives by seconding their own staff to projects, and it may be suggested that this is an appropriate way of providing assistance particularly to initiatives which rely very heavily upon professional expertise. In general, therefore, local authority initiatives seem much more likely to be concerned with creating the optimum conditions for economic development and in stimulating the economy rather than entering directly into its operation through their economic initiatives.

Conclusion

The foregoing analysis has presented a series of empirical assessments of the involvement of local authorities in economic development. It has been shown that although the statutory provisions and resource base upon which local government may engage in such work may be a constraining factor, nonetheless this has not prevented local authorities from expanding their role in assisting local economic development in recent years. However, it may be argued that the contemporary trends in such activities are rather more complex in their nature and operation than has been suggested by Young (1985), who presented a threefold series of processes. The first of these, rippling out, involved a shift of activity levels from the older conurbations and assisted areas to the more prosperous and non-urban regions. There is evidence to support the operation of such a process reflected in the changing patterns of local authority expenditure on economic development, and this has been particularly the case in the years since the early 1980s. However, despite the increasing resource commitment of the non-metropolitan authorities to economic development, growth of expenditure levels has also continued within the metropolitan areas. In terms of the activities in which authorities are engaged, there has been a notable growth of all forms of assistance. However, the analysis of the regional patterns of activity did seem to suggest more widespread involvement by authorities in areas with more acute economic problems.

The second process described by Young (1985) was filtering down, through which it was argued that a growing concern was being shown for economic development by the minor authorities. The evidence from the analyses in this chapter provides two insights into the operation of this process. The first concerns the relationship between the major (county and regional) authorities and the minor (district or borough) authorities, since it appears that in resource terms the relative financial commitment from each tier of local government has remained fairly constant over time. In addition, evidence has been put forward to suggest the potential role of the upper and lower tiers; that is with the county (or regional) authority acting in a strategic, policy formulation role, and the district (or borough) authority serving to implement policy; any shortfall is compensated for by the upper tier authority. The theoretical basis for such a pattern of activity has been proposed and some empirical evidence has been provided to indicate its existing implementation. The second aspect of the filtering down process is the very clear indication of an increasing diversity and more widespread uptake of a variety of economic development measures, noted in the analysis of data drawn from the Industrial Development Guide.

In order to assess the nature of the diversification process proposed by Young (1985) it is necessary to return to the findings and reservations expressed above concerning the operation of rippling out. Diversification relates in particular to the development of more interventionist strategies and it has been argued that these have been developed in particular by those authorities which espouse the theoretical tenets of local socialism. Mawson and Miller (1986) have noted that it is the Labour-controlled authorities, particularly from the traditionally more depressed areas and other urban industrial areas which have attempted to expand economic development activities. While there has been a rippling out of the activities which have previously been practised in the older urban and industrial areas, within many of these areas new strategies have been developed. Frequently these have been based upon a commitment to explore more radical approaches to economic development. It is argued by Mawson and Miller that in seeking to develop their role, local authorities in these areas have attempted to exploit their own resources (and also those of the local community) to implement policy measures and hence it is possible to account for continued expansion in the resource commitment to economic development within these areas, thus counteracting changing patterns of expenditure which might be seen to be arising as a consequence of rippling out.

An additional process which may be added to these three is collaboration, that is the joint working of local authorities and other agencies to engage in economic development, undertaken through local economic development initiatives. It has been shown that local authorities are engaged in a wide variety of schemes, either by setting them up or providing financial support to them. Such schemes often exist independently from the authority itself, frequently being registered as companies. The major advantage of working with such initiatives is that it provides a means of circumventing resource and statutory constraints which may impinge upon the authority. In addition, initiatives are frequently able to lever additional resources from a diverse range of sources. It might be argued that with increasing attempts by central government to constrain and control local government, such local initiatives provide a mechanism whereby local authorities can retain a commitment to local economic development.

Notes

1. Chartered Institute of Public Finance and Accountancy (Regular series) 'Statistical Information Service: Planning and Development Statistics', London: Chartered Institute of Public Finance and Accountancy. The analysis excludes those authorities which did not make any expenditure on local economic development or which made a null return. Similarly authorities with no enumerated economic development staff or making a null return were excluded from the analysis of employees.
2. Scottish Office (1982/83–1985/86, Annual) 'Local financial returns: Planning Services'. The analysis excludes those authorities which did not make any expenditure on industrial promotion or which made a null return.
3. The SDA was established in 1975 by Act of Parliament to stimulate industrial development and employment in Scotland. This is combined with responsibilities for environmental rehabilitation and urban renewal. The SDA is an important source of capital for industry in Scotland, providing loans or equity to re-structure existing companies and support new developments.
4. The WDA was established in 1976 by Act of Parliament to promote economic development and environmental improvement in Wales. It provides loan and equity finance for business projects, and has a large programme for investment in developing industrial sites and premises. The Development Board for Rural Wales was established in 1977 with the responsibility for promoting the economic and social development of Mid-

Wales. The Board has a broad range of powers and an annual budget of some £12m which is spent primarily on factories, housing and social and cultural facilities, and in development of manufacturing, tourism, craft, and other enterprises.

5. The Local Economic Development Information Service (LEDIS) is published by the Planning Exchange. It was launched in 1982 and is published ten times a year. Sheets are produced monthly in four series: Initiative giving examples of local initiatives; Overview giving critical reviews of broad subject areas; Bibliography providing concise literature guides; and Research in Progress giving brief accounts of current academic research. It was the Initiatives series from July 1982 to December 1985 which was taken as a sample for this survey. See Sellgren, J. (1987) 'Local economic development and local initiatives in the mid-1980s: an analysis of the Local Economic Development Information Service Database', *Local Government Studies, 13*(6), 51–68.

References

Cambridge Information and Research Services Ltd (1983–1986, Annual) *Industrial Development Guide*, Harlow: Longman.

Chandler, J.A. and Lawless, P. (1985) *Local authorities and the creation of employment*, Aldershot: Gower.

Coulson, A. (1986) *The future role and organisation of local government: Functional Study No.6: Economic Development*, Birmingham: Institute of Local Government Studies.

Craig, G., Foster, J., Green, G., and O'Malley, J. (1979) *The state and the local economy*, Newcastle Community Development Project/Political Economy Collective in association with Publication Distribution Cooperative.

Fothergill, S., Monk, S., and Perry, M. (1987) *Property and industrial development*, London: Hutchinson.

Gilhespy, D., Jones, K., Manwaring, T., Neuburger, H., and Sharples, A. (1986) *Socialist enterprise: reclaiming the economy*, Nottingham: Spokesman.

Greater London Council (1985) *The London industrial strategy*, London: GLC.

Green, D.H. and Foley, P. (1983) 'Making homes for small firms', *Town and Country Planning*, 52(1):17–20.

Harford, I. (1979) 'Restructuring the state and the inner city' in Craig, G., Foster, J., Green, G., and O'Malley, J. (Eds) *The state and the local economy*, Newcastle Community Development Project/Political Economy Collective in association with Publication Distribution Cooperative, 11–18.

Hausner, V. (1986) (Ed.) *Critical issues in urban economic development*: volume I, Oxford: Clarendon Press.

JURUE (1980) *Local authority employment initiatives*, Birmingham: Joint Unit for Research on the Urban Environment.

Local Government Training Board (1986a) *The contribution of local government to local economic development: a discussion paper*, Local Government Training Board.

Local Government Training Board (1986b) *The division of local economic development between counties and districts: a background paper*, Local Government Training Board.

Mawson, J. and Miller, D. (1986) 'Interventionist approaches in local employment and economic development: the experience of Labour local authorities' in Hausner, V. (Ed.) *Critical Issues in Urban Economic Development: volume I*, Oxford: Clarendon Press.

Mills, L. and Young, K. (1986) 'Local authorities and economic development: a preliminary analysis' in Hausner, V. (Ed.) *Critical Issues in Urban Economic Development: volume I*, Oxford: Clarendon Press.

Municipal Yearbook (1987) (Annual) *Municipal yearbook and public services directory*, London: Municipal Publications Ltd.

Perry, M. (1986) *Small factories and economic development*, Aldershot: Gower.

Ramsdale, P. and Capon, S. (1986) 'An analysis of local authority discretionary expenditure 1984–85' in Department of the Environment, Scottish Office, Welsh Office, *The conduct of local authority business*: *Research Volume IV*: *Aspects of local democracy*, Cmnd 9801 London: HMSO.

Widdicombe, D. (1986) *The conduct of local authority business: Report of the committee of enquiry into the conduct of local authority business*, Cmnd 9797, London: HMSO.

Young, K. (1985) 'Organising for economic development', in ESRC Inner Cities Research Programme, *Strengthening local economic development*, London: ESRC.

Appendix 1

Act	*Power*	*Posible initiatives*
Employment and Training Act 1973 S8	Provision of careers advice service for authorities with responsibility for education	Undertake schemes under the MSC's Youth Training programme
Town and Country Planning Act 1971 Ss6,7,11 (Town and Country Planning (Scotland) Act 1972 Ss4,5,9)	Local allocation, survey of area, prepare structure plans, local plans	Allocate land for future development
Education Act 1944 S7 (Education (Scotland) Act 1962 S1)	Duty to provide efficient education for needs of the population	Work sampler courses
Education Act 1944 S8 (Education (Scotland) Act 1962 S1)	Provision of primary schools (inc. nursery schools and classes)	Nursery school provision
Education Act 1944 S42 (Education (Scotland) Act 1962 S4)	Preparation of Further Education schemes to be submitted for approval to Sec. of State	Training courses
Housing Act 1985 S8	Duty for LA to consider the housing needs of their areas with respect to provision of further housing accommodation	Housing for incoming workers Allocation policies to improve intra housing authority labour mobility
Local Government Act 1972 S203 (Local Government (Scotland) Act 1973 S151)	Provision of co-ordinated and efficient systems of public transport to meet the needs of the County	New roads Road improvement Traffic management schemes
Local Government Act 1972 S203 Local Government (Scotland) Act 1973 S151)	Grants towards costs incurred by persons carrying passenger transport undertakings Powers to subsidise public transport by County or districts to make grants to transport undertakings	Specific route subsidies General fare subsidies
Transport Act 1968 S34	Assistance for rural bus and ferry services	Grants for upkeep of services. Provide support for train services
Transport Act 1968 S37	Power for local authorities to acquire or dispose of public service vehicle undertakings	

Act	*Power*	*Possible initiatives*
Transport Act 1968 S56	Powers to assist provision, improvement or development of public transport facilities to benefit the local area	
Transport Act 1985 S63	Powers for counties to secure provision of public transport and devising policies for such provision	
Transport Act 1985 S106	Grants to assist in the provision of public transport facilities	
Local Government Act 1972 Ss120,121,122,123 (Local Government (Scotland) Act 1973 Ss70,71,72,73,74,75)	Powers for principal councils to deal with land transactions, acquisition, disposal and appropriation of land	
Town and Country Planning Act 1971 S124 (Town and Country Planning (Scotland) Act 1972 S114)	Development of land held for planning purposes by LA or in association with another authorised association, or to undertake repairs and maintenance and general management	Provision of a variety of serviced sites for industrial development
Town and Country Planning Act 1971 S29 (Town and Country Planning (Scotland) Act 1972 S26)	Determination of applications for planning permission Development control	Development control policies Decrease time taken to process applications
Town and Country Planning Act 1971 S51 (Town and Country Planning (Scotland) Act 1972 S49)	Order of discontinuance of use, alteration or removal of buildings or works	Review of policies to re-locate non-conforming uses
Town and Country Planning Act 1971 S52 (Town and Country Planning (Scotland) Act 1972 S50)	Agreements regulating development and use of land to restrict or regulate use either permanently or for a fixed period of time This may include financial incentives	
Town and Country Planning Act 1971 S112 (Town and Country Planning (Scotland) Act 1972 S102)	Power to compulsorily acquire land in connection with development and for other planning purposes	
Town and Country Planning Act 1971 S122 (Town and Country Planning (Scotland) Act 1972 S)	Power to appropriate any land held for planning purposes	

Town and Country Planning Act 1971 S123 (Town and Country Planning (Scotland) Act 1972 S113)	Power to dispose of land held for planning purposes	
Town and Country Planning Act 1971 S250 (Town and Country Planning (Scotland) Act 1972 S237)	Power for the Sec. of State to grant aid to local authorities for the acquisition of land	
Local Authorities (Land) Act 1963 Ss1,2,3,4	Loans for erection of buildings on land sold or let by LAs serviced by a mortgage of the land in respect of which the advance is made (up to 75% valuation). Loans in pursuance of building agreements for buildings on land owned by LA. Sale of LA land to the developer	Loans for building
Local Authorities (Land) Act 1963 S2	LA development of land; erection of buildings or construction works upon land (subject to Minister's consent) to improve the land. Also to repair, maintain and insure any building or works erected or constructed	Provision of advance factories, warehouses and small units
Local Government Act 1972 S137 (Local Government (Scotland) Act 1973 S83)	Power to incur expenditure in interests of the area or its inhabitants up to a maximum of a 2p rate product	
Local Authority Superannuation Regulations 1974 & 1984	Power to invest up to 10% of superannuation funds in unquoted securities	Invest funds in local firms
Local Government Act 1972 S111 (Local Government (Scotland) Act 1973 S69)	Power to do anything conducive to the discharge of their functions	Create economic/industrial development units
Local Government Act 1972 S142 (Local Government (Scotland) Act 1973 S88)	Provision of information on matters relating to local government	Promotion, land and property registers
Local Government Act 1972 S112 (Local Government (Scotland) Act 1973 S64)	Appointment of staff	Industrial development officers
Local Government Act 1972 S141 (Local Government (Scotland) Act 1973 S87)	Power for county authority to undertake research and collect information relating to the County	Survey of local economy
Local Government Act 1972 S90 (Local Government (Scotland) Act 1973 S90)	Power to encourage tourism and provide conference and exhibition facilities	Promote tourism

Act	*Power*	*Possible initiatives*
Local Government Act 1972 S135 (Local Government (Scotland) Act 1973 S81)	Provision for LAs to make standing orders with respect to contracts for supply of goods or materials or execution of works	Contract compliance schemes
Local Government (Miscellaneous Provisions) Act 1976 S28 (Local Government (Scotland) Act 1975 S16)	Allows unlimited discretionary spending from unspent balances, through the creation of funds	
Local Authority (Miscellaneous Provisions) Act 1982 S45 (Local Government and Planning (Scotland) Act 1966 S11)	Powers to enter into arrangements with the MSC	
Local Government Act 1966 S11 (Local Government (Scotland) Act 1966 S11)	Powers for the Sec. of State to make grants to local authorities who make special provisions for Commonwealth immigrants	
Health Services and Public Health Act 1968 S65	Allows for a wide range of voluntary sector bodies undertaking an activity which could be done by the local authority	
Civic Restaurants Act 1947 S1	An Act to empower local authorities to establish and run restaurants and provide meals and refreshments to the public	Municipal restaurants
Slaughterhouse Act 1974 S15	Provision of public slaughterhouses by local authorities	Municipal slaughterhouses
Food act 1984 S50	Powers for local authorities to establish or acquire markets	Municipal markets
Local Government Planning and Land Act 1980 Ss5,6	Powers to set up direct labour organizations	
Education (Work Experience) Act 1973 S3 (Education (Scotland) Act 1980 S123	To enable local authorities to arrange for children under school-leaving age to have work experience as part of their education	

Local Authorities (Goods and Services) Act 1970 S1	Provision for local authorities to supply materials, goods, professional, administrative or technical services, use of equipment and the carrying out of works to other local authorities or public bodies
Race Relations Act 1976 S71	Duty of local authority to eliminate racial discrimination and to promote equality of opportunity and good relations, between persons of different racial groups
Employment and Training Act 1973 S8	Provision of careers services by education authorities
Industrial and Training Act 1964 S16	Facilities for further education provided by a local education authority should include facilities for vocational and industrial training
Education Act 1944 S41 (Education (Scotland) Act 1962 S1)	Provision of adequate facilities for further education by local education authorities

Provisions relate to Great Britain. Where separate legislation exists for England and Wales and for Scotland the latter are given in brackets.

Revised and extended from JURUE (1980) and Coulson (1986).

11

Public policy and local development: the case of Stevenage New Town[1]

J.C. Philpott

Introduction

In constructing the legislative framework for establishing Urban Development Corporations (UDCs) in designated inner city areas under the Local Government, Planning and Land Act (1980), the first Thatcher administration took as its model the New Town Development Corporations (see Buck *et al.* 1986; Klausner 1987). The latter date back to the New Towns Act (1946) which initiated a State financed programme to build self-contained centres of population and employment within designated areas outside Britain's major conurbations.[2]

An independent Development Corporation was set up to plan each New Town. These were appointed by a Minister of State but retained autonomy over planning and day-to-day affairs and were independent of existing local authority in the designated areas. In order to fulfil its remit a Development Corporation was given extensive powers of land purchase and disposal, and was provided with public finance sufficient to build houses, factories and essential infrastructure. These powers and resources were to be maintained until the town reached roughly 75 per cent of its designated population, at which point the Corporation was to be wound up, the management of outstanding public assets transferred to a national body (The Commission for New Towns), and authority to plan the town's further expansion given to elected local councils.

Many of the twenty-eight New Towns developed in this way in Britain since 1946 today exhibit the benefits of outer city prosperity, providing homes and jobs in pleasant semi-rural environments. The contrast with inner city locations deprived of investment is stark, and the role of the UDCs is thus to replicate the new town success in the older urban areas. Ironically, however, the ideological foundations of the UDCs are vastly different from those of their New Town forebears; they are not to be an adjunct of planning but rather a means to override planning constraints and thus underpin the market.[3] It is often suggested, therefore, that the attractiveness of the Development Corporation model to a Conservative Government lies primarily in the Corporations' ability to avoid interference from elected local opposition (see, for example, Duncan and Goodwin, 1985).

Unfortunately, it is precisely this feature of Development Corporations that may prove the least conducive to successful economic management since it often allows the short-term interests of participants in both public and private sectors to prevail over the longer-term needs of the local economy and community. This is well documented in studies of individual New Towns (e.g. Grieco 1984) and is clearly demonstrated by the example of uneven development in Stevenage which highlights the error of pursuing public policy in the absence of local accountability.

Stevenage 1946–80: from balanced to imbalanced development

The initial (or Mark 1) phase of the New Towns programme consisted of eight towns situated in the London-ring with the purpose of attracting people and jobs away from the congested metropolis. Stevenage, some thirty miles to the north of London and close to developing transport and communications networks, was chosen as the site for the first of these, and the town of 75,000 inhabitants which has subsequently developed represents to many the archetypal New Town.[4]

The original Stevenage Master Plan drawn up by the Development Corporation certainly exhibits the classic New Town ideals and aspirations (see Orlans, 1952; Mullan 1980). Stevenage was to be a self-contained social and economic community, devoid of significant numbers of commuters. There was to be a balance between jobs and households, the growth of which would be planned so as to ensure the maintenance of equilibrium as the town matured. The concept of balance extended in turn to the characteristics of both the economic and social structures: there was to be an 'ideal mix' of social classes, and a balanced industrial structure, the latter requiring the Development Corporation to endeavour to avoid specialization by accommodating a broad range of sectors.

In hindsight, Stevenage, along with many other New Towns, has failed to realize these aspirations to their full extent. Explanation for this in part lies in the New Town ideals themselves which were sometimes vague and often contradictory (Cooke 1983). More important, however, is the fact that many New Towns came to depend upon a fairly limited range of industry and employment (in extreme cases one sector or even an individual company) giving rise to what Grieco has called 'imbalanced development'.

Sectoral imbalance, for example, was clearly evident in Stevenage by the early 1970s (Table 11.1) and reflected the pattern of

Table 11.1 The employment structure of Stevenage, 1971

SIC 1968		*Stevenage Total*	*Stevenage %*	*GB %*	*Location Quotient*
I	Ag., For., Fish.	295	0.87	1.94	0.45
II	Mining, etc.	16	0.05	1.81	0.03
	All primary	311	0.92	3.26	0.28
III	Food, etc.	122	0.36	3.33	0.11
IV	Coal, etc.	–	–	0.20	–
V	Chemicals, etc.	–	–	2.00	–
VI	Metal Man.	294	0.87	2.57	0.34
VII	Mech. Eng.	1,623	4.80	4.79	1.01
VIII	Inst. Eng.	3,640	10.77	0.75	14.48
IX	Elec. Eng.	1,847	5.46	3.69	1.49
X	Shipbuilding	–	–	0.84	–
XI	Vehicles	6,665	19.72	3.72	5.34[(a)]
XII	Metal Goods nes.	370	1.09	2.64	0.42
XIII	Textiles	–	–	2.68	–
XIV	Leather, etc.	23	0.07	0.21	0.31
XV	Clothing, etc.	136	0.40	1.98	0.20
XVI	Bricks, etc.	79	0.23	1.39	0.16
XVII	Timber, etc.	725	2.14	1.21	1.78
XVIII	Paper, etc.	737	2.18	2.72	0.85
XIX	Other Manufacturing	2,047	6.06	1.52	4.01
	All manufacturing	18,308	54.20	36.40	1.50
XX	Construction	1,081	3.20	5.54	0.58
XXI	Gas, Water, Elec.	96	0.28	1.20	0.23
XXII	Trans./Comm.	820	2.42	7.13	0.34
XXIII	Distributive T.	4,041	11.96	11.80	1.02
XXIV	Insurance etc.	594	1.75	4.44	0.39
XXV	Prof. and Sci.	4,966	14.78	13.47	1.10
XXVI	Misc. Servs.	2,304	6.82	8.80	0.77
XXVII	Public Admin.	1,266	3.74	6.80	0.55
	All services	13,991	41.40	54.07	0.75
	All industry	33,787	100.00	100.00	–

Source: Annual Census of Employment (ER II) Returns, Department of Employment.
Note: (a) The location quotient for MLH 383 (i.e. Aerospace) is 22.9.

development experienced in the town's formative years. Throughout these years manufacturing accounted for an above average proportion of total employment, much of it concentrated in a limited number of sectors (notably aerospace, instrumentation and electrical engineering).

This was in part the consequence of a curious lack of co-ordination at the national level between government departments responsible for related elements of policy. Conflict emerged between those departments responsible for the New Towns programme (which formed part of intra-regional and physical planning policy) and those responsible for industrial location and regional policy (see Aldridge 1979).

In several cases, for example, New Towns including Stevenage faced difficulty in attracting mobile industry because of the existence of incentives given to firms to locate in Britain's depressed areas and controls upon industrial development in the South East. Particularly important in this respect were Industrial Development Certificates (IDCs) which had to be obtained by manufacturing firms before they could build plant in excess of a specific floor-space limit (the limit in the 1950s being as low as 5,000 sq.ft.).

In certain cases, however, exemptions would be granted to exceed these limits if the production in question had considerable technological and export potential and/or contributed to the national defence capability. Moreover, it gradually became clear to firms engaged in such activities that exemptions to build extensive plant would be granted more freely if located in New Towns (Aldridge, 1979; Balchin, 1980).

The 1950s thus witnessed large-scale investment in Stevenage by firms such as English Electric Ltd and De Havilland (later BAC and Hawker Siddely and more recently consolidated into British Aerospace Dynamics), ICL, British Visqueen (ICI Plastics), Kodak, Marconi and Taylor Instruments. Of these the aerospace companies, primarily involved in the production of guided weapons, were the largest and their dominance in employment terms served to harness the fortunes of Stevenage to the level of State defence expenditure.

In addition to the limited sectoral distribution of this investment, the sheer size of the plants established and their corporate status gave rise to other forms of imbalance. Plant size imbalance, for example, has been an enduring characteristic of Stevenage's industrial structure. By the mid-1970s, two aerospace plants accounted for a fifth of total employment in the town whilst the ten largest manufacturing plants together accounted for well over a third.

Perhaps even more important than size *per se*, however, is the fact that the majority of these large plants occupied subsidiary positions in the spatial structures of production of their respective corporations. With the exception of aerospace, Stevenage's major manufacturing plants have tended to be branch plants or wholly owned subsidiaries of UK or foreign companies (see Stevenage Borough Council 1982); in general, Stevenage has lacked headquarters activities, and given this corporate imbalance the town has taken a subordinate role in what Massey (1984) calls firms' 'spatial divisions of labour'.

The consequences of imbalance

The effects of such forms of imbalance extended beyond the manufacturing sector to other aspects of the town's social and economic structure. The social structure, for example, has to a large extent been conditioned by the employment needs of the town's major employers.

The initial populations of New Towns consisted of workers imported from elsewhere and, in order to achieve this without disrupting other objectives, Development Corporations operated 'key worker' housing policies. In most cases housing was therefore made available only to workers moving in with a re-locating employer or whose skills were those required by existing employers. In Stevenage, the requirement was predominantly for skilled and semi-skilled manual workers, most employers having relatively little need for professional and managerial staff given the lack of headquarters functions in the town.

The result was a social structure which by the mid-1960s was noticeably different from that observed in the South-east as a whole (Table 11.2), and this in turn influenced the rate of structural change within the New Town's economy by affecting the pattern of local demand for services.

It had, of course, been expected that it would take time for indigenous service sectors to develop in a New Town, for reasons associated with the town's immaturity and the age structure of the population. What was surprising, however, was the slow rate of growth of such sectors.

The private consumer services sector, for example, developed particularly slowly, Stevenage being one of only seven Metropolitan Economic Labour Areas identified by Marquand (1983) as being acutely deficient in a range of consumer services in 1971. Marquand suggests that such a deficiency is likely in areas (typified

Table 11.2 Economically active males[a] by socio-economic group, 1966

SEG	*Stevenage* %	*South East* %	*England and Wales* %
Employers and Managers	8.4	12.3	10.1
Professional Workers	7.5	5.9	4.6
Intermediate Non-Manual	7.8	5.4	4.5
Junior Non-Manual	14.4	15.7	12.7
Foreman and Supervisory Manual	4.0	3.3	3.6
Skilled Manual	33.5	27.8	31.3
Semi-Skilled Manual	16.3	12.5	14.9
Unskilled Manual	4.6	7.2	8.1
Personal Service and Own Account	2.8	5.5	4.6
Farmers, Forces and Indefinite	0.7	4.4	5.6
Total	100.0	100.0	100.0

Sources: Census, 1966; Mullan 1980.
Note: (a) Males aged 15 and over.

at the time by Stevenage) lacking significant numbers of professional and managerial workers.

The service sector did, however, improve in the 1970s, as Annual Census of Employment returns illustrate (Table 11.3). Service employment expanded both absolutely and relative to manufacturing, and by 1981 accounted for roughly half of the town's total employment. The rate of growth was far greater than that in the economy as a whole particularly, toward the latter part of the period, in financial services. More generally, Stevenage has shared in the relative prosperity of the South-east where employment in personal services and distribution grew rapidly throughout the 1970s (SERPLAN 1985). Having said this, of course, one should note that the proportion of service employment in Stevenage by 1981 was still lower than that found in Britain as a whole; Stevenage continued to exhibit the characteristics of a 'manufacturing' town.

Service sector growth in the 1970s and early 1980s was, however, paralleled by a severe recession in local manufacturing. A town with such an imbalanced industrial structure was bound to face difficulty in the wake of national and international recession, and Stevenage thus suffered two waves of manufacturing redundancies. The first, in 1975–6 resulted in the loss of 2,000 manufacturing jobs (i.e. an 11 per cent reduction) and was the cause of a 7 per cent decline in total employment. This was followed by a further 6,000 redundancies between 1977 and 1982

Table 11.3 Employment change 1971–81 by industrial orders: Stevenage and Great Britain

SIC 1968		*% Change 1971–81* *Stevenage*	*Great Britain*	*Location Quotient 1981*
I	Ag., For., Fish.	−35.6	−11.8	0.28
II	Mining, etc.	512.5	−15.0	0.15
	All primary	24.6	−13.4	0.24
III	Food, etc.	366.4	−15.5	0.49
IV	Coal, etc.	–[(a)]	−36.4	–
V	Chemicals, etc.	–[(a)]	−7.4	–
VI	Metal Man.	−27.9	−43.5	0.36
VII	Mech. Eng.	−41.1	−26.1	0.68
VIII	Inst. Eng.	−64.2	−18.9	5.34
IX	Elec. Eng.	−7.1	−15.6	1.39
X	Shipbuilding	–	−21.3	–
XI	Vehicles	23.6	−26.9	7.63
(MLH 383	Aerospace)	16.7	−12.3	27.09
XII	Metal Goods nes.	−41.6	−22.2	0.26
XIII	Textiles	–[(a)]	−45.7	0.05
XIV	Leather, etc.	−0.1	−34.8	0.35
XV	Clothing, etc.	−94.8	−38.2	0.01
XVI	Bricks, etc.	178.5	−29.2	0.56
XVII	Timber, etc.	−7.4	−18.2	1.69
XVIII	Paper, etc.	−21.4	−13.6	0.62
XIX	Other Manufacturing	−68.4	−25.5	1.41
	All manufacturing	−12.3	−24.9	1.65
XX	Construction	−17.2	−10.8	0.46
XXI	Gas, Water, Elec.	−9.4	−8.4	0.22
XXII	Trans./Comm.	21.7	−8.2	0.38
XXIII	Distributive T.	17.3	6.4	0.95
XXIV	Insurance etc.	435.8	35.9	1.32
XXV	Prof. and Sci.	−44.8	23.5	0.46
XXVI	Misc. Servs.	61.7	32.7	0.90
XXVII	Public Admin.	45.5	2.9	0.74
	All services	23.2	15.3	0.79
	All industry	2.3	−2.3	

Source: Annual Census of Employment, Department of Employment.
Note: (a) There were no workers recorded in these Orders in 1971. By 1981, however, there were 42 employees in Order IV, 622 in Order V, and 31 in Order XIII.

(i.e. one in seven of all jobs available in Stevenage in the former year) many of them associated with the closure of manufacturing branch plants.

Several of the biggest plants (e.g., the Kodak plant, ICI Plastics, and Bowaters Packaging) were closed as companies rationalized or restructured in response to falling demand and rising international competition. Most of the other manufacturing plants shed labour without full closure, although in some cases this entailed the re-location of entire production divisions (Platignum, for example, retained its plastics division in Stevenage whilst re-locating pen manufacture).

The one exception amongst the dominant manufacturers was British Aerospace which actually expanded employment by 9 per cent during the recession period 1979–81. The success of this company reflects the influence of support from the central government; the Thatcher administration considerably increasing expenditure on guided weapons and electronic equipment. Somewhat ironically, Stevenage's extreme dependence upon defence, whilst always a potential source of vulnerability, has thus in recent years proved to be its greatest strength.

Indeed it was largely the resilience of aerospace which sustained the growth of local services referred to earlier, and assisted a 4 per cent increase in total employment in Stevenage between 1979 and 1981. This, however, merely disguised the magnitude of the manufacturing recession, the effects of which are more readily monitored by the figures for unemployment.

Registered unemployment in Stevenage rose from 1,500 to 5,000 in less than a year between 1981 and 1982, the impact of recession being exacerbated by Stevenage's high labour supply characteristics. 'High supply' in Stevenage in the late 1970s and early 1980s resulted from the emergence onto the labour market of the town's 'second generation', i.e. the children of those, mainly young, families that originally settled in the New Town in the 1950s and 1960s. When combined with substantial job losses in manufacturing, this 'bulge' of young workers was sufficient to produce a 'job shortfall' (Owen *et al.* 1984) in the town.

The official unemployment rate in Stevenage reached 12.6 per cent in 1982 (roughly half the total consisting of individuals aged under 25). This was higher than the average for the South-east (10.5 per cent) and similar to the GB average (13 per cent); thus in spite of being located in the relatively prosperous South-east region Stevenage might well have joined the list of Britain's unemployment 'black spots' had it not been for the hidden subsidy of State defence contracts.

In addition to unemployment, 'job shortfall' has resulted in a substantial increase (13 per cent over the decade to 1981) in the level of out-commuting from Stevenage. Moreover, the most recent population estimates indicate that there was net out-migration from Stevenage between 1983 and 1984; the first time that this has occurred in the New Town's history (Stevenage Borough Council 1985). Clearly, therefore, the initial failure to ensure balanced development in Stevenage has, under the influence of economic recession and structural change, served to undermine the town's self-containment, one of the basic ideals of the original New Town planners.

Imbalanced development: the role of the development corporation

One might ask why the Stevenage Development Corporation (SDC), charged with the task of balanced industrial development and backed up by considerable injections of public resources, managed instead to preside over the creation of structural imbalance?

One possibility is that the constraints upon the SDC reduced its ability to fulfil its task as expected. For example, the policy conflicts at national level referred to earlier seem to have conditioned the types of industry able to locate in Stevenage. Given this one can hardly criticize the SDC for accepting whatever industry it could obtain in the town's formative years; it had, after all, been given the responsibility to develop a new industrial town and was eager to fill sites within the designated area as quickly as possible.

Criticism of the SDC is perhaps more justified when directed at its failure to adjust policies once the signs of imbalance began to emerge in the 1960s and 1970s. Even here, however, it can be argued that the SDC faced constraints, most particularly from local physical land use policy.

Whilst the SDC had planning authority within the New Town's designated area, it had to ensure that its plans fitted into County Development and Structure Plans. This meant having to conform to the planning strictures of Hertfordshire County Council, an authority which maintained a policy of restraint upon development in order to protect the County's rural Green Belt (see Wray *et al.* 1974; Hertfordshire County Council 1986).

The strength of this constraint was evident throughout the 1960s and 1970s: the County Council opposed any significant expansion of Stevenage and was supported in this by a strong environmentalist lobby (as frequent Public Inquiries into expansion plans for Stevenage illustrate, see Mullan 1980). In such a context the SDC was forced to pursue its own policies within a finite area of some

2,500 hectares, less than 10 per cent of which was zoned for industrial or commercial development.

Somewhat ironically, therefore, Stevenage exhibited a poor 'urban structure'; a feature normally associated with the cramped inner cities rather than outer city locations such as New Towns (Fothergill and Gudgin 1982). This created awkward problems for the SDC. It was forced to choose between either re-designating available land to provide sites for more diverse forms of industry, or instead providing land for the expansion of its established employers, many of whom frequently submitted proposals arguing that their floor space requirements were increasing.

The overriding tendency was for the SDC to choose the latter option, since there were short-term advantages to be gained from responding to the needs of local vested interests. Mullan (1980), for example, suggests that the SDC fell prey to the strong lobbying influence of the town's dominant manufacturing firms, i.e. its main source of investment and jobs. According to Mullan, whilst the SDC realized the need to broaden the town's economic base it also recognized that an ardent policy of diversification might threaten its relations with the town's main employers or undermine their confidence in its ability to manage the town's affairs.

The SDC thus avoided action (although not policy rhetoric) on the issue of diversification which would have required setting limits on established firms' expansion plans. This not only resulted in a failure to improve the town's sectoral imbalance, but also (as Wray *et al.* 1974 indicate) exacerbated the problem of plant size imbalance since the expansion of the large established firms served to displace smaller firms or prevented them from growing. As this occurred, of course, the importance of the large employers to the SDC became ever more entrenched; as Mullan puts it, the major employers, in the guise of the Stevenage Industrial Employers Group (the chairman of which was on the board of the SDC), had the SDC 'over a barrel'.

It remains unclear as to whether an active policy of diversification at the time would have protected Stevenage from the ravages of recession in the late 1970s and 1980s since this would have depended upon the types of sectors and firms involved. The simple introduction of a broader range of manufacturing branch plants, for example, would probably have had little beneficial effect. A greater emphasis on services, however, might have produced more employment stability, particularly given the apparent buoyancy of service employment in the town in spite of the considerable restructuring in manufacturing.

Moreover, the failure of the SDC to reduce its dependence upon manufacturing appears even greater when one considers the relative performance of the town's manufacturing sector in the 1960s and 1970s. When set against figures for manufacturing employment change by different types of areas covering the period 1960–78, the relative performance of Stevenage appears poor (Table 11.4).

Table 11.4 Manufacturing employment change by type of area, 1960–78

Area type	*% Change in manufacturing employment 1960–78*	
London	−42.5	
Conurbations	−26.5	
Free Standing Cities	−13.8	
Large Towns	−2.2	(7.2)[b]
Small Towns	15.7	(18.7)[b]
Rural Areas	38.0	(43.7)[b]
New Towns	26.0	
Stevenage[a]	9.0	
Great Britain	−11.5	

Sources: Figures other than those for Stevenage have been taken from Fothergill *et al.* 1983. Figures for Stevenage obtained from Annual Census of Employment (ERII) Returns, Department of Employment.
Notes: (a) Figure for Stevenage calculated for period 1961–78.
(b) Figures in brackets refer to change exhibited by these areas if situated in Southern England. It should be remembered that the fastest growth in Stevenage will have occurred in the 1950s.

Stevenage achieved only half the average rate of manufacturing growth attained by 'small towns' (i.e. districts including at least one settlement with between 35,000 and 10,000 people) in Southern England (Fothergill *et al.* 1983). Stevenage thus benefited less than one might have expected from the so-called 'urban-rural shift' in the location of manufacturing that took place in Britain from the late 1950s onward. Moreover, although (as Table 11.3 illustrated) employment decline in Stevenage was less than the national average over the decade to 1981, the 10 per cent decline in manufacturing employment suffered during the sub-period 1974–78 was far greater than that experienced in Britain as a whole (−2.6 per cent), and well above the rate for the New Towns (−3.5 per cent) (Fothergill *et al.* 1983).

To some extent, of course, this relatively poor performance reflects the fact that Stevenage experienced growth most rapidly during its formative years in the 1950s (i.e. a period for which suitable comparative data are not available). Similarly, in later years Stevenage may have been disadvantaged *vis-à-vis* similar towns by its location in an area of restraint, the resulting poor urban structure being somewhat less conducive to employment growth. None the less, the reality of this performance when added to the sheer structural vulnerability of the town's industrial structure highlights the degree to which the SDC failed in its initial objective of creating a balanced and robust local economy.

Stevenage after the development corporation

The decision to begin winding-up the Stevenage Development Corporation was made in 1977, just at the time when the more serious consequences of the town's structural weaknesses were beginning to appear. It was, of course, always intended that this would occur once the DC had fulfilled its development brief, although the announcement came as a surprise. The decision did not, however, serve as an indictment upon the SDC but reflected instead a reduction in the level of resources available to the New Towns programme by the Labour Government. This echoed a general change in urban policy from the late 1970s: the focus of attention switched to the inner cities, finding expression under Mrs Thatcher's 'New Right' Conservative Administration in the form of such bodies as the Urban Development Corporations referred to earlier (Employment Institute 1987).

The legislation heralding the UDCs reached the statute book in 1980 at about the same time that power was finally transferred from the Stevenage Development Corporation to the Labour controlled local district council, i.e. Stevenage Borough Council. The latter, relatively inexperienced in managing economic development after forty years in the shadow of its powerful predecessor, could hardly have taken charge at a more inopportune time with the town facing serious difficulties.

In pursuing its own 'interventionist' development strategy the Borough Council has proclaimed the need to learn from the errors of the Development Corporation era by endeavouring to accommodate a wide range of local interests in the policy making process and ensuring that the power of vested interests is contained. Policy statements thus state the need to control 'market forces':

> Some control of market forces is essential. They are after all not immutable but rather the result of the conscious decisions and actions of many interested parties. It would be an abdication of responsibility by the agencies and authorities concerned to allow Stevenage to suffer the consequences of others actions

> without attempting to manage the situation to the town's best advantage.
>
> (Stevenage Borough Council, 1986:5)

This is a clear reference to the need to avoid a repetition of the experience of 1977–82 when the town suffered from corporate restructuring on the part of a few firms, and underlies a more general realization of the need to tackle corporate and plant size imbalance as well as the problem of sectoral imbalance.

This approach has not, however, been pursued amidst a mood of hostility toward local industrialists. On the contrary, the Borough Council has continued to maintain close relations with major local firms. The prevailing attitude has been that co-operation with industry is vital if policy objectives are to be realized (an attitude confounding the general portrayal of Labour local authorities as 'militant' or 'anti-business').

To some extent this attitude reflects a mood of pragmatism in the face of financial and legal constraints; the Borough Council simply could not afford to finance an independent development strategy. A policy of 'Keynesianism in One Borough', or direct investment in local enterprise, would require far more expenditure than currently permitted by the Local Government Act (1972) (i.e. the product of a 2p rate which in Stevenage would raise roughly £250,000 per annum).

In addition, the Council has had difficulty in acquiring land for development given that ownership of public assets left undeveloped by the SDC was transferred to a central authority, the Commission for New Towns. The Commission has constrained the Borough Council's room for manoeuvre and even at times frustrated its plans; the Commission has been slowly releasing assets for development to the private sector (as part of the Central Government's privatization policy), often with little regard as to whether the activity concerned conformed with the Borough Council's view of local development.

Faced with such constraints, the Borough Council has been forced to fight the kind of rearguard action typical of many smaller local authorities in the 1980s by, for example, relying on national advertising campaigns to attract public and private investment, providing support for small firms' initiatives, and encouraging the development of co-operatives, etc. It is in these latter activities in particular that the Borough Council has sought co-operation with local firms in order to secure a degree of financial leverage. In so doing it has exploited an important element of the New Town inheritance, i.e. the network of formal and informal contacts between policy makers and local industrialists which flourished under the SDC.

One might interpret from this that Mullan, writing in the late 1970s, was justified in his fear that the Borough Council would simply find itself in the same position as its precedessors, i.e. 'in the pocket' of local industrialists. This remains a possibility, although what Mullan failed to anticipate was the strength of 'localism' (Cooke 1986) in the 1980s. This has resulted in the integration into the policy process of other groups within Stevenage (such as trade unions and community groups) alongside employers and elected representatives, and led the Borough Council to instigate co-operation between like-minded authorities in the South-east region under the umbrella of the South East Economic Development Strategy (SEEDS 1986).

Whether such general localism will be sufficient to reduce the power of the industrial lobby in Stevenage remains unclear, as does the effect of current policy upon the problems of imbalance, although in this latter respect recent trends indicate some improvement.

Borough Council surveys of the period 1980–85, for example, indicate absolute and relative growth in the service sector (Table 11.5). Services accounted for nearly 55 per cent of total employment in Stevenage by 1985, and although comparatively low (the service sector accounting for well over 60 per cent of total employment in Britain as a whole) this reflects the fact that Stevenage is sharing in the expansion of growth sectors such as financial services.

Stevenage has, for example, experienced an influx of investment by foreign (mostly Canadian) insurance companies, some of which have been re-locating UK headquarters activities previously situated in increasingly expensive London premises. Indeed an 'insurance centre' is developing in North Hertfordshire with Stevenage at its pivot. The significance of this (particularly when allied to similar re-locations by multi-national companies in other sectors such as pharmaceuticals) is that it is altering the town's corporate imbalance, given that the activities being established are likely to be more secure than those performed by Stevenage's original generation of branch plants.

One of the interesting aspects of this development is that it indicates a change in the attitude of insurance companies to a Stevenage location. Boddy *et al.* (1986), for example, in their study of Bristol, found that those insurance companies which had re-located from London to Bristol during the mid-1970s had explicitly rejected the alternative of a move to Stevenage: the New

Table 11.5 Stevenage 1980–85: employment change by industry orders

SIC 1968		*1980 No.*	*1985 No.*	*1985 %*	*Change 1980–85 %*
	All primary	60	42	0.11	−36.6
III	Food, etc.	620	585	1.64	−5.6
IV	Coal, etc.	40	34	0.09	−15.0
V	Chemicals, etc.	–	524	1.47	–
VI	Metal Man.	250	18	0.05	−92.8
VII	Mech. Eng.	1,220	961	2.69	−21.2
VIII	Inst. Eng.	1,850	663	1.86	−64.1
IX	Elec. Eng.	1,890	2,080	5.83	10.0
X	Shipbuilding	–	–	–	
XI	Vehicles	7,530	8,639	24.24	14.7
XII	Metal Goods nes.	300	172	0.48	−42.7
XIII	Textiles	40	58	0.16	45.0
XIV	Leather, etc.	na	na	–	–
XV	Clothing, etc.	40	27	0.07	−32.5
XVI	Bricks, etc.	70	60	0.16	−14.3
XVII	Timber, etc.	570	409	1.14	−28.2
XVIII	Paper, etc.	830	631	1.77	−24.0
XIX	Other Manufacturing	1,030	277	0.77	73.1
	All manufacturing	16,280	15,138	42.40	−7.0
XX	Construction	230	761	2.13	230.8
XXI	Gas, Water, Elec.	190	184	0.51	−3.2
XXII	Trans./Comm.	1,060	1,171	3.28	10.5
XXIII	Distributive T.	5,160	5,195	14.58	0.7
XXIV	Insurance etc.	1,270	1,790	5.02	40.9
XXV	Prof. and Sci.	2,713	3,031	8.50	11.7
XXVI	Misc. Servs.	2,996	3,257	9.14	8.7
XXVII	Public Admin.	5,061	5,059	14.19	−0.04
	All services	18,260	19,503	54.70	6.8
	All industry	35,020	35,628	–	1.7

Source: Stevenage Borough Council, Annual Surveys of Employment.

Town was too close to the London labour market and apparently unattractive to re-locating staff. Something has evidently changed, although any number of factors could be responsible.

Borough councillors, perhaps not surprisingly, point to the change in policy emphasis as being important. Alternatively, companies may have been attracted by changes in the availability or price of factors such as land and labour. While, for example, all grades of labour were scarce in Stevenage in the 1960s and early 1970s, this is now only true of highly skilled technical workers: some firms may thus have been attracted by the prospect of a labour surplus, particularly of youth labour.

Another possibility, however, is that firms have simply found it easier to locate in Stevenage in the 1980s because of a reduction in spatial constraints. One million sq.ft. of industrial floorspace (i.e. one fifth of the total available in 1979) became vacant in the course of the town's severe manufacturing recession. This not only released land for plant and offices, but also led to adjustments in local planning controls.

Hertfordshire County Council, for example, has altered its Structure Plan and allowed policy relaxations to encourage the redevelopment (by such agencies as institutional investors) of obsolete industrial sites and premises in Stevenage so as to accommodate both large and small scale manufacturing and service activities (Hertfordshire County Council 1986). This has been quite important in so far as the Commission for New Towns has been reluctant to speed up the release of undeveloped land even to the private sector for fear of flooding a surplus land market.

The author's interviews with firms moving to Stevenage certainly indicate the importance of site availability (as opposed overtly to labour market factors or Borough Council promotion, etc.) to their final decision to locate in Stevenage, although this should not be taken to suggest that this was their only consideration. Firms' primary requirements in the mid-1980s appeared to be for locations that offered easy access to London and other national and international transport and communication networks. Only once these requirements were met did site availability become important.

Stevenage's advantage therefore lies both in its favourable regional location and its ability at present to provide space for development. Whilst firms are clearly aware that the latter exists elsewhere (for example in towns further north of London, such as the more recent New Town of Milton Keynes) the overall locational advantages of other areas appear at present to be less attractive. Clearly, since the town's location has not changed in recent years, it seems fair to conclude that what distinguishes the Stevenage of the 1980s from that of the 1970s is its ability to accommodate growth. How long this can continue before constraints become evident again will of course depend upon the ability of local policy makers to ensure that space for new investment is readily available (the importance of this for local development being highlighted in the study by Fothergill *et al.* 1987). In addition, as the South-east labour market tightens, labour supply considerations may also become important once more.

Local policy initiatives

Ironically, the improvement in industrial balance associated with Stevenage's ability to accommodate incoming investment in the 1980s has run counter to attempts to alter the town's plant size imbalance. This is because the contribution to employment of a small number of large incoming firms has swamped that made by small firms. Thus, in spite of the degree of local attention placed upon small firms initiatives, and some increase in the number of small firms, the proportion of total employment in Stevenage accounted for by large firms has actually increased in the 1980s (Table 11.6). Whether the small firms sector will increase its share in the future remains to be seen, but for the time being employment in Stevenage will continue to be dominated by a small number of companies.

Table 11.6 Size distribution of firms and employment in Stevenage, 1980–86

	1980				*1986*			
Emp.	*Firms*		*Emp.*		*Firms*		*Emp.*	
Size Band	*No.*	*%*	*No.*	*%*	*No.*	*%*	*No.*	*%*
1–24	777	83	5,878	17	1,027	87	5,916	16
25–99	113	12	5,948	17	103	9	4,832	13
100–249	30	3	4,638	13	24	2	3,599	10
250+	20	2	18,560	53	20	2	21,788	61
Total	940	100	35,024	100	1,174	100	36,135	100

Source: Stevenage Borough Council, Annual Employment Surveys.

Conclusion

In November 1986 Stevenage celebrated the fortieth anniversary of its designation as a New Town. The anniversary slogan, 'Stevenage First *and Best*', evoked a feeling of civic pride and expressed a growing mood of confidence far removed from the depression of 1977–82. Employment is now growing (at a rate of 1,000 jobs per year since 1983) and there has been some improvement in the problem of 'job shortfall' albeit that the town's unofficial unemployment rate of nearly 10 per cent in mid-1987 was well in excess of the average for Hertfordshire.

Whether these changes and the slight improvements in the town's industrial balance would have occurred irrespective of recent local policy initiatives remains a subject of debate; it is likely that to some extent the recent experience of Stevenage reflects no more than the 'natural' restructuring of a local economy in the wake of a severe industrial dislocation.

Having said that, however, recent initiatives have at least attempted to break both the policy and structural moulds set by the Stevenage Development Corporation. In so doing they have drawn considerable support from various local groups and provided a focus for community interest in solving the town's adjustment problems. Moreover, one now observes a more open and responsive 'partnership' between industry and local authority. Overall, localism in Stevenage has thus served to restore something of the original New Town optimism which in many ways the Development Corporation failed to realise.

One hopes that the Urban Development Corporations will be more successful in this respect, although as the case of Stevenage has demonstrated, it may be symptomatic of non-elected and locally unaccountable organizations such as these that they fail to serve the widest interests of local communities. It is, therefore, somewhat disturbing to contemplate the consequences of public policy in the inner cities if this is to be exercised without the strictures of effective local control.

Notes

1. The research for this contribution was conducted at the Local Economy Research Unit, The Hatfield Polytechnic. The normal disclaimer applies.
2. For a detailed account of the background to the New Towns programme and its development see Schaffer (1970), Champion *et al.* (1977), and Aldridge (1979). Please note that whilst many studies highlight the importance of social aspects of the programme, particularly housing, the present account concentrates upon industrial and economic development. Evaluation of the 'success' or 'failure' of the programme (or an individual New Town) in terms of these latter aspects of New Town development should not, however, be interpreted as applying to other aspects. Indeed, in terms of housing provision the programme is widely recognized as having been fairly successful.
3. Both the New Towns Programme and the UDCs represent examples of 'property-led' intervention financed by Central Government. In the case of the UDCs, however, the express aim of policy is to use public funds to develop or redevelop infrastructure so as to provide a base for the leverage of investment in predominantly private sector initiatives. Unlike the New Towns, for example, which originally provided public housing for rent, in areas administered by UDCs private sector housebuilders are to provide housing for owner occupation. Similarly, there are to be few

controls and stipulations over the extent and nature of inward industrial and commercial developments.

4. Broader accounts of the social and economic development of Stevenage New Town are provided by Orlans (1952), Balchin (1980), and Mullan (1980).

References

Aldridge, M. (1979) *The British New Towns: A Programme Without a Policy*, London: Routledge & Kegan Paul.

Balchin, J. (1980) *First New Town: An Autobiography of the Stevenage Development Corporation*, Stevenage: SDC.

Boddy, M., Lovering, J., and Basset, K. (1986) *Sunbelt City? A Study of Economic Change in Britain's M4 Growth Corridor*, Oxford: OUP.

Buck, N., Gordon, L., and Young, K. (1986) *The London Employment Problem*, Oxford: OUP.

Champion, A.G., Clegg, K., and Davies, R.L. (1977) *Facts about the New Towns: a Socio-Economic Digest*, Newcastle: RPA Books.

Cooke, P.N. (1983) *Theories of Planning and Spatial Development*, London: Hutchinson.

(1986) (Ed.) *Global Restructuring, Local Response*, London: ESRC.

Duncan, S.S., and Goodwin, M. (1985) 'The Local State and Local Economic Policy: Why the Fuss? *Policy and Politics*, 13:227–53.

Employment Institute (1987) 'Government and the Inner Cities', *Employment Institute Economic Report* 3, 1 October.

Fothergill, S. and Gudgin, G. (1982)*Unequal Growth: Urban and Regional Employment Change in the UK*, London: Heinemann.

Fothergill, S., Kitson, M., and Monk, S. (1983) 'The Impact of the New and Expanded Towns Programme on Industrial Location in Britain, 1960–78', *Regional Studies* 17:251–60.

Fothergill, S., Monk, S. and Perry, M. (1987) *Property and Industrial Development*, London: Hutchinson.

Grieco, M.S. (1984) 'Corby: New Town Planning and Imbalanced Development', *Regional Studies* 19:9–18.

Hertfordshire County Council (1986) *Ten Years After: A Monitoring Study 1974–84*, Hertford: HCC.

Klausner, D. (1987) 'Infrastructure Investment and Political Ends: the Case of London's Docklands', *Local Economy* 1(4):47–59.

Marquand, J. (1983) 'The Changing Distribution of Service Employment', in Goddard, J.B. and Champion, A.G. (Eds) *The Urban and Regional Transformation of Britain*, London: Methuen.

Massey, D. (1984) *Spatial Divisions of Labour: Social Structures and the Geography of Production*, London: Macmillan.

Mullan, B. (1980) *Stevenage Ltd: Aspects of the Planning and Politics of Stevenage New Town, 1945–78*, London: Routledge & Kegan Paul.

Orlans, H. (1952) *Stevenage: A Sociological Study of A New Town*, London: Routledge & Kegan Paul.

Owen, D.W., Gillespie, A.R., and Coombes, M.G. (1984) '"Job Shortfalls" in British Local Labour Market Areas: A Classification of Labour Supply and Demand Trends, 1971–81', *Regional Studies* 18:469–88.
Schaffer, F. (1970) *The New Town Story*, London: Paladin.
South East Regional Planning Conference (SERPLAN) (1985) Regional Trends in the South East: the South East Regional Monitor 1984–85: London, SERPLAN, RPC 369.
South East Economic Development Strategy (SEEDS) (1986) Aims and Objectives Broadsheet, Stevenage: SEEDS.
Stevenage Borough Council (1982) Stevenage's Major Employers – Their Relationship to other Companies. Article in Stevenage *Trends* (Quarterly) August 1982, Stevenage: SBC.
(1985) *Trends*, December, Stevenage: SBC.
(1986) Employment Action Plan, third edition, Stevenage: SBC.
Wray, M., Markham, R., and Watts, D.R. (1974) 'Location of Industry in Hertfordshire: Planning and Industry in the post-war Period', Hatfield Polytechnic.

12

Never mind the planning . . . feel the initiative: local government policy and worker co-operatives

M.S. Lowe

Introduction: restructuring, local government policy and localism

This chapter is concerned with the worker co-operative as an alternative local authority initiative. It illuminates specifically the policies relating to co-operatives in Birmingham, Cambridge, and Leicestershire in the context of the late 1980s – recognized as a period of comprehensive change in all spheres – an era of 'restructuring' (Martin 1987).[1] As a result of such re-organization, conventional policies to deal with the particular problems of local areas, be they nationally or locally conceived, are now considered to be inadequate (Martin 1986a, 1987). It is recognized, however, that restructuring is felt most powerfully by the local areas where it is played out (Cooke 1986), and for this reason it is timely to rethink policy for these places. The chapter is intended as a contribution to such a re-evaluation. It suggests that co-operatives – in their capacity as a component of local economic and employment strategies – are a viable alternative to the polices being pursued at present by national and local governments. Co-operatives are advocated here as a strand of a broad 'localism' movement. However, it is argued that care should be exercised in the promotion of localism *per se* as a policy goal. For instance, it is clear that many radical local authorities have adopted co-operatives as a strand of their grassroots, bottom-up economic strategies ('never mind the planning . . . feel the initiative'). But, in addition, as the idea of co-operatives as 'alternatives' recedes and as they gain widespread acceptance – having been legitimized by central government (see Cunningham 1986) – they are increasingly becoming adapted to the strategies pursued by a number of local authorities of many different political persuasions, conservative through to radical. This could lead to precisely the dangers that Bennington has warned against for local economic strategies more generally; that is the possibility of such alternative approaches becoming 'part of the mainstream components of local government' (of whatever political persuasion) rather than 'testing components of a national strategy' (Bennington 1986).[2] The support of co-operatives in many local areas is now recognized as nothing more than a general 'small firms' initiative, whilst the phrase 'never mind the planning . . . feel the initiative' could apply quite readily to the emphasis of the present government on enterprise and individual initiative (such as the emphasis on enterprise zones, see Archer (1987)). 'Localism'[3] is hence not simply a restructuring 'from the bottom up' or a 'local socialism' in which radical local initiative is seen as a panacea. Indeed, 'the development of economic initiatives by local government over the last few years is only one aspect of the burgeoning 'localism' movement that is under way' (Martin 1986b:287). Localism can also refer to the following:

1. Enterprise localism, i.e the way that the Conservative Government is encouraging a climate of self-help in localities – by its withdrawal of regional aid (see Martin 1986b) and its leaving local areas and the authorities responsible for them to work out their own fate.
2. Corporate localism, i.e. the tendency for large private companies to get involved in their local economies in the form of community redevelopment schemes or enterprise agencies and trusts.
3. Community localism, i.e. broad community alliances at either a national or local level identified by O'Connor, 1984.[4]

   (See Lowe and Martin, (forthcoming) for a more detailed account of these strands).

Both the more radical (local socialism) and the conservative (enterprise localism) strains of localism are valid responses to the economic crisis of the 1980s but for very different political and ideological reasons. Community and corporate localism fall on a broad continuum between the two.

Localism in the 1980s has thus arisen in many guises, largely in response to the perceived 'failure' of present policy formulations to be effective in coping with changed conditions. The way different organizations perceive this failure has important implications for the particular strand of localism they adopt. In addition, the way in which localism is played out cannot be perceived as a purely economic issue, since the political persuasions of the various bodies involved are inevitably reflected in their particular localist stance. In the same way that Duncan and Goodwin (1984) have pointed to the way in which local policies are political as well as economic in nature,[5] central government, private enterprise, and the community all have their many and diverse motivating forces. This chapter will document local government policies concerning co-operatives as part of these new localist ideals. It will attempt to show how differing political ideologies and local conditions impact on an area's 'localist' stance and will draw some conclusions from the co-operative case for the role and future development of local authority initiatives more generally. First, however, it will outline the growth of co-operatives in the present period and the approach of national government to these co-operatives.

The national level: growth and support of co-operatives

> Producer co-operatives are a form of free enterprise, and as such we are anxious to encourage them
> (David Mitchell, Under Secretary of State for Industry *Hansard* 973, 12 November, 1979:882)

> We are convinced that the CDA represents . . . a small but significant addition to our general policy to small business
> (Norman Lamont, Minister of State, DTI, *Hansard* 53, 7 February 1984:778)

> We have more resources than the national CDA . . . – its philosophy is totally in line with small firms entrepreneurship
> (Personal Communication, Roger Dicker, Deputy Director, West Midlands Enterprise Board)

A vast number of co-operatives have been set up in the UK in the last few years (Lowe 1988). Whereas there were only 305 co-ops in 1980, today there are over 1,400 (Carter 1986; Nesbitt and Tonks 1986). Indeed from June 1984 to June 1986 alone there was an increase of 62 per cent in the number of co-operatives (the *Guardian*, 26 January 1987). Despite this massive explosion in numbers there has been a dearth of support for co-operatives in concrete financial terms. Most recently, the Conservative Government has pledged its support for co-operatives, as long as they are self-financing. In this respect the Government views co-operatives as just another method of organization for the small firm.

The lack of national level finance for co-operatives has led Whyatt (1983) to call for a concentration of support at the local level. An examination of local government policy towards co-operatives in three local areas follows. The three areas should be viewed as individual studies in their own right (see Lowe 1988). The cases presented here do not, therefore, 'stand for a larger category . . . (they are not) . . . statistical members of an aggregated class, nor significant representatives of general propositions' (Lemert and Gillan 1982:30–31).

Localism in action: local government policy and worker co-operatives

Different areas have their own distinct approaches to localism. Such approaches are influenced by local contextual factors of an economic, social and political nature. For example, the West Midlands County Council which practised 'local socialism' during its period of operation, had a very different approach to co-operatives to that adopted today by Cambridgeshire County Council which sees co-operatives as 'less conventional small firms', and thus practises 'enterprise localism'. Figure 12.1 attempts to illustrate the localist stance adopted by the various local governments involved in this study. However, the co-operative – because of its diverse origins and aims – essentially transcends these boundaries. Thus, for example, the co-operatives in Cambridge and the local government co-operative initiative intended to support them grew up in response to 'community localism' which has since evolved more along the lines of 'enterprise localism'. More about this later, but here it is useful to reiterate that it is difficult to divide the various initiatives along political party lines, for both the 'left' and the 'right' have adopted co-operatives for various reasons. The chapter will now attempt to make some sense of the complex situation with reference to localist and co-operative policy. It is salient then to begin by examining the various 'contextual' factors that influence the pace and politics of co-operative development in the particular localities studied.

Economic and social context

The three areas studied differ markedly in terms of their economic experience over the last few years. It is impossible to go into detail here, but suffice it to say that Birmingham – central to the West Midlands conurbation – has experienced a rapid turnaround in economic status in the period since 1979. Cambridge, most famous for the recent success of its high technology industries, is a city

Figure 12.1 Localism in action: local government's localist stance in Birmingham, Cambridge, and Leicestershire

*Localism spectrum**			
Local Socialism	Community Localism	Corporate Localism	Enterprise Localism
West Midlands County Council ----	--------		
West Midlands Enterprise Board	----------------	--------	
Birmingham City Council ----	--------		
Leicester City Council ----	--------		
	Leicestershire County Council		
Cambridge City Council ----	--------		
			Cambridgeshire County Council

* For a full account of the various types of localism see Lowe and Martin (forthcoming) *Local Economy*.

which has, to a large extent, escaped the debilitating effects of recession, and has remained comparatively 'buoyant' throughout the 1980s. Leicestershire, meanwhile, includes both areas which have 'escaped' from the recession as well as those which now contain high percentage unemployment rates.

Birmingham

The scale and impact of industrial demise has obviously had important implications for the corrective policies pursued by the various local governments involved. Thus in the West Midlands there has been no room for the 'niceties' of the co-operative option. As Martin Hockley – Industrial Common Ownership Finance Officer (ICOF) for the West Midlands – has noted, 'most of the co-ops in the West Midlands are businesses first and then co-ops – they are different to co-ops elsewhere. . . . The thing you have to remember about West Midlands co-ops is that they are funded as an employment initiative rather than a co-op initiative. . . . It was just another way of putting money into employment' (Personal Communication, Martin Hockley, ICOF Officer for the West Midlands). Moreover, because of the severe situation in which Birmingham finds itself, 'unless people are doing something that is entirely hostile to co-operative ideas . . . (the County) . . . would tend to fund it' (Personal Communication, Lewis Scott, Head of Co-ops Team, West Midlands Enterprise Board).[6] Indeed, Lewis Scott suspects that 'there are a lot of co-ops out there that people in the old 1970s movement wouldn't "touch with a bargepole". On the other hand, they are probably very good businesses' (Personal Communication, Lewis Scott). Birmingham CDA, as Table 12.1 shows has the highest percentage of full-time workers (83 per cent); it also has the highest percentage (21 per cent) of people earning over £100 per week in their co-operative (Table 12.2). Further, although union membership (an indication of employment stability from the point of view of the worker) is low (21 per cent) (Table 12.3) it is higher than that provided in Leicestershire or Cambridge.

Table 12.1 Employment in co-operatives[1]

	Birmingham	*Cambridge*	*Leicestershire*
Total	47	22	57
Full time	39 (83%)	18 (82%)	43 (75%)
Part time	8 (17%)	4 (18%)	14 (25%)
Black people*	13 (27%)	2 (9%)	11 (19%)
Women*	12 (25%)	8 (36%)	26 (46%)
Disabled	1 (2%)		

Source: Personal interviews.
**N.B.* There is obviously some overlap between these two categories.

The Birmingham Co-operative Development Agency (CDA) was set up in 1982 along with two other West Midlands CDAs in the Black Country (Wolverhampton) and Coventry. 'The wholesale decline in the West Midlands economy was the spur to the development of the co-operative initiative in an attempt to create a favourable climate of self-help' (Birmingham CDA, 1984:4) and the three co-operative development agencies were one of the many schemes started 'with the intention of getting people back into work' (West Midlands County Council, 1984:3). The establishment of the CDAs together with other supportive services

Table 12.2 Remuneration per week (full-time equivalent) in co-operatives

	Birmingham	*Cambridge*	*Leicestershire*
< £35*	11%	33%	37%
£35–£49**	21%	33%	35%
£50–£64	6%	17%	2%
£65–£79	–	–	–
£80–£94	11%	–	–
£95–£109	30%	–	7%
£110–£124	–	–	7%
£125–£139	–	–	–
£140–£154	21%	17%	12%

Source: Personal interviews.
**N.B.* This calculation makes no allowance for the quality of working life which is discussed in Lowe (1988). In addition, it does not allow for collective childcare provision and such-like to be taken into account.
***N.B.* This category includes many co-operatives which have been set up under the enterprise allowance scheme, paying its participants £40 per week for one year. In addition, this analysis takes no account of the setting up date of the co-operative; in general terms wages increase over time.

Table 12.3 Union membership, unemployment and political factors in co-operatives

	Birmingham	*Cambridge*	*Leicestershire*
Union membership	21%	5%	16%
% Unemployed before joining co-operative*	77%	64%	91%
% in a co-operative for political/ideological reasons	35%	83%	42%

Source: Personal interviews.
**N.B.* This category includes some people who had just left university and were unable to get a job.

resulted in 'the most comprehensive support system for worker co-operatives outside London and arguably in the whole of the UK' (Titley 1986:xi) and the launch of the West Midlands co-op initiative was accompanied by the largest media campaign of its kind. 'The fact that there were no co-operatives in the West Midlands meant that it was possible to develop an integrated approach' (Personal Communication, Roger Dicker, Deputy Director, West Midlands Enterprise Board) with a full range of financial and support services available.

Today Birmingham CDA sees itself as 'part of the "unemployment industry" – the initiation of the Agency was part of the economic development strategy developed in response to the crisis that had hit Birmingham . . . (it) must be seen in that context' (Personal Communication, Charles Edwards, Development Worker, Birmingham Co-operative Development Agency). Thus the West Midland's situation reflects Boddy's comment that 'as the cold winds of recession were felt in . . . traditionally more prosperous areas . . . the shortcomings of mainstream policy became increasingly obvious' (Boddy 1984:165–6). It was for this reason, along with others discussed below that there was a change in policy emphasis.

Figure 12.2 West Midlands County Council: economic development principles

1. The future prosperity of the West Midlands lies in the survival and strengthening of its traditional industries.

2. There is an urgent need to increase the flow of investment into the West Midlands.

3. There is a need to ensure public accountability where public funds are used to support private industrial and commercial activity.

4. There is a need to invest in human skills as well as buildings and plant.

5. The committee recognises that there are within the community a whole series of energies and talents which can be brought together to create employment opportunities.

6. The committee recognises that despite the very best efforts of the County Council to create and secure jobs, problems of unemployment, low pay and poverty will all continue on a large scale within the County area.

Source: West Midlands County Council, 1984

The 'unemployment industry' referred to above was essentially put into operation by the now defunct West Midlands County Council, one of the well-documented 'radical Labour-controlled' councils which came to power following the local government elections of 1981. In the period from 1981 until its abolition in 1986 the County Council pursued an economic development strategy illustrated in Figure 12.2 which became known as 'Action for Jobs'. In general terms, as the document 'Action in the Local Economy' proclaimed,

Local policy initiatives

> In response to the very serious problems of the West Midlands, the County Council has introduced a wide range of radical economic policies aimed at encouraging investment, stimulating the growth of co-operative enterprises and providing important skill training. These policies recognise the role that a major authority like the County Council can play in the local economy . . .
>
> (West Midlands County Council, 1984:5)

The Campaign for Jobs 'launched a major fight to defend jobs, firms and living standards' within the West Midlands and to pull together 'the wide range of skills and energies' which were present in the Midlands but which were being wasted by economic recession (West Midlands County Council, 1984:5). The preservation of skill mentioned here is indicated in that 25 per cent of Birmingham co-ops are in manufacturing industry, reflecting the past industrial heritage of the region.

In addition, the West Midlands has been keen to respond to the specific problems of disadvantaged groups within its labour market. This has become an important part of CDA policy which has included such things as investment in human skills and attention being paid to women, the handicapped and members of the black and Asian community. The CDA stress:

> We are available to deal with enquiries from all over Birmingham, all age groups, all ethnic groups, all sexes, but we give more intensive marketing to inner city areas, ethnic minorities and women. We have just taken the initiative of organising a joint training scheme with Handsworth Employment Scheme, we are not doing that in Solihull. We have also been involved in the ICOM women's link-up training programme
>
> (Personal Communication, Charles Edwards)

Having pointed to this emphasis placed on 'marginalized groups', it is nevertheless important to recognize that the West Midlands County Council, unlike the GLC 'don't believe the . . . system of extra points for different groups — ideas must be viable. They have to be enterprises that sustain jobs and, if possible, provide money for re-investment. That's not always possible with a group with social objectives'. It is ultimately recognised to be 'a lot easier to set up a co-op if you are well-educated, know about business, are white and a man – people are prepared to take you more seriously. You can therefore only make exemplary advances you can't change things dramatically' (Personal Communication, Lewis Scott). This sentiment is reflected in the fact that 27 per cent of workers in co-operatives in Birmingham are black, 25 per cent are women and 2 per cent are disabled (Table 12.1). Moreover, 38 per cent of co-operators have no qualifications — an indication of the emphasis placed on the disadvantaged. The contention that it is easier to set up a co-operative if you are educated, however, is reflected in the high percentage of people with degrees or higher degrees who work in co-ops – 45 per cent in total (Table 12.4).

Table 12.4 Qualifications of co-operative workers

	Birmingham	*Cambridge*	*Leicestershire*
None	38%	18%	53%
'O' levels	11%	18%	2%
'A' levels/HND	6%	27%	12%
Degree	28%	37%	28%
Higher Degree	17%	–	5%

Sources: Personal interviews and Nesbitt and Tonks (1986).

The abolition of the West Midlands Metropolitan Authority in April 1986 has had important implications for the development of the co-operative initiative. These implications will be discussed in detail on p.303 – for the moment note that the other Council responsible for co-operative development in Birmingham – Birmingham City Council, had no strategy prior to 1985. Although the City was experiencing severe malaise it was perceived to be unnecessary to engage in direct action in the economy. Instead the City followed the County in its support of various initiatives, the CDA being one of them. Since 1985, in the context of various political developments outlined below, the City has become more involved. Nevertheless its approach is distinct from that of the County and in economic terms it is still concerned with the preservation of the traditional industrial structure of the City – witness, for example the reference made to British Leyland:

> The City believes that the thrust of economic intervention will remain assistance to traditional businesses. However, we feel that we should try and address some of the problems of the inner city through self-help activities. In the case of the CDA we see it as city-wide in coverage and accept the jam to be spread fairly thinly. . . . You are talking about a response to BL (British Leyland) and we need people who have ambitions and want to grow. You should assess people not just by the viability

> of their business plan – but their ability to make it work . . . find a group of people that want to co-operate and have a viable idea that will grow into a fifty-man (sic) co-op. . . . The CDA must be more hard-nosed and determine whether a project is a winner in practical terms. A co-operative is – at the end of the day – a different type of business structure – but it has to be viable in a commercial sense
>
> (Personal Communication, Jim Cocker, Deputy Head of Economic Development Unit, Birmingham City Council)

It is likely therefore that in the long-term the response of Birmingham CDA will become more commercial as a result of the increasing role and impact of the City Council.

However, as already stated, the development of policies cannot be reduced to economic explanations. It is of paramount importance to examine the political developments encapsulated in the region in order to examine the policies of Birmingham City and the West Midlands. Such developments have been viewed as more important than the sheer force of economic decline in determining future policy outcomes. More about this later; first it is important to examine the economic context of the other areas chosen.

Leicestershire

Like the West Midlands, Leicestershire has experienced a rapid and significant deterioration in its local economy since 1979. Until then the East Midlands had always been viewed as a region of relative economic prosperity. However, in the depths of the recession even the 'prosperous' East Midlands has been hard-hit – particularly those areas of Leicestershire which have been reliant on a few major employers. The diversity of the Leicestershire economy is reflected in the sectoral spread of the co-operatives (Table 12.5). In Leicester City itself over 15 per cent of the workforce are unemployed whilst in most of the County towns there are pockets of very high unemployment rates. It is as a result of such variations that the CDA in Leicester and County has delineated a series of 'county priority areas' for particular policy targeting – Loughborough, North West Leicestershire, and Hinkley are seen as in need of specific policy responses.

Within Leicester City, which has experienced severe malaise in the period since 1979, the emphasis from the council is on 'drawing together the experiences and energies of working class people in order to provide alternatives to capitalist methods of production

Table 12.5 Sectoral distribution of co-operatives

	Birmingham	*Cambridge*	*Leicestershire*
Building	–	17%	–
Fishing, agriculture and forestry	–	–	6%
Manufacturing	25%	–	32%
Services	75%	66%	56%
Retail and wholesale	–	17%	6%
Transport	–	–	–

Source: Personal interviews Nesbitt and Tonks (1986).

and job loss' (Leicester City Council 1985:2). The County sees its targets in spatial terms – Inner Leicester, the priority zones of North Braunstone, and the Leicestershire coalfield (Leicestershire County Council 1984). Leicester City

> has a whole range of projects which are social but they are considered 'economic' within the terms of reference of the employment unit[8] . . . The value of 'social enterprise' is seen to lie in its ability to meet a wider set of objectives than those normally pursued through private enterprise. What the Unit is looking for is ethnic minority co-ops, working class co-ops and co-ops with women
>
> (Personal Communication, Tom Cosh, CDA Liaison Officer, Leicester City Council)

Leicester and County CDA aims to be particularly sensitive to the needs of marginalized groups – young people, women, black

Table 12.6 Age of co-operative workers

	Birmingham	*Cambridge*	*Leicestershire*
16–20	15%	14%	2%
21–25	15%	9%	42%
26–30	19%	54%	17%
31–35	21%	18%	16%
36–40	13%	5%	9%
41–45	–	–	–
46–50	2%	–	–
51–55	6%	–	9%
56–60	9%	–	–
60+	–	–	3%
Unknown	–	–	2%

Source: Personal interviews

people, and the handicapped. The commitment to the black population is exemplified by the fact that the CDA produces all its leaflets in four languages. The CDA has also been particularly successful in the involvement of women (46 per cent of all co-operative workers [Table 12.1]). In addition it has managed to attract black people into co-operation but not to the same extent as Birmingham CDA. The presence of 25 per cent of part-time work would be regarded as a failure to create 'real jobs' by Birmingham CDA but Leicester see the provision of flexible work – to allow time for other commitments – as important in their general scheme. Leicester and County CDA's concentration on marginalized groups is also noticeable in the high percentage of co-operators who have no qualifications (53 per cent, see Table 12.4) – there are also a large number with degrees but Leicester acknowledge the fact that in the present economic situation even these people are unlikely to find work – and the high percentage of young people (44 per cent under 25, see Table 12.6). Like Birmingham's co-ops, those in Leicester are full of people who were unemployed before they joined the co-operative – 91 per cent in this case (Table 12.3). A reflection in part of LCCDA's concentration on 'deprived' members of society is the great deal of workers earning less than £50 per week (72 per cent, see Table 12.2) although it must be remembered that many of these people are at present earning the statutory £35 on the Government's 'Enterprise Allowance Scheme' and also that in any business it takes a while for wages to be built up. In many ways it is impossible to fully analyse the 'success' of the co-operative initiative until it is out of its infancy.

Figure 12.3 Leicestershire County Council: themes and policies for economic development

Objective 1	To assist the long term health of the Leicestershire economy.
Objective 2	To help individuals to improve their chances of securing conventional and unconventional employment – includes helping the unemployed to set up all forms of business, including co-operatives and alternatives to traditional forms of employment such as community ventures.
Objective 3	To lessen the problems of unemployment for the individual and for particular communities.

Source: Leicestershire County Council, 1986.

In Leicestershire co-operatives fall within 'Objective 2' of the 'Themes and polices for economic development' (see Figure 12.3). That is 'to help individuals to improve their chances of securing conventional and unconventional employment'. The County recognizes the likelihood of a substantial 'job gap' and therefore encourages innovatory ideas and more permanent solutions to the problem through alternative and less conventional forms of employment. In general it is recognized that 'the CDA started very much along the lines of any other business advice agency . . . but, as it developed it has moved away from this central core – it has its own client groups which are very different to those that the other advice agencies deal with' (Andy Griffiths, CDA Liaison Officer, Leicestershire County Council). However, the County stresses that 'such initiatives . . . give local people a start, but it is for them to build on' (Personal Communication, Pam Chivers, Employment Unit, Leicestershire County Council). In this way the County is falling into the 'community localism' mould. How far this is along the lines of local socialism or an enterprise localism is difficult to distinguish.

Cambridge

Like the lucky parts of Leicestershire, Cambridge is a city which has to a large extent escaped the debilitating effects of recession. Nevertheless, both Cambridge and Cambridgeshire are classic examples of the way in which all local areas now feel compelled to become involved in their local economies 'because everyone else is doing it'. Throughout the 1970s neither authority had any economic development policy but in the 1980s the City's promotion literature proclaims: 'Despite a local unemployment rate of about half that which prevails nationally the creation and diversification of job opportunities continues to be one of the Council's top priorities' (Cambridge City Council, undated).

The relatively advantaged economic situation in Cambridge and Cambridgeshire has had an impact on the amount of attention which is paid to economic development, but it is significant that recently both the Labour controlled City and the Conservative County have supported the co-operation option. It is interesting to note here the fact that the first co-operatives set up by the CDA in Cambridge came about in 1984 and were, therefore, established much later than those which fell under the initiative of Leicester and Birmingham CDAs. Both authorities remain committed to co-ops as part of their more general 'small firms' initiatives. The City supports co-ops and is Labour-controlled, meanwhile the County sees the CDA as 'complementary to, and performing a similar function to the enterprise agencies' (Personal Communication, Chris Green, Cambridgeshire County Council). The county's main priority is Fenbet – the enterprise agency in the Fens; meanwhile the City has located its CDA in the same building as the enterprise agency and has encouraged the CDA itself to liaise with the enterprise agency. Cambridge CDA is thus an example in action of the way in which the motivations for co-operative support become confused and yet can lead to the same end result. 'Community localism' has been utilized to the advantage of both the 'left' and the 'right'.

In both the case of Cambridge and Cambridgeshire the policies concerned with co-ops are distinct from those detailing training and support for the unemployed. This is reflected in the fact that in comparison to 91 per cent in Leicestershire and 77 per cent in Cambridge only 64 per cent of co-operators were unemployed immediately prior to joining their co-op (Table 12.3). On the other hand, the development of the co-operative initiative in this area has been seen as a response to community activation on the part of the Co-operative Retail Society. The Society feels that 'as the old dinosaurs of the movement . . . it is important for us to be involved with them as the newest and most vigorous part of the movement' (Personal Communication, Melanie Johnson, Member Relations Officer, Cambridge Co-operative Retail Society). The member relations committee of the Cambridge co-op were interested in setting up a CDA 'for political and ideological reasons'. It is probably this commitment to the 'alternative' rather than the 'employment' side of co-operation which has led to a large number of people joining co-ops in Cambridge for political and ideological reasons (Table 12.3). The fact that a lot of the workers in co-ops are graduates – 37 per cent (from Cambridge or elsewhere) adds to this trend (Table 12.4).

Fewer women and black people are employed in co-operatives in Cambridge than in co-ops elsewhere in my study (Table 12.1). Obviously, in the case of blacks, this reflects the social milieu – unlike Birmingham and Leicester, Cambridge does not contain large numbers of black people. The close relationship between the Co-op Society and the CDA is indicated by the fact that the Member Relations Officer acted as Secretary of the CDA for some time – another example of community localism. The Cambridge co-op still has a member on the CDA Board.

The Cambridge CDA takes a much more ideological standpoint than the Councils which fund it. The CDA workers see

> as their natural clients . . . those who are unemployed and who don't have ready access to large amounts of money. Women and those who are more inclined or interested in working in co-ops anyway . . . (but) because of limited resources . . . (the CDA) take co-operative development from where it comes and take the view that setting up successful co-ops is the best way of promoting them . . . targeting comes much later
>
> (Pete Hannan, Development Worker, Cambridge CDA)

The CDA has a specific commitment to 'learning new skills and work patterns as well as unlearning some other patterns' (Cambridge CDA, 1983:1). The CDA will only recommend that a business should get a loan if it is a bona fide co-operative and in addition it (the CDA) is closely involved with the broader co-op movement locally and nationally. There is a conflict here between the 'community localism' that the CDA sees itself involved in and the more right-wing community entrepreneurship that the County Council, in particular, is promoting. The 'alternative' nature of the Cambridge co-ops is reflected in their commitment to 'a cause' or to their own quality of work rather than to high wages – 83 per cent of Cambridge co-operators earn less than £65 per week (Table 12.2).

Political context

As I have indicated the specific effects of economic and social circumstances on local areas is only part of the reason for their involvement in particular initiatives. The politics of local government, and indeed local politics more generally outside of that formal sphere will have an impact on the policies of the authorities in question. The West Midlands County elections in 1981, for example, signalled a new departure for local economic strategies in the region. As Boddy has noted, 'the political development encapsulated therein was more important than the economic situation in which the new radical labour group came to power' (Boddy 1984:166). In a similar fashion to that followed by the Greater London Council (GLC) and Sheffield City Council (SCC) the West Midlands developed a radical local economic strategy. Central to policy was a demonstration to the Government that there were alternatives to its economic policies (Mawson *et al.* 1984). Further, 'there was a democratic reaction to planning from on high', it was felt that 'people should be involved in the creation and development of plans – and planning should take place in the community and within individual enterprises' (Personal Communication, Roger Dicker). The emphasis on community here, however, was not to the extent that local government could abdicate responsibility for the people living in its area – but such that the community should be involved in the planning process – and should be provided for.

The abolition on 'All Fools Day' 1986 (Titley 1986) of the GLC and the Metropolitan Authorities could have been disastrous for West Midlands Co-operatives – it signalled a loss of £8m in Section 137 finance (see Sellgren, this volume) and led Dick Knowles, leader of Birmingham City Council to comment that 'the scrapping of the economic planning role of the County Council will hinder local development and economic growth' (quoted in Wolmar 1986). In reality the situation has not yet been as bleak. The incorporation of the West Midlands Co-operative Finance Company (WMCOF) – which was set up by the County – as a subsidiary of the Enterprise Board and the continued financial support of the district councils has meant that the CDAs are safe for the time being. However, the transfer of the control of co-operative support from West Midlands County Council to Birmingham City Council is bound to have implications for the future development of the co-operative initiative in the city.

It is interesting to remember at this point that Birmingham City Council had no economic development strategy until April 1985 (Birmingham City Council 1985). The City was Conservative controlled from 1982 and yet supported the co-operative initiative throughout this time – an indication of the appeal that co-ops have to all political persuasions. With the control of the City falling to Labour in 1984, the City's economic development strategy was outlined. It is, in many senses, operated in parallel with what were the County's priorities (those which now fall under the head of the Enterprise Board) – full support is given to the co-operative development agencies. However, there is a greater emphasis placed on the small business and the need for viability – community enterprise goes hand in hand with small business (Birmingham City Council 1986a). Thus there has been a subtle shift from 'local socialism' to a mixture of 'community localism' and 'enterprise localism' – the community has been involved from a 'left' perspective.

The Labour controlled council in Leicester is – in a similar vein to West Midlands County – committed to 'alternatives to capitalist methods of production'. The co-operative development agency was established as a result of a move made by City Councillors – a genuine political commitment to developing co-ops as an alternative form of working. When the CDA was established by the City Council it was not only to 'support and assist worker co-ops in Leicestershire' but also, 'to promote and encourage the idea of co-operation at work' – in a broad type of local socialism. Development is seen as a primary function and the remit of the CDA is, therefore, wider than sheer job creation – for example, it is accepted that it (the CDA) attracts 'a lot of people . . . who are working but who want to stop working and form a co-op (Personal Communication, Dorothy Francis, Development Worker, Leicester and County CDA). This is reflected in the type of co-operatives that have been set up (see Tables 12.1 and 12.4).

With reference to the development of co-ops in Cambridge, I have already mentioned the community agitation on the part of the Co-operative Retail Society which led to the establishment by the City Council of the CDA. Thus the CDA was essentially developed in an informal local political arena. Both the Labour-controlled City and the Conservative County support the co-operative option in very flimsy terms — little attention, financial or otherwise is paid to the co-ops. Co-operatives in Cambridge most resemble the type of non-party 'social movement' identified by Castells (1983) – a result of the development of an 'alternative culture' in the 1970s.

Co-operative support

The political persuasion and the emphasis placed on co-ops as a result of economic and social contextuality has fed into the availability of assistance for co-operatives (in financial terms and otherwise). Birmingham is fortunate, a series of factors mean that the CDA 'don't debar people on the basis of them having no cash and . . . frequently find 100% of the package between (themselves) and ICOF' (Personal Communication, Lewis Scott).

In the West Midlands generally the new co-operator can expect to receive in-depth assistance from the CDA, training and feasibility by external consultants, product development, and financial help. In addition to the on-going assistance provided to support the CDAs, a grant of £500,000 was made to the financial arm of ICOM (ICOF) in 1982 for administering a revolving loan fund for West Midlands co-ops. In 1984 a new company (WMCOF) was set up and given a budget of £1.25 million to act as an effective mechanism to provide investment funds for co-ops.

Such investment was mainly in the form of grants but also loans and equity. Training is financed in part through EEC funding – in particular for women through the ICOM women's link-up training programme. Further, as a component of its expanded role, Birmingham City Council provides feasibility grants so that 'groups with an idea have some resources to find out if it will work' (Birmingham CDA 1986:6). It has also financed the provision of a worker at the CDA with sole responsibility for marketing. In this way the city is aware of the need to become more 'hard-nosed'. The move of the CDA to the Co-operative Enterprise Centre, the Zair Works, including the provision of units for co-operatives and workspace for groups shows the emphasis that will shortly be placed on co-operative success, first and foremost, before 'co-operative' and social methods.

In Leicester co-ops are seen as

> a useful vehicle for many different groups in society who are marginalised by the labour market but, at the same time (it is felt that) it has to be done well, there has to be a lot of support and you can't do it on the cheap. . . .With minimal resources you are setting people up to fail
>
> (Personal Communication, Tom Cosh)

As a result substantial finance has been provided to the CDA which enables it to employ six development workers, run compulsory development courses and to allocate feasibility grants to co-operatives. Unlike Birmingham, though, the CDA is fundamentally interested in the 'education' rather than the 'job-creation' process, *per se*. This is successful in terms of the number of disadvantaged groups that the CDA reaches (see Tables 12.1 and 12.4), but it is also reflected in terms of the poor financial returns, low levels of unionization, and so on, accruing to co-operative workers.

By contrast, Cambridge CDA has few resources to allocate to the development of co-operatives, it sees itself mainly as fulfilling an educational role. 'Success is a non-quantifiable product. What others have failed to do in resuscitating the local economy, local CDAs cannot be expected to do single-handed. . . . Our job is mainly educational with the ultimate aim of job-creation' (Cambridge CDA 1983:2). The poor support for co-operatives in Cambridge is reflected in terms of the number and type of co-operatives that are set up; most people in co-ops are graduates, earn very poor wages and only 5 per cent are in a union.

Conclusions: implications for policy

> CDAs and local authorities funding co-operatives have been around for about five years and in the first flush there has been a massive expansion of co-operatives, but it will be interesting to see how much open-ended funding remains
> (Personal Communication, Tom Cosh, CDA Liaison Officer, Leicester City Council)

> Those reflecting on the importance of long-term investment and the need for a hard-headed approach are the best friends of the future of the co-op movement
> (Blunkett, 1987)

As has been stressed throughout this chapter, the different approaches to 'localism' adopted by local government will result in a diverse range of co-operatives – employing different people, having different aims and securing different returns to their workers. It is difficult to reach any conclusions about the co-operative option through a strict quantitative analysis. However, with regard to policy, it is perhaps pertinent to draw some conclusions from the study. It must be said, for instance, that the Birmingham CDA appears most 'successful' in setting up viable (economic) co-operatives. However, it is necessary to comment on the more 'social' achievements of the CDAs, such as the way in which Leicester and County CDA reaches a large number of disadvantaged people. Moreover, the very fact that the Leicestershire co-operative seeks to deal with the problems of those who are already fundamentally disadvantaged is bound to affect their 'economic' success rate, and as a result we should not, therefore, be surprised by the apparent 'failure' of the Leicester co-ops to secure such economic goals as a minimum wage for co-operators.

What is clear is that, in common with Whyatt's (1987) claim, there is a correlation between the amount of money that a local authority puts into co-operative development and the number of co-operatives that are established. But, this correlation need not follow with respect to the nature of co-operative jobs. Adequate capital investment remains essential (Macfarlane 1987), but, this is not enough, and there is still a pressing need for there to be a comprehensive co-operative support structure similar to that which existed under West Midlands County Council before abolition. In many ways this support would be better provided by national government, and yet all the present government does is promote a particular kind of localism that effectively abdicates responsibility for the regions. A radical increase in national-level funding of the CDA is required (Woodcock 1986), whilst at the regional level there is a need for supportive administrative bodies which provide finance for the co-operatives that they support.

This need obviously has implications for the potential of local government initiatives more generally. The present Conservative Government is antithetical to local initiative and yet has supported co-operatives as 'small firms'. There is a danger that local government is doing likewise. It is important therefore that such policies do not reduce the potential of more alternative forms of localism.

Notes

1. The term 'restructuring' is taken here to mean 'the broad process of economic, technical, social and political reorganisation associated with the decline since the early 1970s of the post-war phase of economic development and the restabilisation of the socio-economy around a new structure of production, work and welfare' (Martin 1987:2).
2. This is one of many reservations that Bennington (1986) has for local economic strategies. More specifically, if they are co-opted into what are known and accepted as 'conventional' local responses they lose most of their 'clout' concerning them setting themselves up as alternatives to the politics and policies being peddled by the Conservative Government.
3. 'Localism' as a term is often used but little defined. The most workable definition is that of O'Connor (1984) that is 'Localism or populism is a catch-all term which includes diverse local social, economic and political initiatives'.
4. Castells (1983) and O'Connor (1984) are examples of the way in which localism as a concept has emerged from a wider conceptual field concerning 'urban social movements' and 'non-aligned local politics'.
5. Their example of Sheffield drew on many sources of explanation for the way local economic policy was worked out. For example 'Local economic policy is not directly about economic change, it is about the way in which political demonstration and organisation support economic change' (Duncan and Goodwin 1984:11).
6. The West Midlands Enterprise Board has basically adopted the policies earlier pursued by the West Midlands County Council's Economic Development Unit. For the remainder of the Chapter the policies of the two must be regarded as synonymous.
7. As regards the tables, it is important to emphasize that as Richard Macfarlane has commented, a quantitative evaluation of 'policy outcome' is inadequate since in the co-operative sector social and political – as well as economic – criteria are important. 'A survey of co-operatives that gathers both quantitative and qualitative information is necessary' (Macfarlane 1986). For this reason it is clearly inadequate solely to examine quantitative data concerning 'Local Government and Worker

Co-operatives'. Those interested in a more comprehensive analysis must consult Lowe (1988b).

8. Leicester City Council has no economic development strategy. Tom Cosh is therefore speaking personally rather than as a representative of the Council.

References

Archer, D. (1987) 'The Context of "Metrocentre"; A Tale of the Benevolent Capitalist', unpublished B.A. Dissertation, Department of Geography, University of Cambridge.

Bennington, J. (1986) 'Local Economic Strategies: Paradigms for a Planned Economy', *Local Economy* 1:7–24.

Birmingham City Council (1985) 'An Economic Strategy for Birmingham', April.

(1986) Review Economic Strategy.

Birmingham Co-operative Development Agency (1984) Annual Report 1983/4.

(1986) Annual Report 1985/6.

Blunkett, D. (1987) 'The Third Way', *New Socialist* 46, 3 February.

Boddy, M. (1984) 'Local economic and employment strategies' in M. Boddy and C. Fudge (Eds) *Local Socialism*, London: Macmillan.

Cambridge City Council (date unknown) *Cambridge: A Centre of Excellence.*

Cambridge and District Co-operative Development Agency (1983) First Annual Report.

Carter, N. (1986) 'Co-operatives – the state of play', *Political Quarterly* 57, 2:182–7.

Castells, M. (1983) *The City and the Grassroots*, London: Edward Arnold.

Cooke, P. (1986) The Context (1) The Changing Urban and Regional System, paper presented at *Joint IGU/RTPI Conference Local Economic Development: Context and Policy Initiatives Royal Geographical Society*, 15 May 1986.

Cunningham, J. (1986) 'The workers co-op movement wins new political friends', *Guardian*, 6 November.

Duncan, S.S. and Goodwin, M. (1984) 'The Local State and Local Economic Policy: Why All The Fuss?', *Urban and Regional Studies, Working Paper* No.40, University of Sussex.

Leicestershire County Council (1984) 'Policies for Employment and the Economy', April.

Leicester City Council (1985) 'Making Leicester Work', An economic strategy for Leicester, Report of the Chair and Vice Chairs Policy and Resources (Employment and Urban Policies) Sub-committee, 14 August.

(1986) Policies for Employment and the Economy, Report of the Chief

Executive and County Clerk and the Director of Planning and Transportation Policy and Resources Committee, Wednesday 11 June.

Lemert, C.G. and Gillan, C. (1982) *Michel Foucault: Social Theory as Transgression*, New York: Columbia University Press.

Lowe, M.S. (1988) 'The rise and role of worker co-operatives as agents in local social and economic restructuring', PhD Thesis, Department of Geography, University of Cambridge.

Lowe, M.S. and Martin, R.L. (forthcoming) 'The limits to economic localism', *Local Economy*.

Macfarlane, R. (1986) Council support co-ops, *Centre for Local Economic Strategies Report* 2, CLES: Manchester.

Macfarlane, R. (1987) 'Floating Worker Co-ops', *New Socialist* 46, 9 February.

Martin, R.L. (1986a) 'Getting the labour market into geographical perspective', Guest Editorial in *Environment and Planning A* 18, 569–72.

Martin, R.L. (1986b) 'Thatcherism and Britain's Industrial Landscape' in R.L. Martin and R.E. Rowthorn *The Geography of De-Industrialisation*, London: Macmillan.

Martin, R.L. (1987) 'The new economics and politics of regional restructuring: The British experience', paper presented at International Conference on 'Regional Policy at the Crossroads' University of Leuven, Belgium, 22–24 April.

Mawson, J. *et al.* (1984) 'Economic Regeneration in the West Midlands: The Role of the County Council', *Local Government Policy Making* 11 (2):61–72.

Nesbitt, G. and Tonks, A. (1986) *The National Directory of Co-operatives and Community Businesses*, London: Co-operative Development Agency.

O'Connor, J.(1984) *Accumulation Crisis*, Oxford: Basil Blackwell.

Titley, G. (1986)'West Midlands Co-ops in Action', *Marxism Today* March, xi.

West Midlands County Council (1984) *Action in the Local Economy*, Progress Report of the Economic Development Committee, West Midlands County Council.

Whyatt, A. (1983) 'Developments in the structure and organisation of the co-operative movement: Some policy considerations', *Regional Studies* 17 (3):273–6.

Whyatt, A. (1987) 'A Time for Change', *New Socialist* 46, 5 February.

Wolmar, C. (1986) 'To the slaughter . . . seven metropolitan sacred cows', *Observer* 30 March.

Woodcock, C. (1986) 'Funds Limit to CDA growth', the *Guardian*, 22 December.

Index

Index

For Product Safety Concerns and Information please contact our EU
representative GPSR@taylorandfrancis.com
Taylor & Francis Verlag GmbH, Kaufingerstraße 24, 80331 München, Germany

www.ingramcontent.com/pod-product-compliance
Lightning Source LLC
LaVergne TN
LVHW010630300926
849162LV00001B/108

* 9 7 8 1 0 4 1 1 3 1 5 9 5 *